To Freddie & Suzie with
warmest regards

Yigal & Sylvia
December 1986
5747 חנוכה

Judaism

The Art of World Religions

Judaism

Michael Kaniel

Blandford Press
Poole Dorset

First published in the U.K. 1979
by Blandford Press Ltd,
Link House, West Street,
Poole, Dorset BH15 1LL

British Cataloguing in Publication Data

Kaniel, Michael
Judaism. – (The art of world religions).
1. Jewish art and symbolism
I. Title II. Series
704.948′9′609 N7415

ISBN 0 7137 0972 3

Set in 10/12pt Monophoto Times
Printed and bound in Great Britain by
Butler & Tanner Ltd, Frome and London

Contents

Part One Early Jewish Art

1 Judaism and Art 2
2 Jewish Art in Antiquity 12
3 The Synagogue in Antiquity 21
4 Early Funerary Art 31
5 Hebrew Illuminated Manuscripts 35
6 The Art of the Hebrew Printed Book 50

Part Two Jewish Ceremonial Art

7 The Sabbath in Jewish Art 58
8 Jerusalem and the Jewish Home 88
9 The Art of the Synagogue 90
10 Art for the Jewish Year 106
11 The Life Cycle in the Jewish Tradition 126
12 The Synagogue 142

Acknowledgements 154

Index 155

In Memory of My Parents

ר׳ ישראל אליעזר בר׳ משה מיכאל ז״ל
פריידע בת ר׳ משה ז״ל

Part One
Early Jewish Art

1 Judaism and Art

For centuries the existence of Jewish art was denied, even by those deeply interested in Judaism and Jewish culture. The creative genius of the people who gave the world the Bible, monotheism and the foundations of Western ethics, morality and law was thought to be limited to literature, poetry and music. For it was generally believed that the Second Commandment expressly excluded any kind of art or sculpture among the Jews: 'Thou shalt not make unto yourself any graven image or any likeness of anything that is in the heaven above or on the earth beneath, or in the waters beneath the earth. Thou shalt not bow down to them, nor shalt thou serve them' (*Exodus XX:4*).

It was not until the second half of the nineteenth century when the magnificent medieval illuminated Hebrew manuscript treasures, long preserved in European libraries, were revealed, that the existence of Jewish art began to become known. Then, in the early decades of the twentieth century ancient synagogue mosaics were uncovered, notably those found at Bet Alpha in northern Israel in 1928, which further confirmed the existence of a rich Jewish artistic tradition.

In 1932, the exciting discovery of the magnificent frescoes of the third century AD synagogue at Dura Europos in Syria removed any remaining doubts. Indeed, the Dura wall paintings have reversed the situation, for they have led scholars to conclude that Christian art, and thus the very foundations of Western art, had its origins in Jewish art.

The existence of Jewish art does not in itself, however, resolve the basic dilemma: how can Jewish art be reconciled with the Second Commandment? Was that commandment intended to be interpreted literally? And if not, what was the underlying purpose of this injunction and of the many Biblical prohibitions against representational art? To carry this one step further, why is the *Torah*, the Hebrew Bible, filled with so many denunciations of the creation and worship of idols?

Indeed, it is the special relationship which the Torah sees between idolatry and representational art that provides the essential clue.

This relationship can be characterised by a single word: unity. Throughout history, religion has been the source of virtually all art and the principal subject matter of artistic production. In every ancient civilisation, representational art was essentially religious art, and most of the arts – music, dance, drama, poetry, literature and architecture – developed from activities and objects originally devised for the control of divinities.

As Judaism saw it, God, as the Creator of nature, transcends nature, and His very incorporeality is incomprehensible to man. Since man cannot comprehend the incomprehensible, any attempt at an artistic depiction of God could only mislead and distort. Such depictions were therefore strictly prohibited. The first of the Ten Commandments, the proclamation of monotheism, is therefore immediately followed by a second commandment limiting the graphic arts, which is designed to protect the central concept of monotheism – the keystone of Judaism – and to guard it from corruption. These two commandments, taken together, constitute not only a decisive departure from, but a vehement denunciation of, the prevalent polytheism at the time.

Polytheism is integrally connected with the creation of symbols to express man's veneration and, later, deification of the elemental powers of nature. These symbols, which primitive man painted on the walls of his cave dwellings or formed into objects, were invested with magical powers designed to serve both as objects of veneration and as a means of controlling nature. At a much later stage, the sun, the moon and the stars were extolled and worshipped, and the elemental powers of nature – the wind, the rain, the trees, even the rocks and the regenerative earth – were deemed holy and inspired the creation of representational symbols and objects.

As Judaism saw it, man, by fashioning these representations was in fact creating God in his own image. All the gods were anthropomorphic, exaggerated human beings with human foibles, who lived, loved and died as humans do. The Bible declares that God created man in His own image (*Genesis I: 27*), which Judaism understands as meaning that man was given the spiritual traits of his Creator, and that he is obliged to utilise these traits to elevate himself spiritually and, by his own free will, to achieve a state of holiness. A basic command of the Torah declares Judaism's elemental lofty goal for the Jew: 'And you shall sanctify yourselves and shall be holy, for I your God am holy' (*Leviticus XII: 44, 45*). In the Jewish view, the idol worshipper, rather than conforming to Judaism's ideal of man's elevating himself to God, reduces God, so to speak, to his own diminutive size by worshipping the artistic creation of his own hands.

Judaism taught that man created gods to fulfil the lusts and desires of his own lowest instincts, and by giving divinity to the images of his own creation he gave his base actions the seal of sanctity. Thus, the god Moloch was honoured and worshipped by burning children alive. Astarte was not a 'love goddess', but a figure that debased man by sanctifying his submission to animal-like lust; 'worship' of this goddess was by active participation in orgies of sexual debauchery. Fornication was also the means of worship of Baal Pe'or. It has been said that if Zeus is a god, licentiousness is no sin; if Aphrodite is a goddess, chastity cannot be a virtue.

The uncompromising tone and unparalleled vehemence with which the Torah refers to idolatry – 'burning anger', 'provocation' and 'zeal' are some of the terms used – the rabbis explain, is because idolatry, sexual immorality and bloodshed are the three cardinal prohibitions contained in Jewish law (*Bab. Talmud Sanhedrin LXXIV: A*); and idolatry involved the abolition of all moral restraint and ethical standards since rites of worship included vice, corruption, perversion, sexual immorality and bloodshed. Idolatry thus meant the defilement of man and the extinguishing of the spirituality stamped on man by God when He created him in His own image. Thus, the Jewish sages declared that whoever transgresses the laws relating to idolatry is, as it were, transgressing the entire body of commandments of the Torah (Ibn Ezra on *Exodus XXIII: 24*). Forty-four separate Biblical prohibitions are violated in idolatry, and their gravity is underlined by the fact that martyrdom is enjoined before transgressing the idolatry laws.

The Jewish concept of idolatry includes any corporeal representation of God, the ascribing of divine influence to any intermediary, and the deification of man. Judaism recognises a God who is 'neither corporeal nor possesses any physical properties or who takes any form whatsoever' (Maimonides, *The Thirteen Principles of the Faith*). Despite a long and continuous history of tribulations and suffering the Jews have remained faithful to their pure, pristine concept of the monotheistic ideal. That this ideal has not been extirpated from Judaism is largely because of the Torah's stern and uncompromising attitude towards idol worship. It can be readily seen, therefore, why the Torah prohibited any conceivable graphic portrayal of God, Who was intended to be revealed only by His deeds. Anthropomorphic expressions regarding God's 'organs' and 'attributes' were never intended to be taken literally, but were designed to explain in human terms abstract expressions of Divine actions. The Talmudic principle is that 'The Torah speaks in human language.' The incorporeality of God is emphasised in the Torah: 'And the Lord spoke to you out of the midst of the fire. You heard the voice of words but you saw no form, only a voice ...' (*Deuteronomy IV: 12*).

The Jew saw natural phenomena as but outer manifestations of God's glory and greatness. In the words of King David: 'The heavens declare the glory of God, and the firmament shows His handiwork' (*Psalms XIX: 2*). It was holiness that Judaism demanded of the Jew, and through holiness a constant striving to elevate himself to godliness. The Greek worship of beauty, form and sculpture was anathema to Judaism for it represented a form of idolatry – man's veneration of God's creations or of the creation of his own hands. The great eleventh-century sage, Maimonides concluded in his monumental *Code of Jewish Law* that the sin of idolatry is committed not when the beauty of images is admired, but when they are endowed with divine attributes (*Code, Laws of Idolatry, ch. III, Sect. 6*). But, once it has become clear that a work of art will not itself be venerated, the prohibitions are immediately relaxed. This is best exemplified by the cherubim, the brazen oxen and the molten sea which adorned the Temple in Jerusalem.

Thus, there has been no opposition in Judaism to art *per se* – only opposition to art which could be used for idolatrous worship. Talmudic statements regarding idolatry ranging from severity to liberalism resulted from the responses of the rabbinic sages to the varying degrees of the threats to Judaism by idolatry faced by the people at different times. During periods where there clearly existed no idolatrous instinct amongst the Jews, liberalism reigned in the use of decorative images in art, even in synagogues. It is illuminating that the first-century AD rabbi, Jonathan ben Uziel, explained the Biblical passage prohibiting the creation of idols and graven images as follows: 'You shall not place a figured stone on the ground to worship unto, but a colonnade engraved with pictures and likenesses you may have in your synagogue – but not to worship unto . . .' However, when Ezra and Nehemia built the Second Temple following the Babylonian exile, they did not replace the *cherubim*, the sculptured depictions of winged angels above the Ark of the Covenant, because following the destruction of the first Temple, Nebuchadnezzar's soldiers had carried out the cherubim and exhibited them as the Jewish god.

Even pagan images and symbols have appeared in synagogues in ancient times after they no longer retained their original significance. Hence the Talmudic sage Rabbi Gamliel, who lived in Acre in the first century AD, saw nothing wrong in using the bath of the goddess Aphrodite, pointing out that the bath was not made for the veneration of Aphrodite, as her statue was merely an adornment of the bath (*Bab. Talmud: Avodah Zarah IL LV: B*). In the third century, the Talmudic sages, Shmuel and Rav, the latter himself an accomplished artist, prayed in the Babylonian city of Nehardea in a synagogue in which there stood a royal Roman statue (*Bab. Talmud Rosh Hashana XXIV: B*). Indeed, Byzantine synagogues had mosaic floors which depict pagan goddesses.

The appearance of synagogue decoration in the form of mosaic floors and wall paintings corresponded to events described in a variant manuscript of the Jerusalem Talmud: 'In the days of Rabbi Johanan they began to paint on the walls and he did not prevent them. In the days of Rabbi Abun they began to make designs on mosaics and he did not prevent them' (Epstein, J. N. *'Additional Fragments of the Jerusalem Talmud'*, Tarbiz, vol. III; 193, p. 20). Rabbi Johanan ben Napaha (born at the end of the second century, died 279 AD) was the head of the Jewish community of the land of Israel during much of the third century. He thus lived at the time the magnificent wall paintings at the synagogue in Dura Europos were executed and the Talmudic statement confirms that he gave the rabbinic sanction for their execution. Rabbi Abun lived at the beginning of the fourth century, and thus, as in the case of the wall paintings, provides a date for the introduction of mosaic floors in the synagogue. This is confirmed by archaeological discoveries, as from the fourth century onward we find mosaic floors with representational art in synagogues in Israel and elsewhere in the ancient world.

Judaism, as a total God-oriented and God-directed way of life, encompasses the totality of the life of the individual. Every act in life and every decision must be directed toward his spiritual elevation to a state of holiness and godliness as outlined in the Torah. This principle has traditionally determined Judaism's attitude towards art too. Recognising the human need for visual images in faith, Judaism did not suppress art, but it did circumscribe it. The Tabernacle in the Wilderness and the ritual which surrounded it demonstrated an awareness of the need for these visual images. The *Menorah*, the seven-branched candlestick which was destined to become the most widely used emblem of Judaism, the table with the shewbread, the hangings and the altar – all these were functional ritual objects which also served as visible religious symbols for inspiration and spiritual elevation.

Nor was the aesthetic aspect of the ritual objects neglected. Of the two cornices for the altar, one was utilitarian (that the priest should not slip and fall) and the other was designed for beauty (*Bab. Talmud Zevahim LXII: A*). The valances of the Tabernacle curtain were also designed for beauty (*Rashi* on *Exodus XXVI: 12*), and it is emphasised twice that the priestly garments were made both for glory and beauty (*Exodus XXVIII: 2, 40*). The ritual objects of the Tabernacle were the forerunners of the objects of Jewish ceremonial art which were to surround the Jew in his home and synagogue in later generations.

The Tabernacle and its ceremonial art objects became a significant outlet for the artistic, the talented and the creative. All those capable of executing decorative designs for the Tabernacle and its furnishings were summoned (*Exodus XXXVI*), and the response was so overwhelming that Moses announced the mission to be extraordinarily successful, even to the point of being 'oversubscribed'!

The description given in the Old Testament of the ideal artist, Bezalel, is further evidence of Judaism's positive attitude towards the arts. His name means 'in the shadow of God', and indicates the purpose of his artistry and the use of the talents of the artist as a means of fulfilling the spiritual goal of the Jew. Bezalel, the Bible tells us, was filled with 'the spirit of God, with wisdom, with insight and with knowledge in every craft ... able to devise skilful works in gold and silver and in copper and cutting in stone for setting and in wood carving, and to work all manner of skilled craftsmanship.

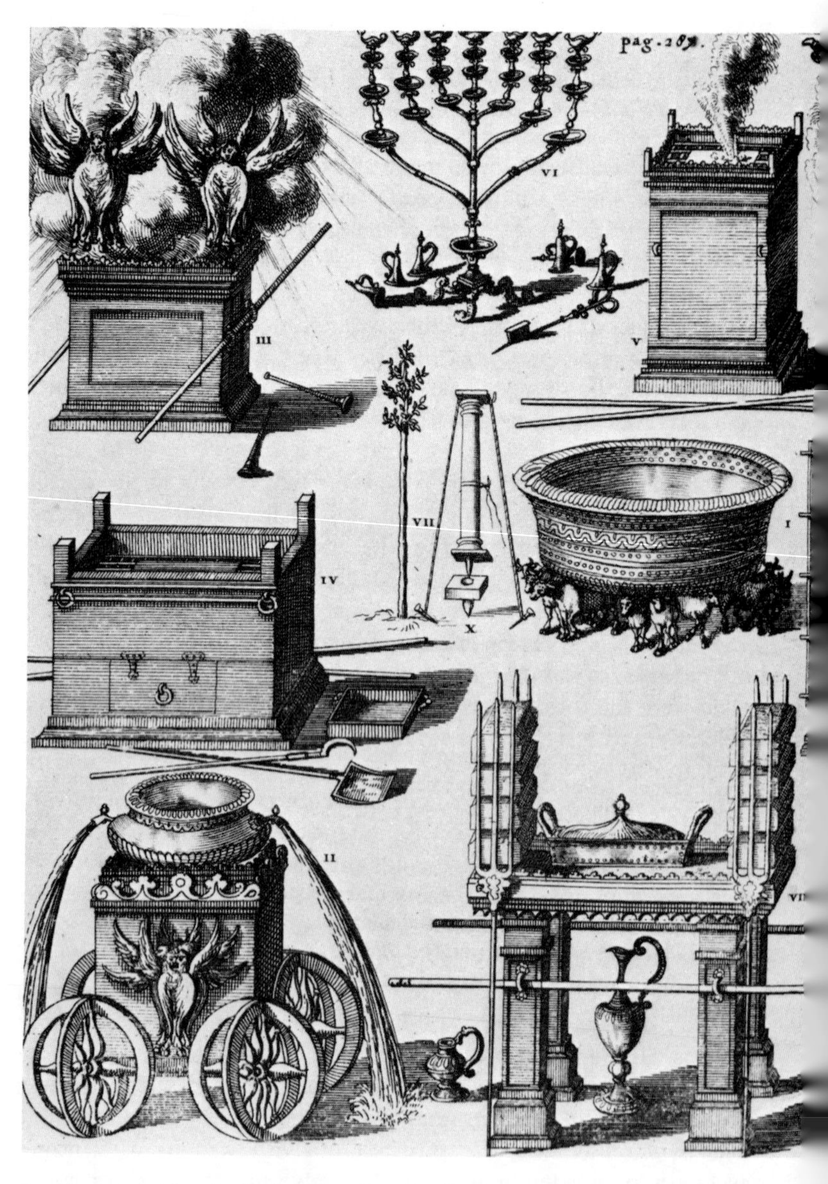

Jewish ceremonial art in the Jerusalem Temple. (Copperplate engraving in Philologus Hebraeo-Mixtus, by Johanne Leusden, Leyden and Utrecht, Holland, 1699.)

And God gave Bezalel and Ahaliav, his associate, the gift of teaching and filled them with wisdom to do skilful works in the crafts and of the weaver of colours in blue and purple, in scarlet and in fine linen . . .' (*Exodus XXXV: 30–35*).

In Jewish lore, God himself is referred to as the Supreme Artist who first designed the world, and from its materials then designed man (*Midrash Sifri*). The rabbis refer to God as a sculptor (*Bab. Talmud Berakhot X: A*); and, indeed, human sculptors are compared to the Divine Sculptor (*Mehkilta of Rabbi Simon Bar Yohai*). To create beauty was considered in Judaism one of the greatest challenges given to man, for it meant participation in the creative character of the Divinity. (Interestingly, this situation is reversed in Islam, where artists are uncompromisingly condemned in the most severe fashion. The Prophet is reported to have said that those who God will most severely punish on the Day of Judgement will be the painters because they thus usurp the creative function of the Creator [Sir Thomas W. Arnold, *Paintings in Islam*, p. 7].) When a Roman official taunted Rabbi Akiva, the great second-century Talmudist, that the Jewish rite of circumcision is evidence that God created man as an imperfect creature, Rabbi Akiva readily agreed that according to Jewish tradition this was a God-given opportunity for man to complete God's work. He then placed a sack of wheat and a row of pastry before the Roman official and asked him to make his choice.

Perhaps the attitude of Judaism towards art and beauty, as compared with the Greek for example, may be best expressed by the Talmudic interpretation of the Biblical blessing to Japhet, one of the sons of Noah. Japhet, whose name means beauty, is considered the progenitor of the Greek civilisation and the cultural progenitor of art and aesthetics in the world. In the Bible he is Blessed: 'God enlarge Japhet so that he may dwell in the tents of Shem' (*Genesis IX: 27*). Simeon ben Gamliel, the president of the Sanhedrin in the first century AD, interprets the blessing to mean: 'May the beauty of Japhet be found within the tents of the Semites' (*Bab. Talmud Megillah IX: B*).

The rabbis thus taught that when the spirit of Judaism prevails over the Greek, beauty is stripped of its pagan sensuality and stands revealed in its pristine glory. The homiletical interpretation was that art and aesthetics cannot be an end in themselves, but must be subject to ethics and morality. As Judaism sees it, art as a Divine gift must be Divinely used. Aesthetics and art go together, but should they ever conflict with ethics and morality, there is no question that the latter takes precedence. Art could never be a serious contender for the central role in the Jewish value system.

While art and aesthetics are not ends in themselves, they are considered to be significant means in helping the individual to achieve spiritual elevation. As the psalmist sings, 'The voice of God is in beauty' (*Psalms XXIX: 4*). Rabbi Israel Baal Shem Tov, the eighteenth-century founder of *Hassidism* – a movement emphasising direct communication with God in prayer through joy and spiritual exaltation, dance and song – saw attributes of God in all of His creations, both animate and inanimate. 'If the vision of a beautiful woman, or of any lovely thing, comes suddenly to a man's eyes, let him ask whence the beauty, if not from the Divine Force which permeates the world. And why be attracted by the part? Better be drawn after the all ... Such perception of beauty is an experience of the eternal' (Tsavaat Ribash, 1797, 18).

Judaism even requires a special benediction to be pronounced upon beholding beauty – when seeing handsome people, a beautiful tree or animal, the first blossoms of spring etc. So important is this aesthetic concept that it is considered the first of the seven rabbinic ordinances which are added to the six hundred and thirteen *mitzvot*, the Biblically-ordained commands which are binding upon the Jew. Aesthetics thus became a vital consideration expressed in the appellation *hiddur mitzvah*, the embellishment or the beautification of the command. The significance of art in the life of the Jew is dramatically emphasised by the stipulation that one is obliged to spend up to one third more than the normal cost in the purchase of ceremonial objects in order to fulfil the mitzvah in a proper aesthetic manner.

'This is my God and I shall glorify (lit. adorn or beautify) Him', sings Moses (*Exodus XV: 2*). The Talmud explains that one 'adorns' God with mitzvot; that the Jew is required to design, create and use beautiful, artistic ceremonial objects in fulfilling the commandments. The Talmud then goes on to list some of the ceremonial objects which should be created in a beautiful manner (*Bab. Talmud – Shabbat CXXXIII: b*). The second-century passage emphasises the antiquity of the Jewish tradition of creating artistic objects for use in ritual practices, and was undoubtedly a significant factor in the development of beautiful Jewish ceremonial art in the home and synagogue. The frequent massacres, pogroms, constant expulsions and forced wanderings of the Jews and the concurrent confiscation of their belongings resulted in the destruction and melting down of uncountable treasures of Jewish art and the extreme rarity of Jewish art objects today, especially those from the eighteenth century and earlier.

We see, then, that there is no fundamental tension between Judaism and art. Misconceptions about Jewish hostility to art originated either from a basic misunderstanding of the Second Commandment or from a disregard of its main meaning which clearly links the prohibition against artistic creation with idol worship. They may also have originated from ignorance of Talmudic and other Jewish traditional interpretations of the prohibition, together with a lack of awareness of material evidence which indicates a rich tradition of Jewish creative activity. The Biblical restraints were successful in inhibiting, to some extent, free artistic creativity among Jews, lest it lead to direct or indirect worship of the creation of human hands; and the Biblical tenets guided the development of Jewish art in an ethical direction. However, Judaism does not oppose visual or represensational art, which was found even in ancient Jewish houses of worship. Artistic activity was encouraged, provided that it did not lead to idolatry or impair the unsullied belief in a non-corporeal Creator. The artistic embellishment of Jewish ceremonial art was especially encouraged.

Art was seen by Judaism not as something detached or compartmentalised, but as a vital part of life itself. Judaism, therefore, was unable to accept obeisance to purely human values expressed in the supposedly pristine concept of 'art for art's sake', for this was thought to be akin to idolatry. The traditional Jewish attitude to art over the years was that, as an essential part of life and as a means of enhancing life, art should ideally have a moral content and convey an elevating message. The function of art in the Jewish tradition is to elevate and ennoble man.

2 Jewish Art in Antiquity

In the autumn of 1932, a group of young archaeologists, part of a joint Franco-American expedition in Syria, stood before a long, dirt-encrusted wall. They were halfway through the fifth season of excavations at Dura Europos, an ancient trading city on the Euphrates dating back at least to Assyrian times, the middle of the first millennium BC. The expedition had already made some notable discoveries, including the earliest known Christian chapel which contained Christian paintings, but they had no idea that they were on the verge of a discovery whose magnitude could be compared to that of Pompeii. Clark Hopkins, head of the expedition, gave the following account of what they saw after the layer of dirt had been carefully cleared away from the wall: 'The dirt fell and revealed pictures, paintings, vivid in color, startling, so fresh it seemed they might have been painted a month before. There was a mighty series of painting, the scenes continuing from the north corner along the whole forty feet of wall ... It was a scene like a dream! In the infinite space of the clear blue sky and bare grey desert there was a miracle taking place, an oasis of painting springing up from the dull earth ... the extraordinary array of figures, the brilliant scenes, the astounding colors ...' They were startled and delighted, but bewildered by their amazing discovery. Their hope for a key to unlock the secret of their find was soon to be fulfilled. As the excavators enthusiastically continued to clear away the dirt, suddenly a magnificent wall painting was uncovered. A tall figure was seen leading a large group from the wall of a city; below it, like a 'heaven-sent gift' (ibid.), was an Aramaic inscription which read 'Moses leads out of Egypt'.

What the stunned, incredulous group of archaeologists had discovered were the remains of a synagogue dating from the third century AD. It was in an extraordinary state of preservation; its four walls were adorned with the most remarkable wall paintings, the like of which had never been seen before, featuring the central figures of the Bible.

The synagogue, built during 244–45 AD above an earlier syna-

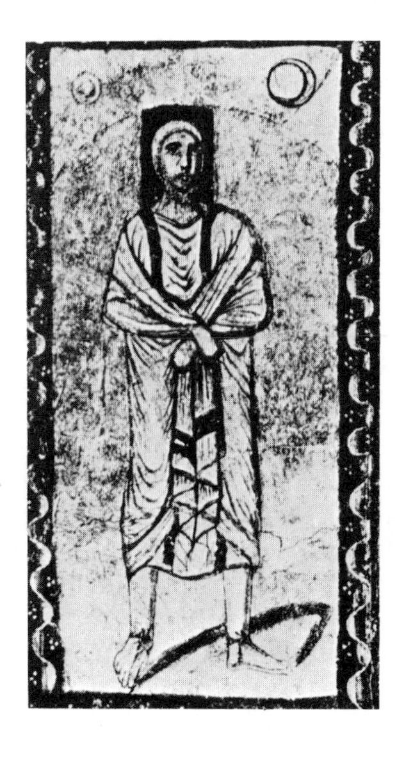

Wall painting of a prophet, possibly Abraham or Moses, from the west wall at Dura Europos.

gogue dating from half a century earlier, lay just inside the wall of this frontier city of the Roman Empire. In 256, in an attempt to strengthen the exposed city wall against the advancing Sassanian army, the inhabitants had removed the roofs of the buildings adjacent to the walls and filled the shells of the buildings with sand from the desert; thus the synagogue had been protected as effectively as the lava had protected Pompeii. Indeed, thirty separate panels of wall paintings have survived in incredibly good condition, including virtually all of the west wall, substantial portions of the north and south walls and a small part of the east wall. The west, or Jerusalem-oriented, wall contains a niche which served as a Torah-shrine flanked by two columns, and was surmounted by depictions of the seven-branched *menorah* and other Jewish symbols and ritual accessories typical of those found in Jewish art in the late classical period.

The exciting discovery of the Dura wall paintings is of such magnitude that its significance for the study of both general and Jewish art history can be compared with that of the Dead Sea Scrolls and their significance for our knowledge of Judaism. For, as the sheets of dirt fell away so did the support for the long-held convictions that there was no Jewish representational art in antiquity. These convictions had been based on the flimsiest of theories, but had far-reaching implications. Here was a Jewish community in the Diaspora, some 250 miles (400 km) from Nehardea, an important Talmudic centre of Babylonian Jewish learning, where Jews not only profusely decorated the walls of a synagogue, but also made abundant use of the human form in figurative art.

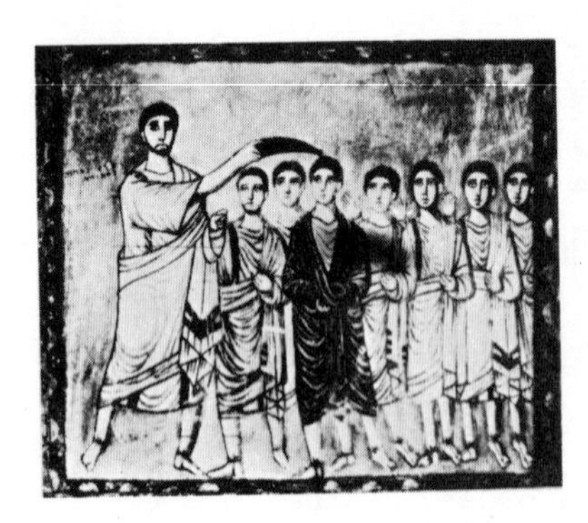

Wall painting of Samuel anointing David King of Israel in the presence of his brothers. From the west wall at Dura Europos.

The discovery of the Dura synagogue paintings is of primary significance in the history of art as well, at the very least because of the dimensions of the discovery. The synagogue not only preserved the oldest surviving Old Testament paintings, but also the largest single group of ancient wall paintings outside Italy from the classical period, and thus provides an extraordinary opportunity to examine and study the development of art in the middle of the third century.

But, as significant as Dura is for an understanding of the Jewish origins of Christian art and hence Western art, it is even more important for an understanding of Jewish art, and possibly even of certain aspects of Judaism itself. For these extraordinary wall paintings may be said to be the embodiment of the essential features of Jewish

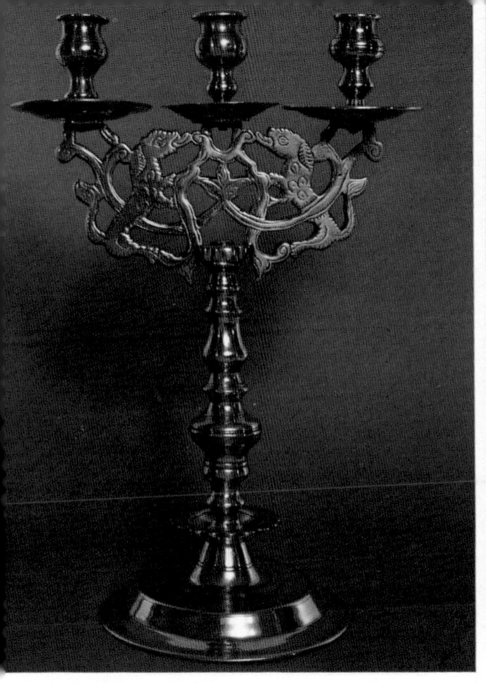

Bronze Sabbath candlestick. Poland, 17th century.

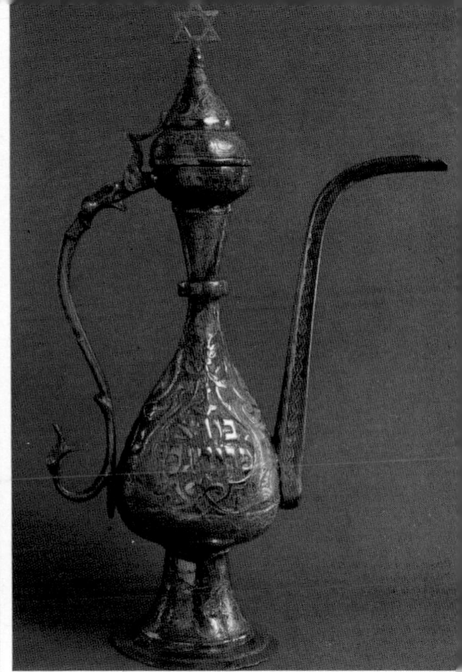

Brass wine decanter with Hebrew inscription. Damascus, 19th century.

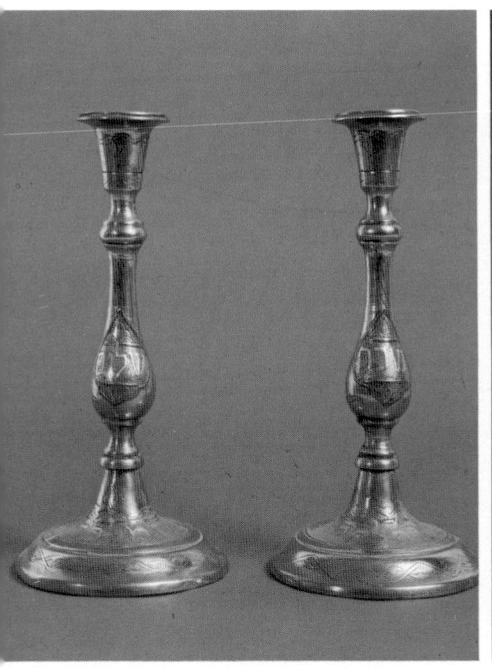

Pair of brass and silver Sabbath candlesticks. Damascus, 19th century.

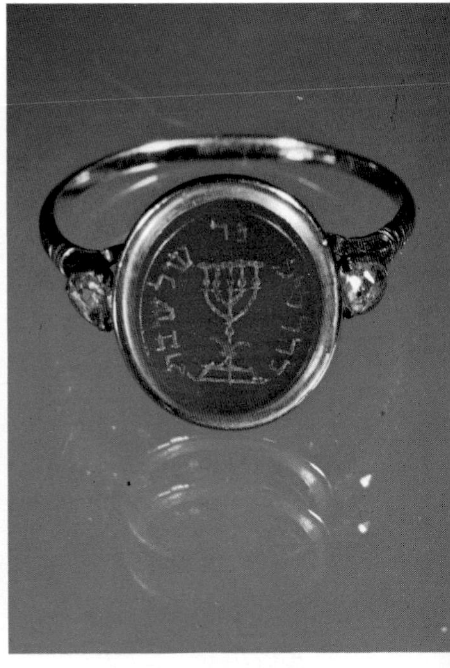

Gold and cornelian Sabbath ring inscribed 'To kindle the lamp of the Sabbath'. Central Europe, 18th century.

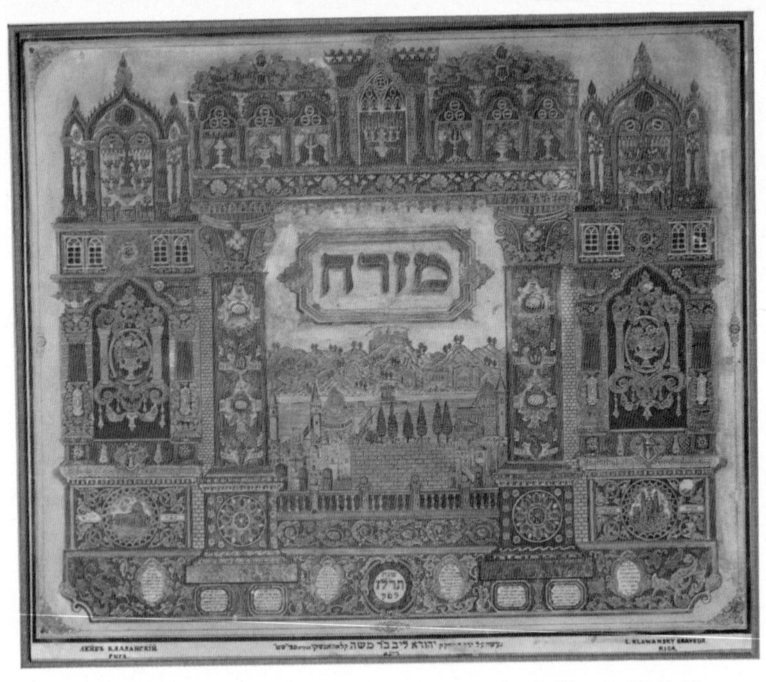

Engraved and coloured mizrach tablet featuring Jerusalem's Western Wall. Kiev, Ukraine, 1877.

Mizrach tablet, painted on glass, featuring in two scenes the Binding of Isaac which took place on Mount Moriah in Jerusalem. Jerusalem, 1912.

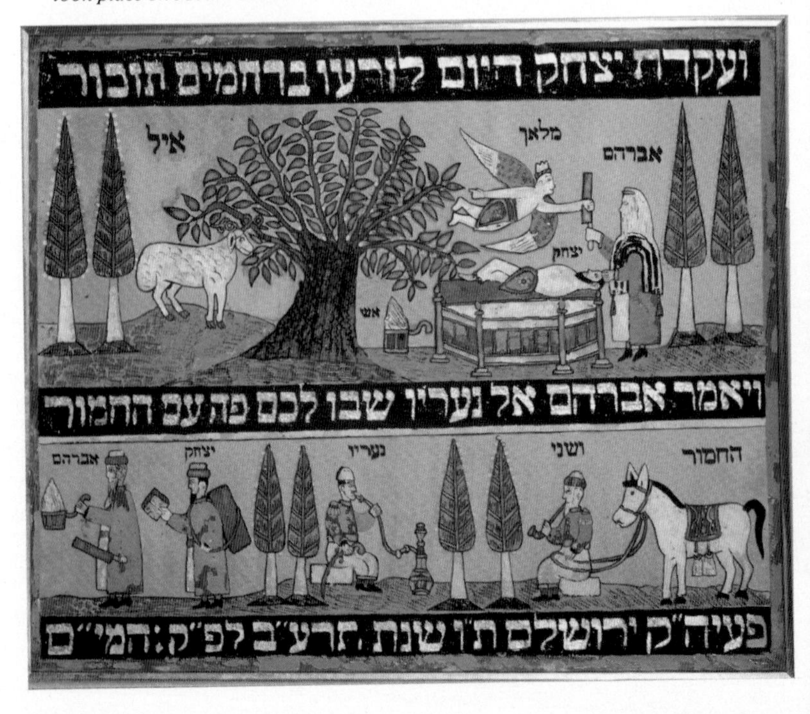

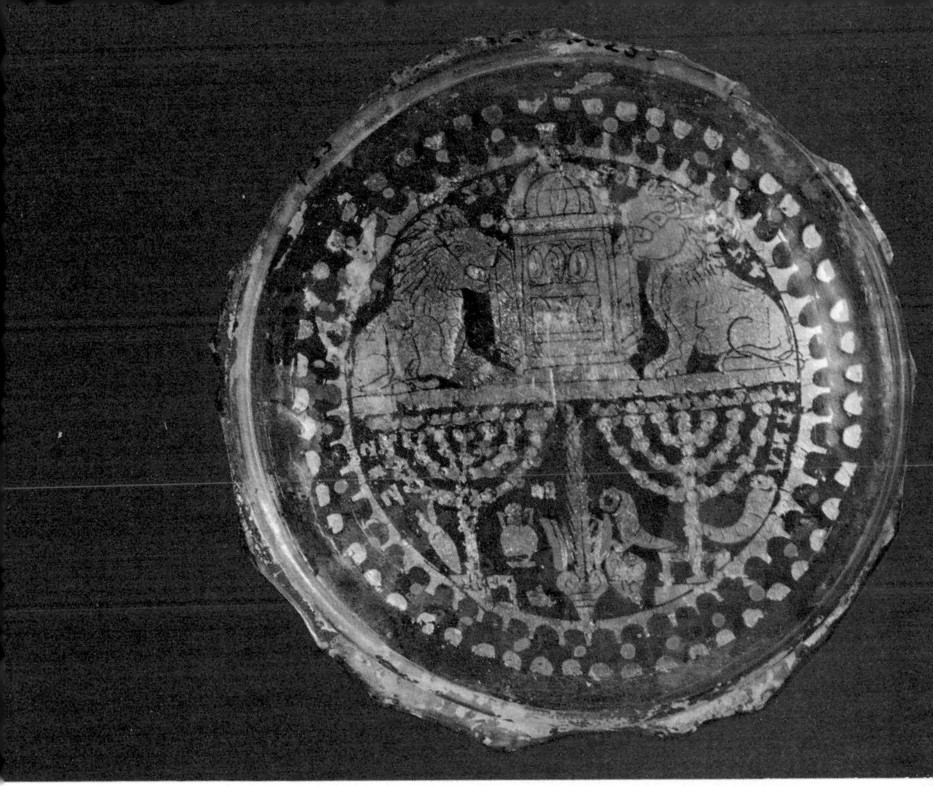

Jewish gold glass. Twin lions of Judah couchant flank an open Torah ark revealing the Torah scrolls within. Also depicted are menorahs, shofars and a lulav and etrog. c. 7th century.

Decorated Esther scroll with copperplate engravings of scenes from the book of Esther, by Francesco Griselini, Venice, c.1740-50.

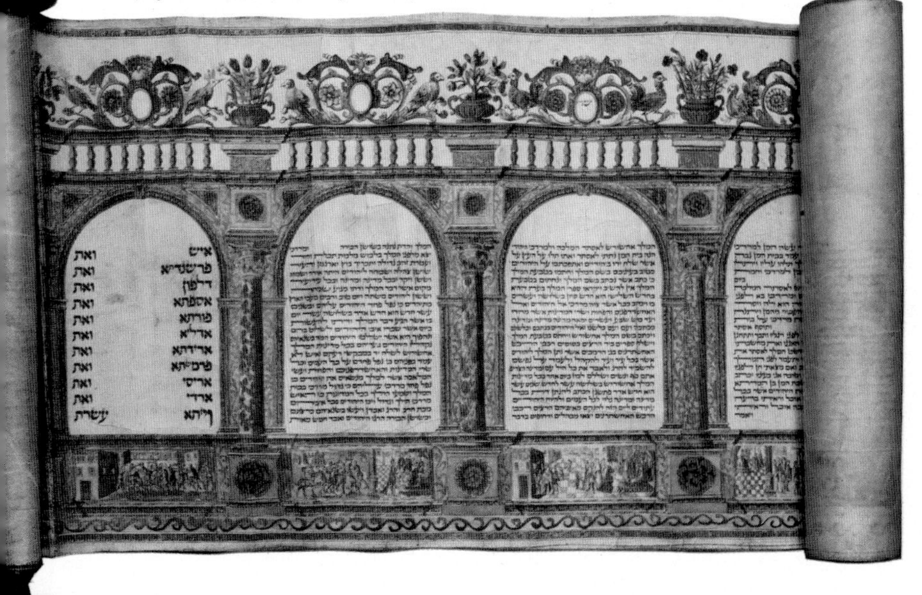

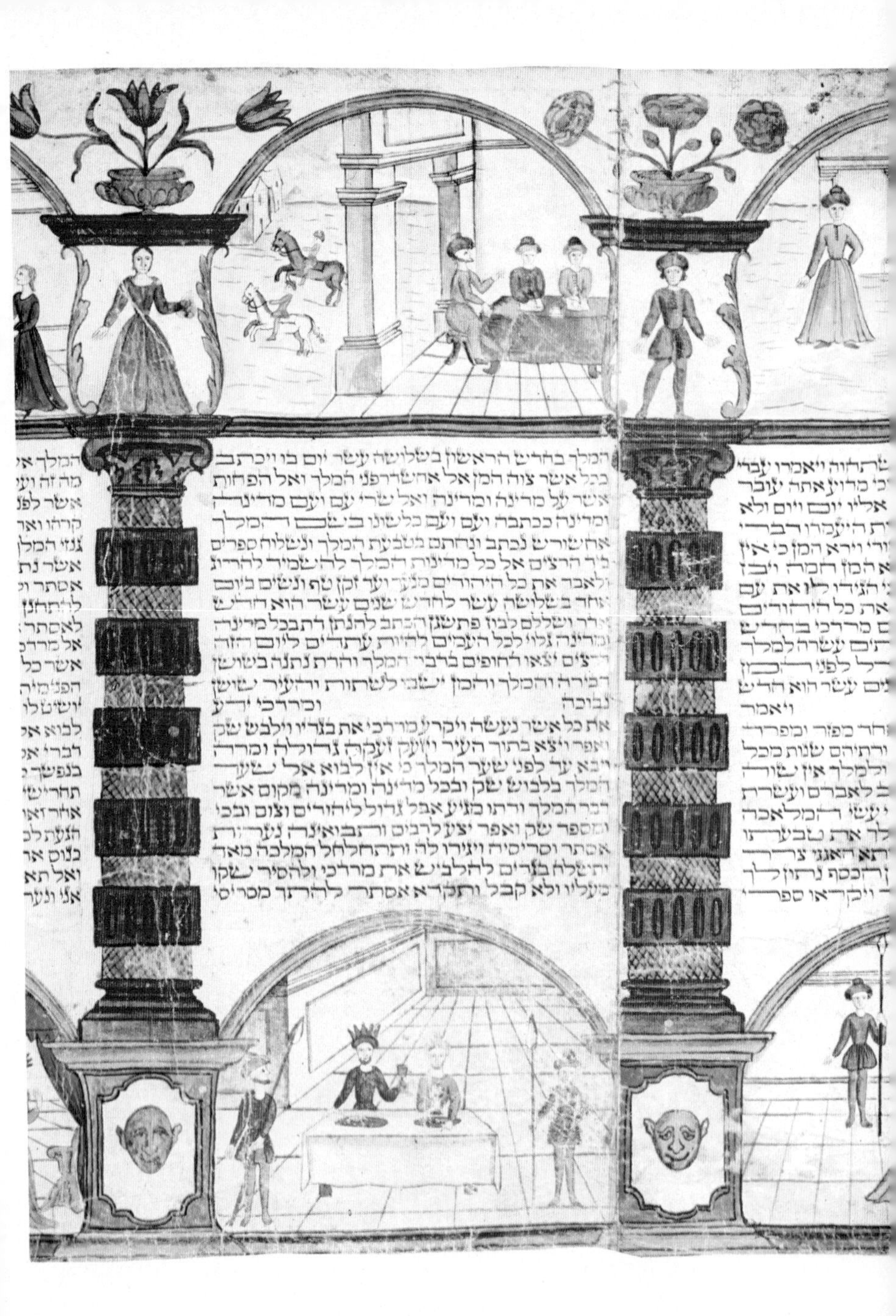

Illuminated Esther scroll (megillah) on parchment. Bohemia-Moravia, c.1700.

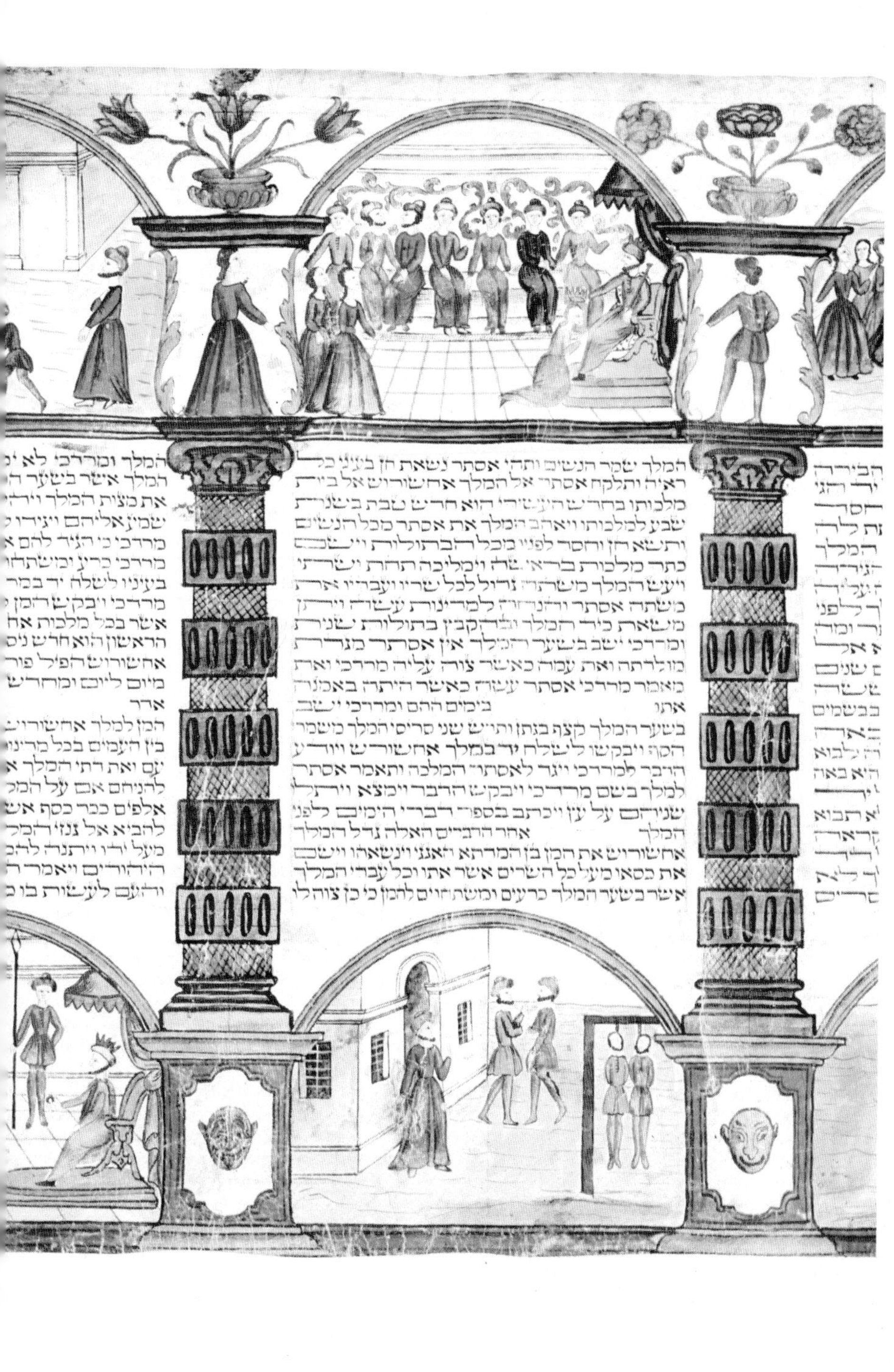

המלך שמר הנשים ותהי אסתר נשאת חן בעיני כל
ראיה ותלקח אסתר אל המלך אחשורוש אל בית
מלכותו בחדש העשירי הוא חדש טבת בשנת
שבע למלכותו ויאהב המלך את אסתר מכל הנשים
ותשא חן וחסד לפניו מכל הבתולות וישם
כתר מלכות בראשה וימליכה תחת ושתי
ויעש המלך משתה גדול לכל שריו ועבדיו את
משתה אסתר והנחה למדינות עשה ויתן
משאת כיד המלך ובהקבץ בתולות שנית
ומרדכי ישב בשער המלך אין אסתר מגדת
מולדתה ואת עמה כאשר צוה עליה מרדכי ואת
מאמר מרדכי אסתר עשה כאשר היתה באמנה
אתו בימים ההם ומרדכי ישב
בשער המלך קצף בגתן ותרש שני סריסי המלך משמרי
הסף ויבקשו לשלח יד במלך אחשורש ויודע
הדבר למרדכי ויגד לאסתר המלכה ותאמר אסתר
למלך בשם מרדכי ויבקש הדבר וימצא ויתלו
שניהם על עץ ויכתב בספר דברי הימים לפני
המלך אחר הדברים האלה גדל המלך
אחשורוש את המן בן המדתא האגגי וינשאהו וישם
את כסאו מעל כל השרים אשר אתו וכל עבדי המלך
אשר בשער המלך כרעים ומשתחוים להמן כי כן צוה לו

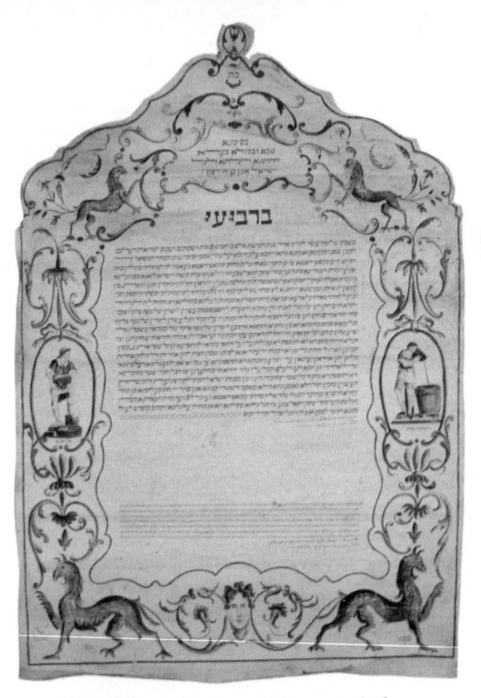

Ketubah on parchment. Ancona, Italy, 1822.

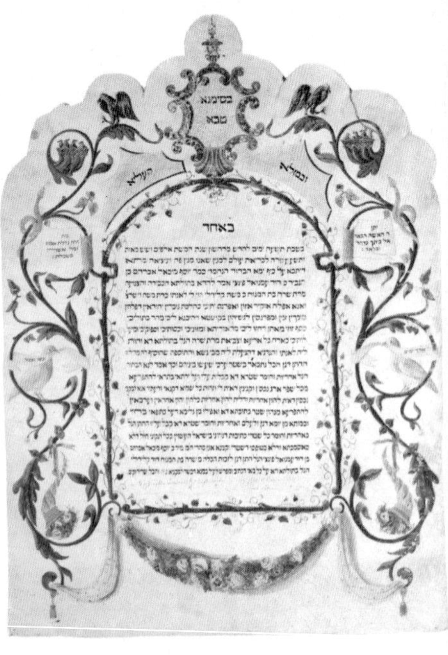

Ketubah on parchment. Venice, Italy, 1858.

Ketubah on parchment. Amsterdam, 1687.

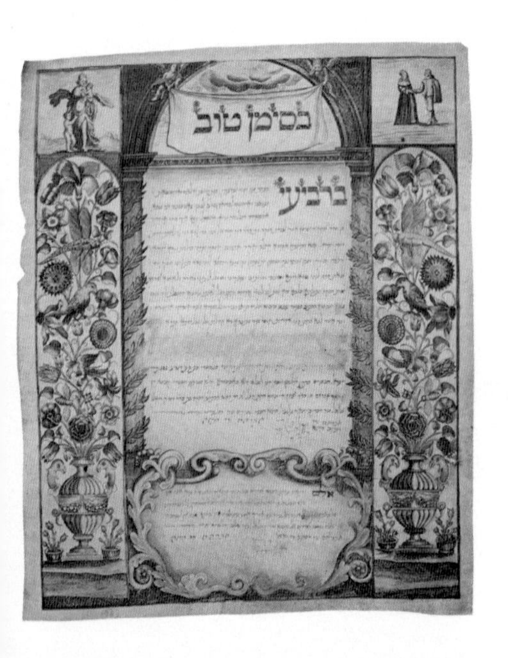

Ketubah on parchment. Rome, 1857.

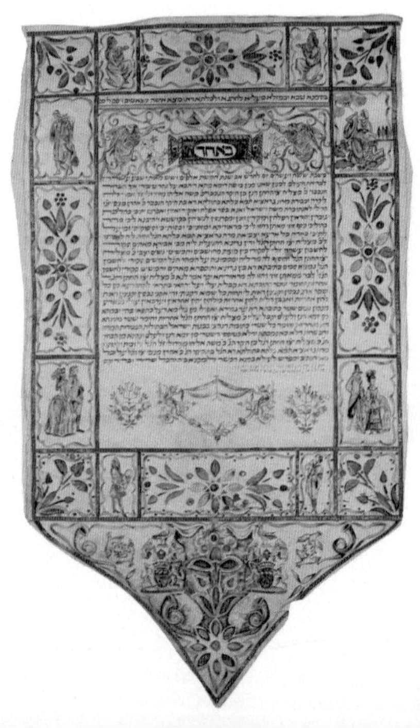

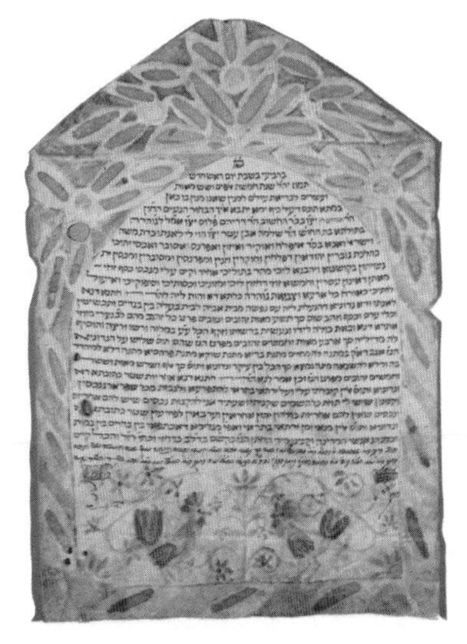

Ketubah on paper. Tunis, 1860.

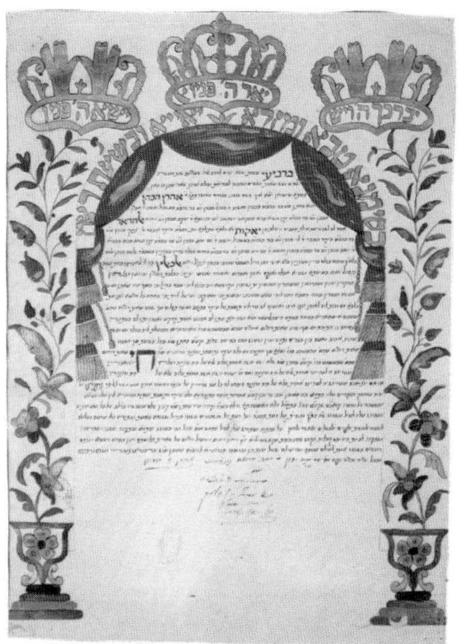

Ketubah on parchment. Tetuan, Morocco, 1902.

Three silver megillah cases with Esther scrolls from, left to right: Turkey, 18th century; Asia minor, 18th century; Poland, 18th century.

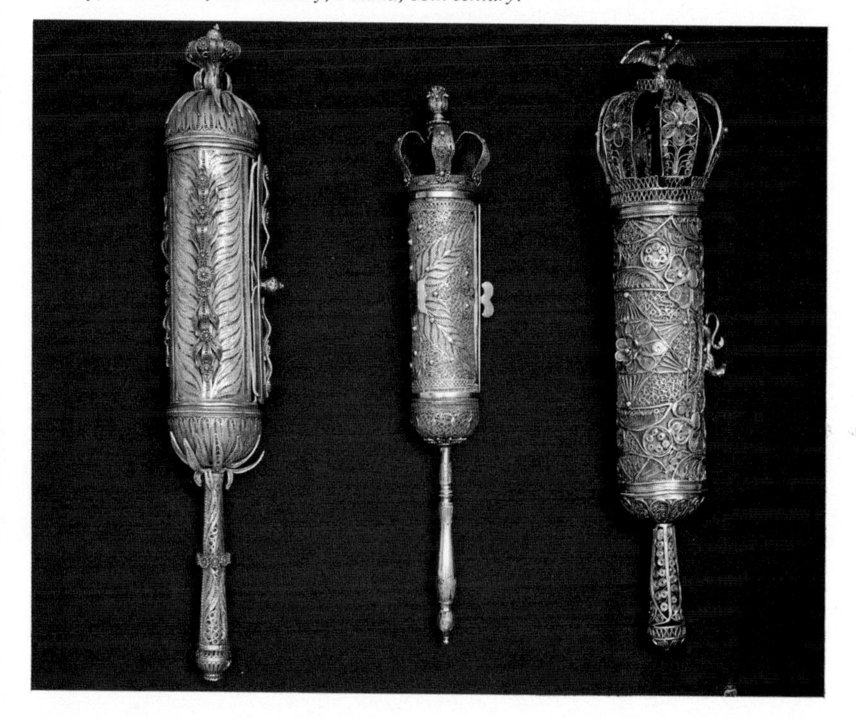

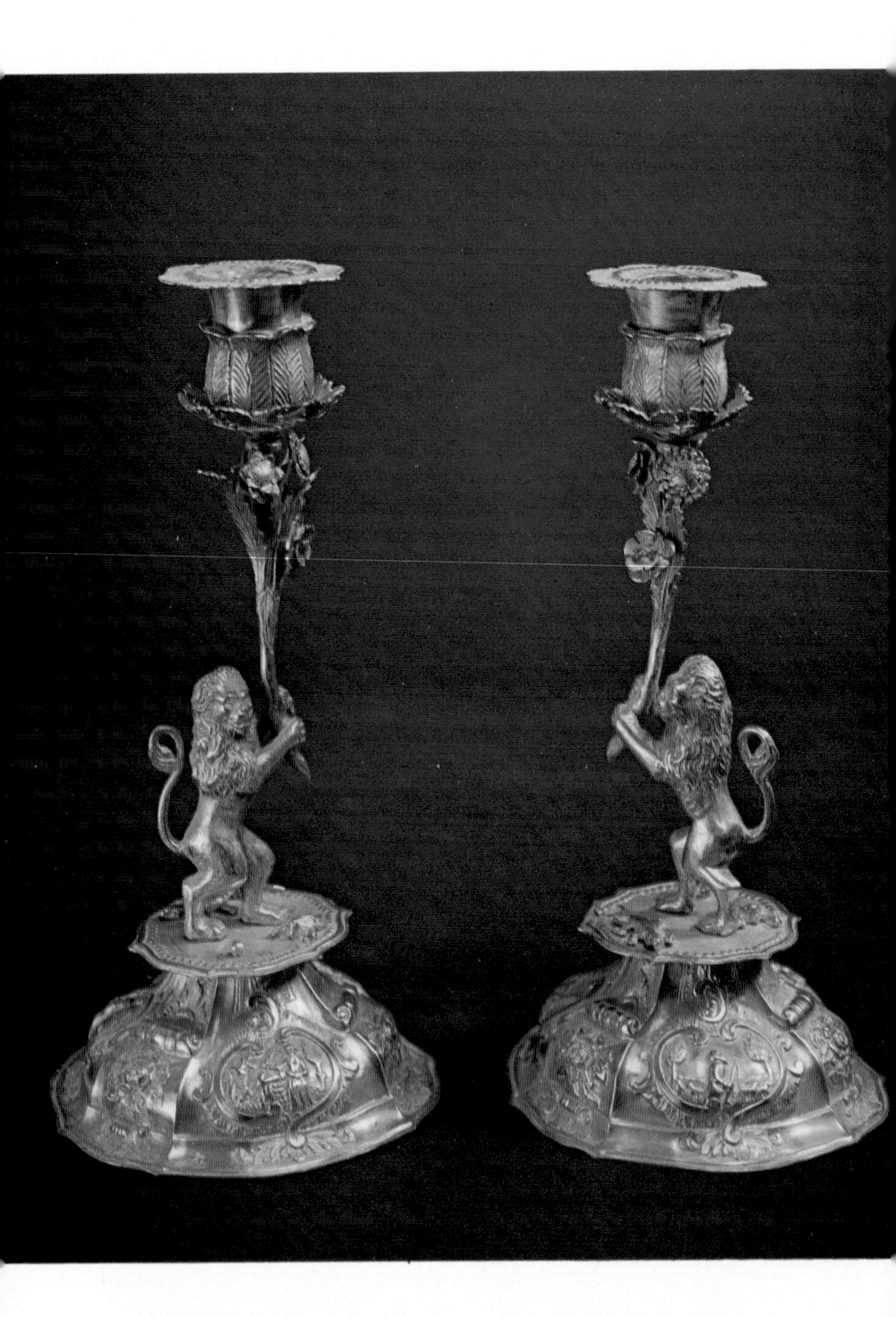

Silver gilt Sabbath candlesticks in the form of twin lions of Judah rampant. At the bases are six Jewish and Biblical scenes. Germany, 19th century.

art. They mark altogether a singular, significant and dramatic divergence from the sensuous realism of the Hellenistic painting of Greece and Rome towards a new spirituality. The emphasis on physical beauty and the perfection of the human body and form, so characteristic of the three-dimensional representation of Hellenistic and Roman art gives way to a lofty spirituality as expressed in the delicacy and grace with which the figures are drawn. Indeed, the portrayals of Moses or Ezra have invited comparison to much later ones of Jesus.

While human figures abound in all the scenes, they are subordinate to the story or action depicted in the scene. The distinctively Jewish style of art of the Dura paintings, emphasised by the continuous narrative sequence of scenes, was homiletical, i.e. they served as instruction to the Jewish community in certain basic tenets of Judaism.

Wall painting of a prophet, possibly Moses or Ezra, reading the Torah. From the west wall at Dura Europos.

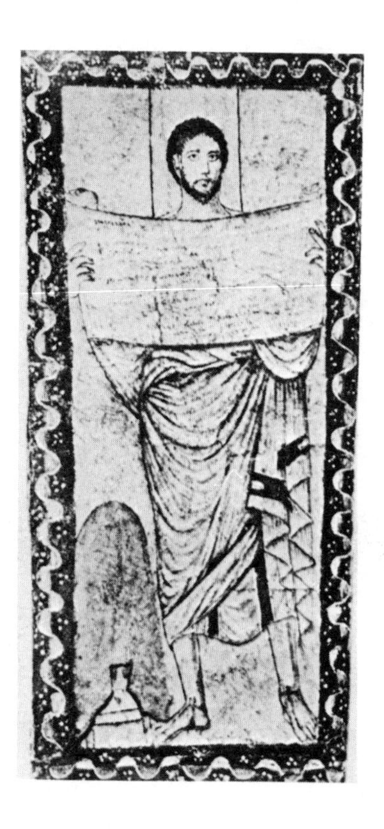

Chief among them was the spiritual message of the transcendental nature of God as manifested in the Torah, through pictorial interpretations of the major events that it describes. There are no representations of God, of course, except for the appearance of anthropomorphic hands in the Ezekiel scenes, but the Divine Will is manifest throughout. This is the significant contribution of the Jewish art of Dura: while the Divine Presence is suggested in all the Biblical scenes, it is His Will, reflected in the visible expression of Divine creativity in the pictorial sequences and the sensitive depictions of the actors in the Biblical dramas which gives the paintings their soaring spirituality and their specifically Jewish character.

These Jewish concepts in art were transmitted to and were reflected in early Christian and Byzantine art in the fourth century and after, and became widely current in Christian art in the middle ages. Jewish and Christian art converged temporarily, but the didactic needs of the Church required substantial revision of the principle of artistic expression of the Divine Will only, and God soon became visible in Christian art. Christian art then tried to combine the expression of the Divine Will with depictions of Jesus. But Judaism and its art could not accept any compromise of the principle of the incorporeality of God expressed in the absolute terms of transcendental monotheism and persisted in giving expression only to the Divine Will in its art.

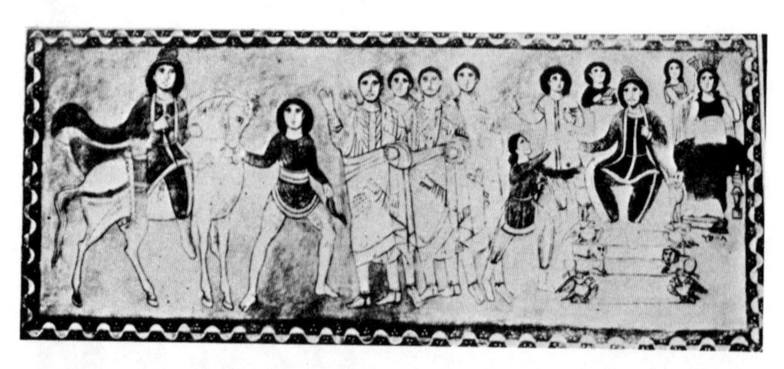

Scenes from the Book of Esther. Left: Haman leads a mounted Mordecai through the streets of Shushan. Right: King Ahasueros and Queen Esther hear a report on the destruction of the enemies of the Jews. From the west wall at Dura Europos.

In certain respects, such as the continuous narrative style, the frontality of the figures and their arrangement in rows and in symmetrical groups, the Dura paintings are classical examples of Byzantine style, but in fact they pre-date similar Byzantine Christian art by perhaps two centuries. Before the discovery at Dura, art historians seeking the antecedents of Christian art, out of which modern Western art developed, erred in taking little or no account of Jewish sources. The discovery of the third-century synagogue at Dura showed this to have been a significant oversight. In the light of the close association of Jews and Christians in the first centuries AD (many of the early Christians recruited throughout the great cities of the Mediterranean world had been Jews) and the knowledge that the Christian liturgy and Church music have their common origins in those of the Jews, it is not surprising to find that Jewish art exerted a profound influence on the development of Christian art as well.

It is now clear that Jewish art served as the antecedent for, and provided the richest source for, Christian art. Until the fourth century, Christian art seems to have been limited, and appeared primarily in burial places. The Christian baptistery in Dura is an exception, and it is believed that the extension of iconoclastic painting to the walls of Christian places of worship was suggested by the contemporary practice of the Jews. (André Grabar, *The Beginnings of Christian Art*, Thames and Hudson, London, p. 26.)

Scholars agree that the Dura synagogue is not unique, and represents what must have been a typical Jewish house of worship in a community of means at that time. It is believed that other synagogues similarly decorated with wall paintings of Biblical scenes, possibly with similar repertoires, existed elsewhere in the ancient Middle East and, if they still survive, may yet be discovered. A considerable number of ancient synagogues of the classical period have been excavated, but none has been found in such a perfect state of preservation as that of Dura. Most have been uncovered with only a floor or a portion of the floor intact, sometimes together with the remains of a wall or a façade and some columns. In a number of synagogues excavated in Israel and elsewhere, dating for the most part from a later period, colourful mosaic floors have been uncovered, but so far none of them has painted walls. But we are getting ahead of our story of Jewish art in antiquity.

Chronologically speaking, the story begins much earlier, in about the thirteenth or fourteenth century BC, with the artist–designer–craftsman Bezalel and the Tabernacle in the Wilderness. Although no Jewish art from this period survives, we do have detailed descriptions and measurements of the Tabernacle and its ceremonial objects to enable us to visualise them and even reconstruct them quite accurately. The Temple of Solomon in Jerusalem, which became the focal point of Jewish artistic creativity about four centuries later, has also disappeared without a trace. Despite extensive excavations at the Temple Mount in Jerusalem, archaeologists have thus far failed to uncover anything that can be ascribed with certainty to the First Temple.

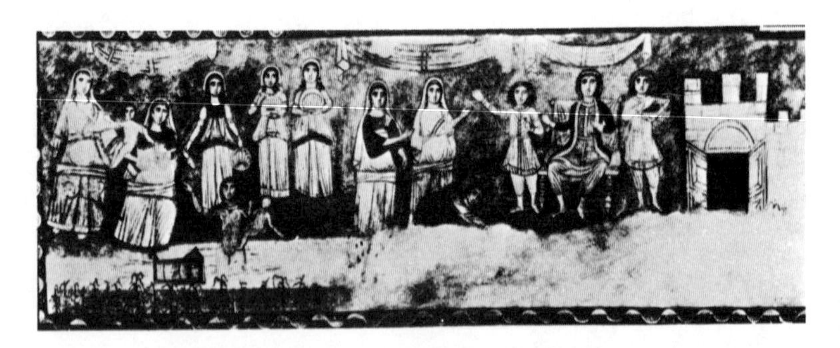

Painting from the west wall at Dura Europos. Left: the discovery of the infant Moses by Pharaoh's daughter. Right: Pharaoh ordering the destruction of all male Jewish infants.

The Bible (*I Kings* and *II Chronicles*), however, allows us to draw some conclusions about the architecture of the First Temple and its ritual objects. We are told that the Temple took six and a half years to build, and that 30,000 Israelites participated in its construction, together with 150,000 Canaanites and 3,300 supervisors. Solomon built the Temple with the help of the king of Tyre and a craftsman from Tyre who served as Solomon's 'Bezalel'. It was a rectangular structure built of ashlar, masonry and timber. It consisted of three rooms – a porch (twenty cubits wide and ten cubits long), a main hall (forty cubits long, twenty cubits wide and twenty cubits high) and the *Sanctum Sanctorum* or Holy of Holies (twenty cubits wide by twenty cubits long by twenty cubits high). A clerestory allowed the penetration of natural light. Inside, the Temple walls and doors were decorated with panelled cedar wood carved with cherubim, palm trees, flowers and chain work, and covered with gold.

The ritual objects in the Temple included ten golden Menorot, a small altar made of cedar and overlaid with gold, and a table holding the shewbread. In the Holy of Holies the Ark of the Covenant was surmounted by two winged cherubim, carved of olive wood and gilded; each was ten cubits high and their four wings had a combined span of twenty cubits. In the Temple court stood the brazen sea, a huge bronze bowl (ten cubits in diameter and five cubits high) supported by twelve oxen. Twin bronze columns stood at the entrance. An impressive, possibly unique structure, the Temple was considered a fitting monument for the monotheistic worship of God.

In 586 BC, Nebuchadnezzar, King of Babylon, destroyed and pillaged the Temple and took the Jews into captivity in Babylon. The construction of the Second Temple by the Jews who returned from Babylonian exile was completed in 515 BC. The Second Temple was modelled after its predecessor and presumably the builders were guided by the Biblical details provided for the construction of the original Temple. There were no major architectural changes, although Ezra writes that those Jews who still recalled the First Temple wept when they saw its modest successor. Cyrus, now king in Babylon, returned the precious vessels taken from the First Temple and, with the exception of the cherubim, the contents of the Second Temple were similar to those of the First.

Much of the Second Temple period, beginning when Judaea came under the suzerainty of Alexander the Great, was marked by a conflict between Judaism and Hellenism – in particular with the Greek concept of the nature of beauty and art. The Seleucids were zealous Hellenisers, and Greek culture gained ground, especially amongst the wealthier, better educated Jews. At first, the Seleucid Kings respected Judaism and even lavished precious gifts on the Temple. However, the attitude changed with the advent of the Syrio-Greek Antiochus IV, who called himself Epiphanes (meaning 'God manifest' in Greek). He carried off the precious Temple vessels, and in 167 BC he instituted the worship of an array of Olympian gods and even installed a statue of Zeus in the Temple grounds. No greater abomination was possible in the eyes of the Jews than the converting of the holy House of God into a pagan temple of Zeus, and the Jews revolted. Led by the priestly Hasmonean family, the revolt ended victoriously for the Jews in 165 BC, and the Temple was purified. Its rededication is today marked by the Jewish festival of *Hanukah*.

Herod (73–4 BC), known as the Great Builder, completed the renovation of the Temple. As a result, the area of the Temple Mount was doubled; the Temple sanctuary itself was raised by forty cubits and broadened by thirty. A new façade of unhewn white stone was provided and many of the gates were covered with gold or silver. A royal basilica now formed a monumental entrance to the Temple: a hundred and sixty-two columns, each over thirty feet (9m) tall, had been set on bases, forming a stoa some one hundred feet (30m) long in basilica fashion along the southern portion of the Temple square. Their richly decorated Corinthian capitals were particularly admired. The Temple walls were covered with gold and decorated. At the entrance to the Temple hall stood a resplendent golden vine, its branches of grapes each as tall as a man.

The legendary splendours of the Herodian Temple can perhaps best be gleaned from the Talmudic statement: 'He who has not seen the Temple of Herod has never in his life seen a beautiful building' (*Bab. Talmud, Bava Batra, IV:a*). Herod's reconstruction of the Temple was designed to enhance his popularity among the Jews. But any credit he may have gained was lost by his murder of his wife and two sons, and by his desecration of the Temple in placing a golden Roman eagle on top of the Temple gates as an object of veneration.

3 The Synagogue in Antiquity

The synagogue (in Hebrew – Bet Haknesset; in Greek – synagoge – meaning a House of Assembly) constitutes one of Judaism's major contributions to the spiritual life of mankind. For the synagogue was built to serve as a place where people could come together to pray rather than to participate in sacrifices. Indeed, the synagogue was to become for the Jewish community what the home was to the individual. The concept of the synagogue as a House of Prayer was subsequently adoped both by Christianity and by Islam.

Already an old and well-established institution by the last decade preceding the destruction of the Temple in 70 AD (one Talmudic passage tells of three hundred and ninety-four synagogues in Jerusalem alone at the time of the destruction, while another counts four hundred and eighty), it became Judaism's central and most important institution only after the Temple ceased to exist. It is then that the synagogue's functions began to include that of a House of Prayer, A House of Study and a Communal Centre, the hub of Jewish religious and community life and an educational centre for young and old. In the words of the English Protestant theologian Robert Travers Herford: 'In all its long history, the Jewish people have scarcely done anything more wonderful than to create the synagogue. No human institution has a longer continous history, and none has done more for the uplifting of the human race.'

The exact origins of the synagogue are lost. Some, including the first-century AD historian Josephus, dated it back as early as the time of Moses, while most others trace the founding of the synagogue to the period of the Babylonian exile in the sixth century BC. The Shef Ve-Yativ Synagogue in Nehardea was said to have been founded by Babylonian exiles under the leadership of King Jehoyachin. An ostracon excavated near Eilat which has been dated back to the sixth century BC, reads '*Bet Kenisa b'Yerushalayim*' – The Synagogue in Jerusalem. The Apocryphal *III Maccabees* mentions the founding of a synagogue at Ptolemais in the reign of Ptolemy IV (221–204 BC).

The earliest positively dated archaeological remains of a syna-

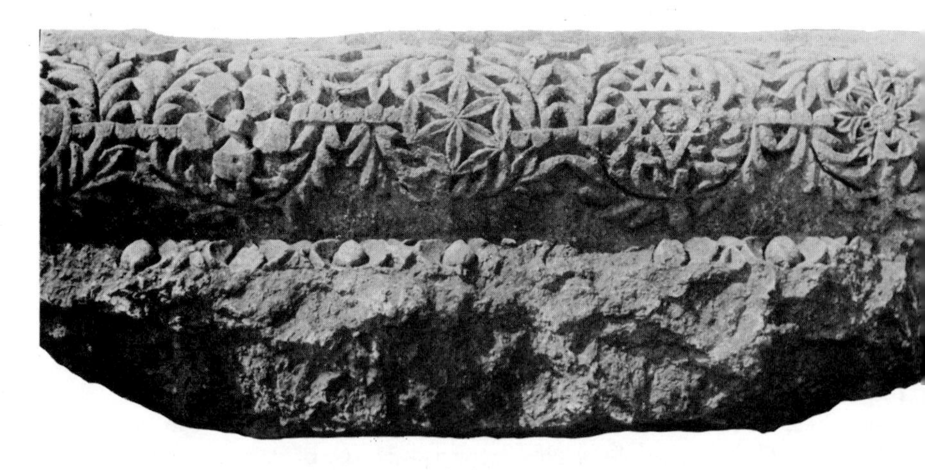

A richly decorated frieze from the interior of the Capernaum synagogue. Acanthus scrolls form medallions with rosettes and a Star of David.

gogue consists of a marble dedicatory slab from Alexandria stating that the Jews dedicated the synagogue to Ptolemy III, Eurgetes (247–221 BC) and his queen Berenice. Unfortunately, this is all that remains of the Alexandrian synagogue. An idea of its magnificence, however, can be gathered from its description in the Talmud which refers to it as 'the great glory of Israel'. It is described as a kind of great basilica, a stoa within a stoa, which contained seventy-one golden chairs, one seat of honour for each elder. Members of different craft guilds sat together. In the middle was a wooden *bimah*, a podium or platform for the reading of the Torah. The synagogue was so huge that the voice of the precentor was inaudible, and in order to communicate with the worshippers he waved a flag to signal congregational responses.

Philo refers to many other synagogues in Alexandria as well, and to synagogues in Rome. At Ostia, near Rome's international airport, the remains of a first-century AD synagogue have been discovered. Josephus refers to a synagogue at Antioch in Syria, possibly the one at which Paul preached. Paul preached in synagogues in Damascus, Athens, Corinth and Thessalonica, as well as in Cyprus. It was from the ranks of synagogue-goers throughout the Mediterranean that the early Christians came.

After the Bar Kochba revolt against Rome (132–135 AD), large numbers of Jews began settling in Galilee, and from the end of the second century and throughout the third century it was a major religious and national centre. Synagogues were built throughout the land of Israel between the second and eighth centuries; the remains of well over a hundred have been found to date, especially in Galilee. Their construction and ornamentation, and the development of Jewish art in later centuries was allowed – even encouraged – by the tolerance of the Roman Severan emperors and their successors.

Generally, these earlier synagogues, especially the Galilean ones, formed a homogeneous group, resembling each other architecturally

Frieze from Capernaum depicting aedicula on wheeels, believed to represent the Ark of the Covenant.

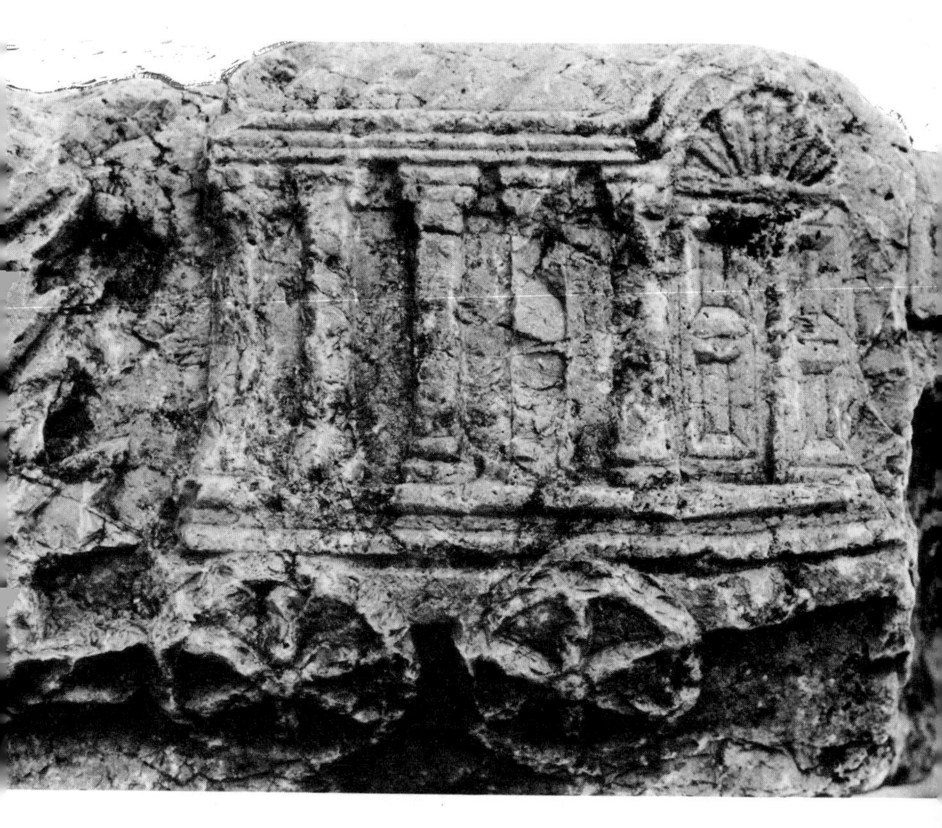

in their plan and method of construction, in the materials used and in the manner of decoration as well as in their imposing appearance. The main room, which served as the assembly and prayer hall, was essentially modelled on the Greco-Roman basilica; that is, it contained two rows of columns along its length to support the roof and divide the room. A third colonnade often ran crosswise, parallel to the façade of the building. The columns, usually not fluted, rested on high square pedestal bases. The capitals were mainly Corinthian, with Ionic and pseudo-Doric rarely being used, and deviated sharply from the classical type, particularly because of the absence of inner spirals. There was usually a second storey to the synagogue which served as an upper gallery for women. The synagogues were oriented toward Jerusalem, in conformity with accepted practice confirmed in Biblical and post-Biblical sources that Jews faced toward Jerusalem when praying. In the early synagogues the Torah scrolls were kept in a chest in a side room and were carried or wheeled into the main hall. In the later Byzantine synagogues an apse in the Jerusalem-oriented wall served as the repository of the Torah; this eventually evolved into a permanent Torah ark.

The synagogues usually had richly-ornamented façades, in contrast to their stark interiors, possibly indicating a desire to attract the people to the synagogue, while not providing distraction from prayer. The upper gallery, however, was frequently decorated with richly-carved stone friezes. A feature of some synagogues was an imposing *cathedra*, called 'The Seat of Moses', which may have been used as a seat of honour or as a place to display the Torah when it was outside the ark and not being read.

By far the most imposing Galilean synagogue discovered is the first century AD synagogue of Capernaum on the shores of the Sea of Galilee. Its architectural splendour and rich artistic ornamentation exceed any other contemporary synagogues excavated in Israel to date. Its bright limestone masonry sets it off from the dark basalt stone houses of the community. It is surrounded by a raised platform and a spacious adjacent courtyard with shaded porticos. The ornamentation in the balustrade and frieze in the upper gallery consists of a richly-decorated stone relief of acanthus leaves. Various symbolic figures appear within the circles of these leaves, such as the hexagram and pentagram, to be called in later periods the 'Star of David' and the 'Seal of Solomon' (but which probably were not yet specifically Jewish symbols), interspersed with clusters of grapes, figs and pomegranates. The lintels of all three doorways bore floral and animal designs, with the central lintel featuring a palm tree and a row of cupids bearing garlands. One frieze shows a representation of the Ark of the Covenant, while one of the Corinthian capitals bears depictions of ritual art objects of the Temple – the seven-branched *menorah*, the *shofar* and the incense shovel. Parts of sculptured lions were discovered in the ruins as well.

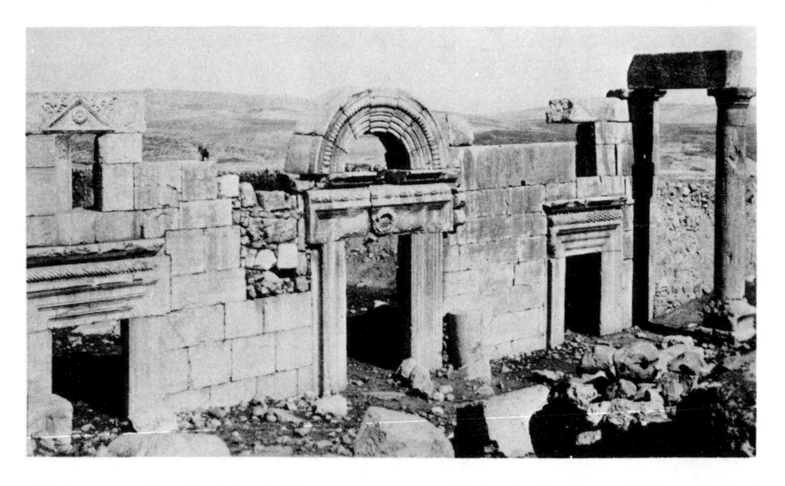

The elaborate façade of the Galilean synagogue at Bar'am before it was fully excavated, showing three ornamented entrances and upper windows, and the remains of the columned porticos fronting it.

In comparing the development of early Christian architecture with the well-developed architecture of the Galilean synagogues, scholars reason that the basilica-type synagogue of ancient Israel and elsewhere served as models for and exerted considerable influence on the development of Christian Church architecture (André Grabar, *The Beginnings of Christian Art*, pp. 171, 172, 173).

The principal ornamentation of the later Byzantine type of synagogue was that of mosaic floors, made with coloured stones or glass fragments. It is believed that some synagogues may have also had wall paintings, but of those few synagogues found to date with their walls intact none has had any painting. But the existence of painting has been attested to by the passage in the Jerusalem Talmud referred to in Chapter 2 (p. 20). Archaeological digs of sites dating from the fourth century onward have uncovered mosaic floors with representational art in synagogues in Israel and elsewhere in the ancient world, but nowhere in greater number or with a richer and more varied repertory of pictorial representation than in Israel.

The subject matter for the synagogue mosaic floors came primarily from nature and from the Bible. The signs of the Zodiac were a recurring theme, often with constellations inscribed with their names and usually depicted in a circular, radial arrangement with the chariot of the sun at the centre, and personifications of the four seasons around it. It has been speculated that this theme originally, and possibly more appropriately, appeared on synagogue ceilings (much as zodiacal signs have appeared on the ceilings of European synagogues in recent times) and at some point moved downward to the synagogue floor. The *menorah* appears very often in these mosaics, usually together with the *shofar* (a horn 'trumpet'), the *lulav* (palm), the *etrog* (citron) and the Temple ritual implements.

The best example of preserved synagogue mosaic pavements, and one of the finest examples of Jewish art of the Byzantine period, is that of the sixth-century synagogue at Bet Alpha, a small Galilean village, unearthed in 1928. Signed by the two rural artists, Marianos and his son Hanina (who are also associated with another local synagogue in nearby Bet Shean), the Bet Alpha mosaic is in the form of an oblong rectangle consisting of three major panels. In the upper one is a Torah Ark flanked by two menorot, two rampant Lions of Judah, two lulavim and etrogim and various ritual objects. The centre panel depicts the zodiac in a circular radial fashion, with four figures on the sides representing the four seasons. In the lower panel there is a single Biblical scene depicting an incident central to

Opposite: *part of the mosaic pavement at the 6th-century Bet Alpha synagogue. Top panel: twin rampant Lions of Judah and various ritual symbols flank a Torah Ark. Centre panel: the signs of the zodiac and the four seasons. Lower panel: the Binding of Isaac showing Abraham, Isaac, Eliezer, Ishmael, the hand from heaven and the ram.*

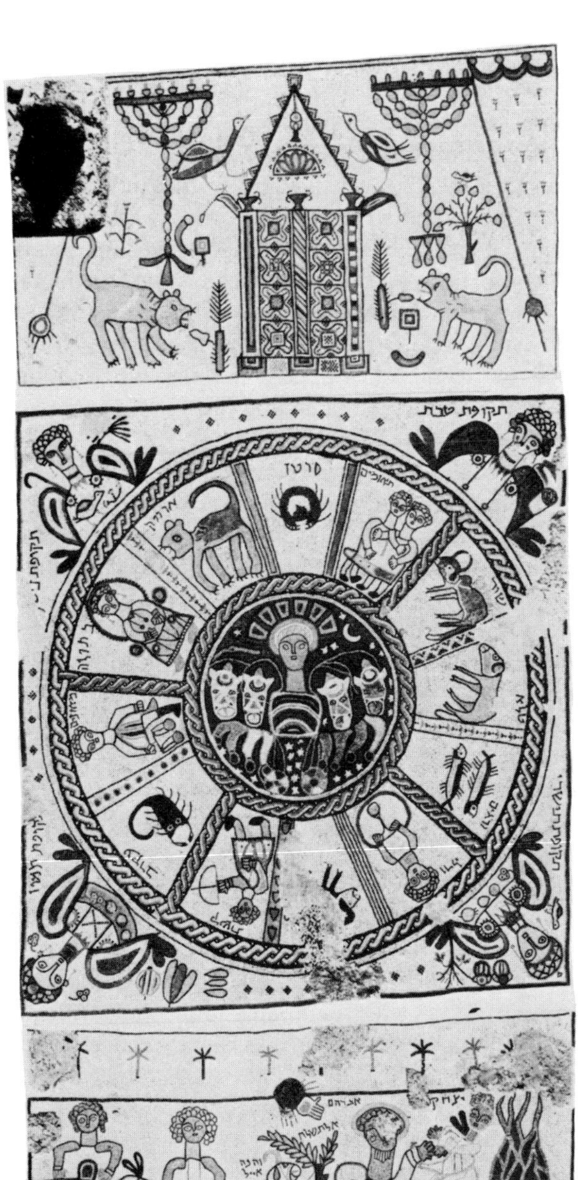

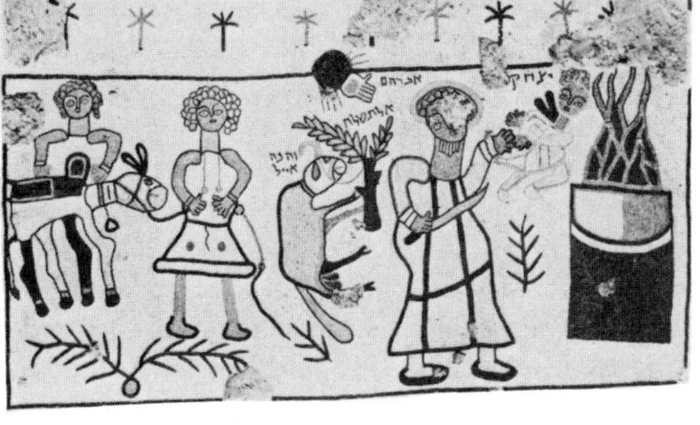

Judaism, the Binding of Isaac, which symbolises the Jew's readiness to sacrifice himself at all cost to fulfil God's will. The scene figures prominently in the Dura synagogue wall paintings and in Jewish art throughout the ages. In typical Byzantine fashion, the faces of the figures are all depicted frontally, no matter how the bodies are turned, with considerable emphasis on the eyes. While the figures are all composed rather primitively, lacking consistent scale, proportion and anatomic expertise, the colourful work speaks with freshness and directness and establishes a personal rapport with the viewer. The three panels are framed in a band filled with geometric ornamentation and depictions of flora and fauna.

The Byzantine synagogue mosaics appear in their richest and most harmonious balance in Bet Alpha, but since the folkloristic artists, Marianos and Hanina, were hardly artistic innovators, it is fairly certain that their work was modelled after many even finer examples. This is borne out by the beautiful mosaic floor of the synagogue of Hamat built in the fourth century at the Sea of Galilee near Tiberias, which was excavated by a team of archaeologists in 1961. It contains a Torah ark and a radial zodiac featuring Helios, the sun god, with a chariot at the centre and menorot, shofarot, lulavim, etrogim and incense shovels, and in general design and arrangement was similar to those executed two centuries later at Bet Alpha, except that the lowest panel has twin rampant lions of Judah instead of a Biblical scene.

Mosaic floors uncovered at Byzantine synagogues at Susiya and Bet Guvrin also feature depictions of the Torah Ark, flanked by twin seven-branched menorot surrounded by shofarot and Temple ritual implements. A mosaic floor in the vestibule of the fifth-century trans-Jordanian synagogue at Jerash features Noah and the animals leaving the ark, and the menorah, etrog, lulav and shafar. Daniel in the Lion's Den is the main subject in a synagogue mosaic in Na'aran which, unfortunately, is only partially preserved. One panel depicts birds and animals and another, the rather poorly preserved zodiac wheel, with Helios driving a chariot in the centre.

The discovery in 1966 of a large sixth-century synagogue in Gaza revealed an imposing figure of David, identified by name, playing the harp. Around him are various wild animals being soothed by the music. Many animals are shown in medallions linked by vines – lion cubs suckling from a lioness, a leopard, giraffes, a zebra, a stag, foxes, peacocks, and a bird in a cage. A contemporary mosaic floor, probably executed by the same hand or at least produced in the same workshop, was discovered in a sixth-century synagogue in Maon, a community neighbouring Gaza. Depicted on the fifty-five medallions (eighteen of which are wholly or partially lost) are elephants, stags, peacocks, hens, a flamingo, partridges, doves, an ibex and baskets of fruit. It also features a seven-branched menorah, along with shofar, lulav and etrogim, twin Lions of Judah and twin palm trees. A similar type of mosaic arrangement is found in a contemporary synagogue floor in Isfiya on Mount Carmel in the north. In addition to grapevines, there are a peacock and other birds, a menorah, a shofar, a lulav and etrogim. It also contains a zodiac wheel, the best designed and best executed, if not the best preserved, of all zodiacs in synagogue mosaics.

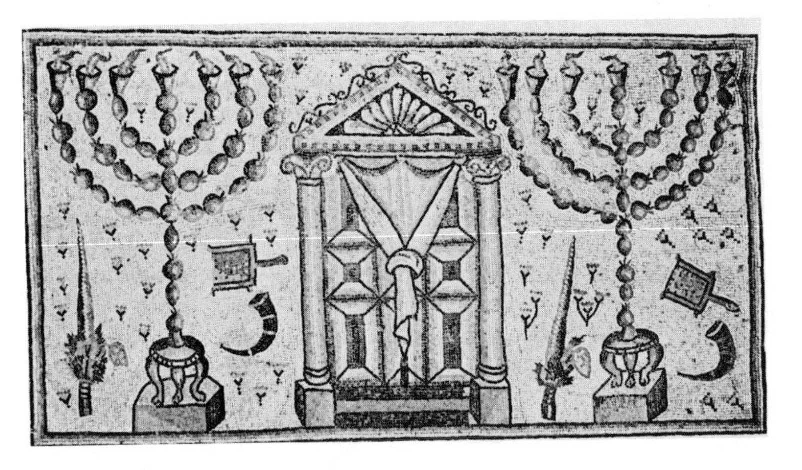

The mosaic pavement at the 4th-century synagogue at Hamat, near Tiberias. Menorahs, etrogs, lulavs, shofars and incense shovels flank a Torah Ark.

Excavations in the Jordan Valley of the synagogue of Bet Shean in 1970–71 uncovered a mosaic floor pavement with similar medallions, nine of them in rows of three, encircled by vine tendrils growing from a vase. Within the medallions are goats, birds, cows and a peacock. At the centre is a menorah flanked by an etrog and Temple ritual implements and the word 'Shalom' (peace) which frequently appeared on ancient synagogue inscriptions. An inscription identifies the artists as Marianos and Hanina, who did the Bet Alpha mosaic. The Bet Shean mosaic is characterised by the phenomenon of *horror vacçui*, with the artists filling in every available space around the border frame with geometric ornamentation and depictions of birds, animals and grape clusters.

At En Gedi, the community by the shores of the Dead Sea near the cave cliffs where David hid from Saul, the remains of a synagogue dating from the late sixth or early seventh century were excavated in 1971–72. A bronze synagogue menorah was found, along with three menorot in the mosaic floor. The central portion of the floor was a tastefully organised decoration consisting of four cranes inside a circle within a square. Twin peacocks flank grape clusters in the corners of the rectangular band framing the central decoration. This is surrounded by a carpet-like geometric ornamentation which makes up the bulk of the mosaic floor.

The animal designs are somewhat reminiscent of those in a beautiful synagogue mosaic at Naro (now Hamam Lif) in Tunisia, which dates back to the fourth or early fifth century. There are two main scenes in the well-arranged four panels, one of fish and ducks swimming in water, another of brightly-coloured peacocks at a fountain flanked by birds and palm trees. The two other panels are decorated with stylised cartouches, each containing birds or flanking animals. At the centre is a Greek inscription, flanked by two seven-branched menorot within ornamental cartouches. The scene has been interpreted in a Messianic vein, with the central theme considered to be a portrayal of paradise.

4 Early Funerary Art

There are three primary sources for the study of ancient Jewish funerary art: the monumental tombs to the north of Jerusalem, the great necropolis in Bet Shearim near Haifa and the Jewish catacombs in Rome.

Outside Jerusalem, on the slopes of the Temple Mount and the Mount of Olives, lies a vast cemetery in use for some three thousand years. Between the two hills, in the Kidron Valley, are a group of imposing tombs. Some are hewn from the solid rock flank at the base of the Mount of Olives and form single architectonic units, whereas others combine the natural mountain rock with ashlars quarried from the mountain. Some are family mausoleums, and some are memorials to individuals.

Monumental in proportion, the imposing tombs with their monolithic columns and pilasters carved out of the solid rock mountainside sometimes resemble the fronts of palaces and temples. In fact, in the second century, Pausanias, the author of the 'Descriptions of Greece', admiringly likened the monument built by Queen Helena of Adiabne in the Kidron Valley at the end of the Second Temple period to the mausoleum of Halicarnassus, one of the seven wonders of the world. Although the turbulent history of Jerusalem has not been kind to many of its above-ground monuments, still the remains of a number of them offer eloquent witness to their early magnificence. Of chief interest is the aforementioned Tomb of the Queen of Adiabne, now known as the Tomb of the Kings in Jerusalem, the Tomb of Zecharia, the so-called Tomb of Absalom, and the Tomb of Jason, to the west of the Old City.

In northern Israel, on the southern slopes of lower Galilee on the Nazareth to Haifa road, Bet Shearim's burial caves provide a rich source for the study of Jewish funerary art as well as Jewish folklore of the period. Beginning at the end of the second century, Bet Shearim became a central burial place for Jews of Israel and throughout the Diaspora.

Within the caves are stone carvings, carved sarcophagi and ossuaries, and graffiti ornamented with geometric and representational art. The latter included animals, ships, flowers and a wealth of Jewish symbols and motifs, particularly the seven-branched menorah. The Torah Ark is also represented, along with the shofar, the etrog and lulav and the Temple ritual implements, all of which are also found in the remains of ancient synagogues. The carved rock includes architectural ornamentation, such as columns, capitals, arches and ornamental stone doors in working condition that imitate wooden ones in every detail, including bolts, locks and keys.

The Roman catacombs play a major role in the study of early Christian art, for although the scenes are primarily Old Testament ones, they provide the only large scale example of early Christian painting. The extensive examples of Jewish painting at the Dura Synagogue places the relative significance of the Jewish art of the catacombs in a decidedly secondary role.

In the six labyrinthine Jewish catacombs discovered in Rome, mainly along the Appian Way, which were used from the first to the fourth century, there are several examples of Jewish funerary art. As in other contemporary examples of Jewish art in Israel and the Diaspora, the menorah was the most extensively employed Jewish symbol. Of some eighty-three decorated catacombs at Monteverde, no fewer than seventy-eight feature the menorah. It is thought that, apart from its deep symbolic significance, the menorah's conspicuous use in Rome during the early centuries relates to its prominent representation on the Arch of Titus in Rome, where it is shown being carried by Jewish slaves to Rome following Titus' destruction of Jerusalem and the Temple in the year 70.

Other Jewish symbols represented in the catacombs are the shofar, the lulav and etrog and a circumcision knife. In addition, birds and animals abound: lions, chickens, sheep, rams, cows, eagles, peacocks and a dolphin on a trident, as well as palm trees, baskets and garlands of flowers and fruit. The sun and the stars are also shown, and interestingly enough, some pagan, mythological figures such as Victory crowning a nude young man and Fortune with the horn of plenty. In the Villa Torlonia catacomb, prominent on an arched wall is a Torah Ark, doors wide open to reveal the Torah scrolls. It is flanked by two imposing menorot and other Jewish religious symbols.

A sarcophagus fragment in the Vigna Randandini catacomb depicts two winged cherubs holding a round medallion with a large menorah between them. Next to one stands a nude figure holding

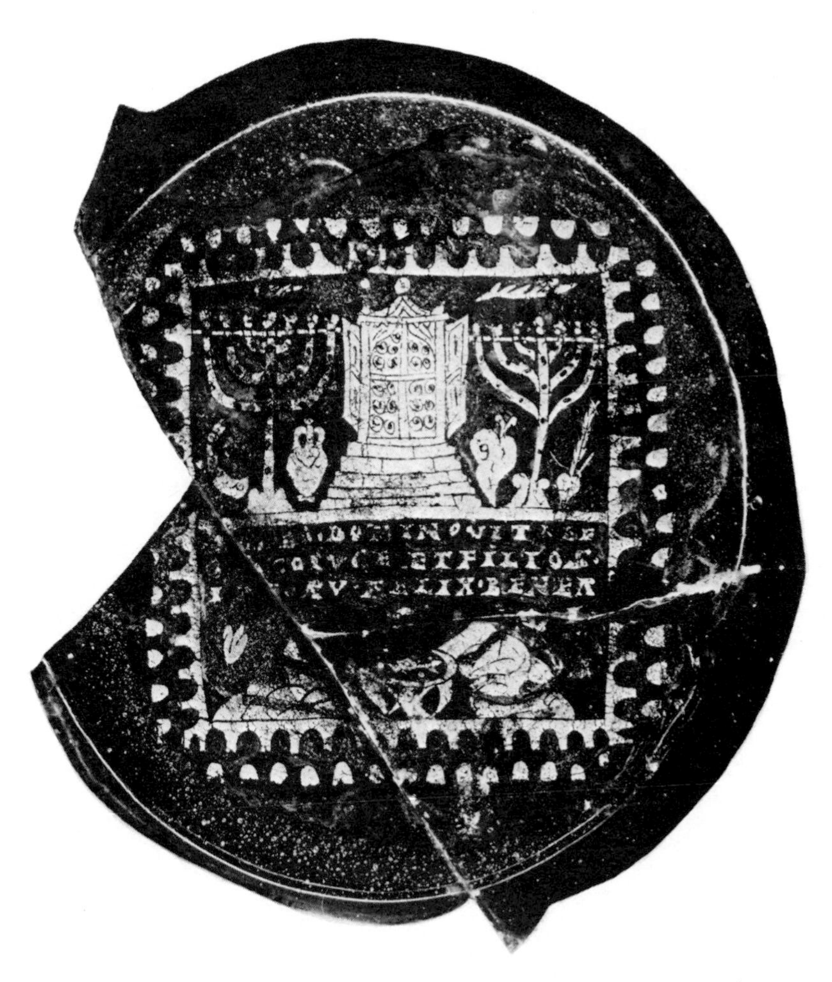

Jewish gold glass, featuring twin menorahs, lulavs and etrogs flanking a Torah Ark, c. 3rd to 4th century.

a basket of fruit in one hand and a pair of geese in the other. Beneath the medallion is a smaller secondary group of three nudes treading grapes in a vat, which has two spouts in the form of lion heads. The existence of possible pagan motifs have given rise to questions about the orthodoxy of those commissioning the works. Some view it simply as pagan motifs having been incorporated into Jewish art, but the predominant view is that the pagan symbols had lost their original meaning and had become commonly accepted decorative themes without their original identification. This was the case with the Helios used in the zodiacal wheels of Byzantine mosaic floors.

The earliest examples of Jewish art known (before both the discovery of catacomb art and the synagogue mosaic pavements, and even before the discovery of the Dura wall paintings) were the Jewish 'gold glasses', consisting of thin pieces of gold leaf with Jewish artistic motifs and symbols on them, laminated between two layers of glass. Fourteen, which are definitely Jewish, have been found; another one hundred and fifty found are Christian, and yet another two hundred and eighty lack positive religious identification. The Jewish ones usually feature a Torah Ark with the doors open revealing Torah scrolls, often flanked by twin Lions of Judah couchant, and there is almost always one or two menorot plus other ritual objects.

It is speculated that the 'gold glasses' may have been the bases of Kiddush cups used at Sabbath and festival meals. Most of the gold glasses, both Jewish and non-Jewish, were created in the early centuries AD and may well have been executed by Jewish craftsmen employed in ancient glass-making centres from Phoenicia to Alexandria to Rome to Cologne.

5 Hebrew Illuminated Manuscripts

'The sword and the book were given from Heaven wrapped together. The Holy One, Blessed be He, said to Israel: If you guard what is written in this book you will be delivered from the sword – and if not, in the end it will kill you' (Midrash-Leviticus Rabah, XXXV). Throughout the history of the Jewish people, great emphasis has been placed on the acquisition and transmission of knowledge. Therefore, it is no coincidence that the Jews, numerically a minute segment of the world's population, have made such an extraordinary contribution to culture, science and medicine.

The book has always been valued and treasured by Jews. Indeed, the *Genizah*, the place of concealment where old sacred books must be hidden away, literally means 'treasury' which indicates the significance attributed to the book in the Jewish tradition even when it was no longer usable. The examination of the contents of several Genizot, notably that of an old Cairo synagogue at the end of the last century which contained hundreds of thousands of manuscript pages, many going back more than a thousand years, has yielded invaluable information to scholars and historians.

Having chosen the book over the sword, the book has been inextricably bound up with the fate of the Jews, accompanying them through all their wanderings and vicissitudes. So much so that the book became one of the principal targets in attacks against the Jews, beginning with the book burnings in Paris on June 17, 1242, in which twenty-four cartloads of Hebrew books went up in flames, and culminating in the mass book burnings of the Nazis when countless millions of volumes were ruthlessly destroyed. But the Jewish people, along with its companion, has survived.

The oldest Biblical manuscripts extant are the Dead Sea Scrolls which date back to the first century BC to the first century AD. None of these was illuminated, which is not surprising, since the *Halacha* (Jewish law) prohibits any form of adornment for Biblical

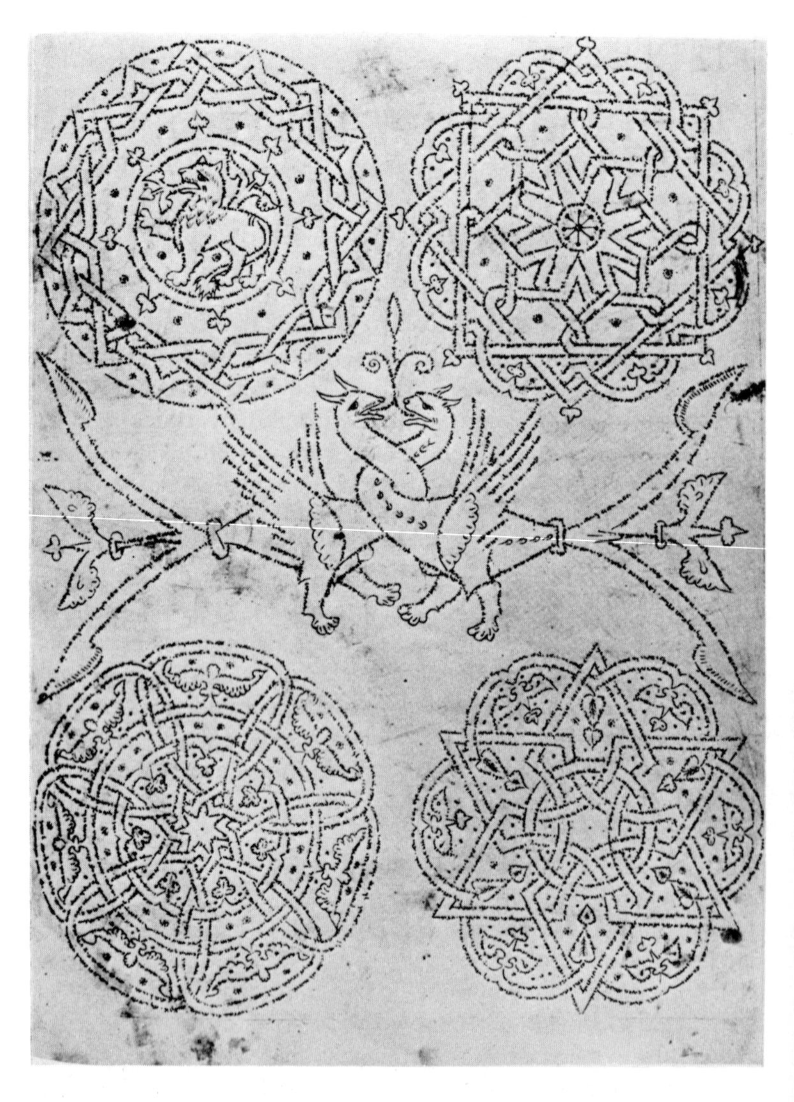

Illuminated Bible, with Hebrew micrography. Germany, 13th century.

scrolls, including vowel signs and punctuation, in addition to laying down exacting requirements regarding format, such as columns and spacing.

There are a number of references which point to the practice of Hebrew manuscript illumination in antiquity. The Talmud declares that if a Torah scroll is found with God's name written in gold it is to be hidden. In a discussion of a Torah belonging to 'Alexandrians', where the name of God was written in gold throughout, the sages in the first half of the second century directed that the Torah be hidden in a Genizah. In the so-called 'Letter of Aristeas', dating from the beginning of the second century BC, the presentation copy of the Septuagint (i.e. the Greek translation of the Old Testament by the seventy scribes of Alexandria) given to King Ptolemy was said to have been written entirely in gold. Talmudic references to a family of *katvanim umanim* (lit. artist-scribes) as well as to the existence of a special class of calligraphers at the time of the Second Temple also point to the existence of Hebrew illuminated manuscripts in the classical period.

The similarity of artistic themes in many of the synagogue mosaics, and in examples of funerary art and gold glasses of the Byzantine period, to those used in medieval Hebrew illuminated manuscripts, as well as in manuscripts dating from the ninth and tenth centuries onward, indicate that Hebrew manuscript illumination flourished from the early centuries AD to modern times. Quite possibly such illuminated manuscripts were used by the Dura artists to guide them in their synagogue paintings of Biblical scenes. However, the only conclusive evidence can be supplied by the actual discovery of some of these manuscripts, a discovery which would rank in importance with the finding of the Dead Sea Scrolls and the synagogue wall paintings at Dura Europos.

As in different forms of Jewish art, the styles and motifs of Hebrew illuminated manuscripts reflected artistic trends prevalent in the countries in which the works were created. Thus, the absence of figurative art in the Hebrew illuminated manuscripts produced in Moslem countries owes less to Rabbinical objection than to the iconoclasm of the Moslem host community which itself can be traced to the influence of early Jewish converts.

The characteristics of the Hebrew alphabet particularly lend themselves to elongation and stylisation. The repetitive, rhythmic nature

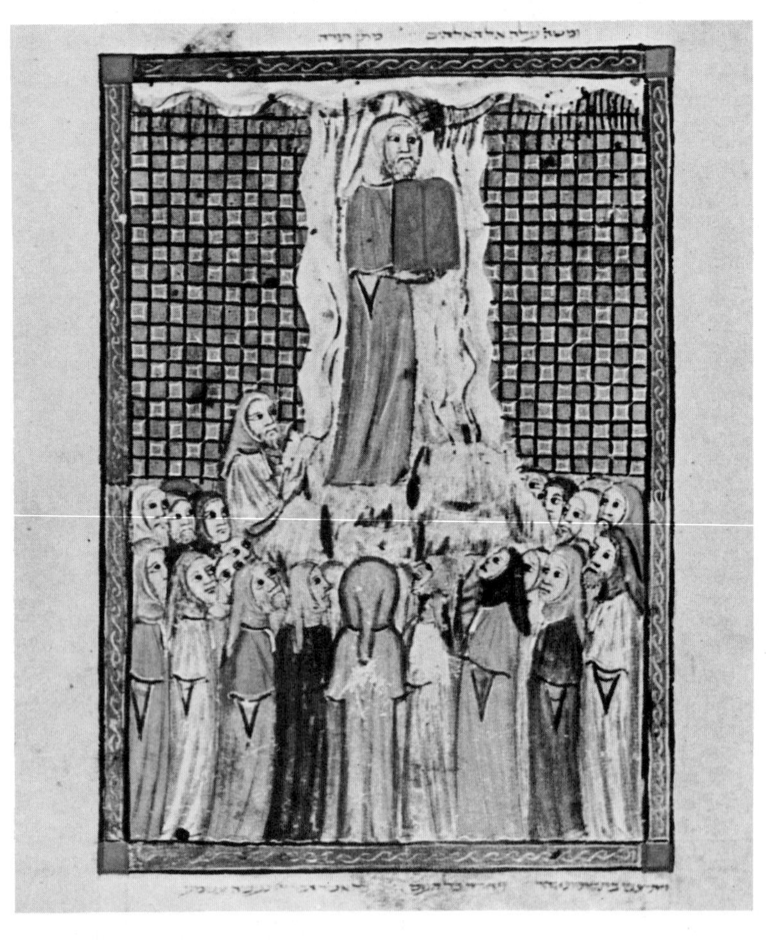

Illuminated page from the Sarajevo Hagadah. Spain, 14th century.

of certain letters along with the ascending and descending lines of others provides material for interesting and decorative motifs. Lacking capital letters, often the whole first word, and at times even the entire opening phrase, was given prominence, rather than initial letters, as is the case with illuminations in the Latin alphabet. Where initial Hebrew letters were elongated, they were often distinguished by colour, usually gold, and filled in with floral or geometric ornamentations or with animals or grotesques.

A characteristic form of decorating Hebrew manuscripts was the use of micrography, a laborious and painstaking art involving the ornamental use of minuscule Hebrew words to form decorative patterns. Often entire carpet pages were decorated in this manner. Sometimes the illumination was done by special artists, but quite often the illuminators were the scribes themselves, for whom beautiful Hebrew calligraphy was but one form of artistic expression.

The Bible, of course, was a major subject of Jewish manuscript illumination, especially in the oriental world. Prayer books, especially *mahzorim* for the festivals, were frequent subjects. Whatever iconoclastic restraints existed regarding manuscript illumination for the holy books used in the synagogue, they were often relaxed when it came to decorating the *Hagadah* – lit. 'the relating' of the Exodus story – read at the festive Passover *seder* feast (see Chapter 10). Legal and philosophical manuscripts such as the major treatises of Maimonides were also illuminated. Occasionally, secular works of general interest, such as astronomical or medical treatises, would be translated into Hebrew and illuminated. The *Ketubah*, the obligatory Jewish marriage contract, was a particularly popular document for illumination, especially in oriental countries and Italy (see Chapter 11).

The styles of Hebrew manuscript illumination can be broadly separated into several major divisions – the Oriental school, the Spanish school, the Italian and the German schools.

The earliest examples extant of Hebrew manuscript illuminations are oriental ones dating from the ninth to the thirteenth centuries. Their ornamentation consists mainly of floral and geometric decoration in carpet pages, often with extensive use of micrography in the opening pages and in the colophons. Figurative art is non-existent and textual illustration of any kind is very rare. The Egyptian and Yemenite manuscripts, in particular, are distinguished by their detailed and patterned micrography of traditional Hebrew commentary alongside the text. Occasionally there is included a page on which Temple ritual implements are depicted.

Spanish Hebrew illuminated manuscripts contain many of the

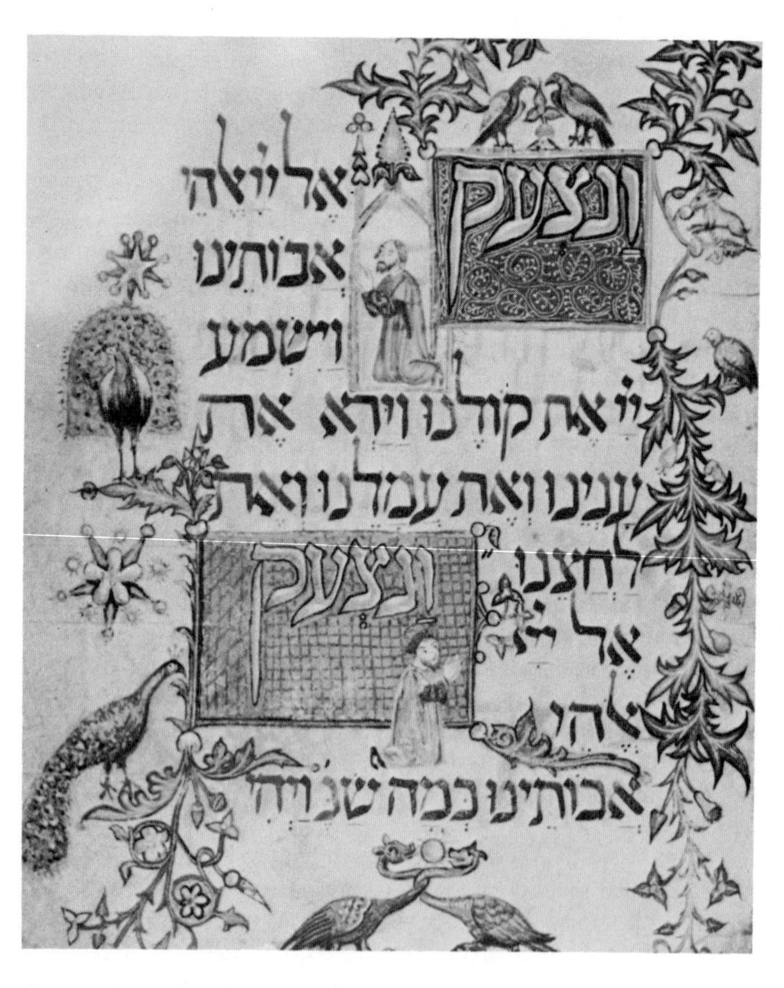

Illuminated page from the Kaufmann Hagadah. Spain, 14th century.

motifs found in oriental ones, and were obviously strongly influenced by them. Depictions of Temple ritual implements appear, sometimes spread over several pages. Micrography prevailed even more extensively than in the oriental manuscripts, especially in

Spanish Old Testaments, often spread over whole carpet pages. Zoomorphic and anthropomorphic letters appear frequently as decorative elements, especially in Hagadot.

An outstanding example of Spanish Hebrew manuscript illumination is the Kennicott Bible, now in the Bodleian Library at Oxford. This Bible was completed in 1475 in Corunna in north-west Spain by the scribe Moses ibn Zabara, who worked in close collaboration with the illuminator, Joseph ibn Hayim. In a virtually perfect state of preservation, the Bible consists of approximately nine hundred pages of the finest vellum, including seventy-seven fully-decorated pages and one hundred and seventy-three pages with marginal decorations. Lavishly illustrated, the work is an admixture of various styles – Gothic, Romanesque and Moorish elements along with those of the Renaissance. These are reflected in the diverse architectural styles forming the framework for many pages of text. It contains numerous examples of delicate interlacing ornamentation which form interwoven borders, as well as many examples of Hebrew micrography set in ornamental patterns, all meticulously and beautifully executed. As in many contemporary Hebrew illuminated manuscripts, zoomorphic elements serve as decorative features; birds and animals, grotesques, dragons and other mythological beasts are frequently represented. The artist's sense of humour is evident in delightful scenes depicting an army of cats armed with swords and shields preparing to storm a castle defended by mice and an army of hares led by their king besieging a wolf in his castle. Human figures are depicted, sometimes even in the nude. Strangely enough, most of the illustrations do not relate to the accompanying text. Exceptions are a stylised depiction of an old King David seated on his throne, and a narrative sequence of the Jonah and the whale story. Most strange is the artist's colophon, in which each letter in the inscription is made up of wild combinations of zoomorphic and anthropomorphic figures and grotesques.

Usually included in the Spanish school, although in some respects stylistically distinguished, are the illuminated Portuguese Hebrew manuscripts from the fifteenth century produced in Lisbon. Characterised in the main by a lack of textual illustrations, they often have beautifully-illuminated borders richly ornamented in geometric and floral patterns, especially in their opening pages or at chapter beginnings. Particularly fine examples of this style can be found in the

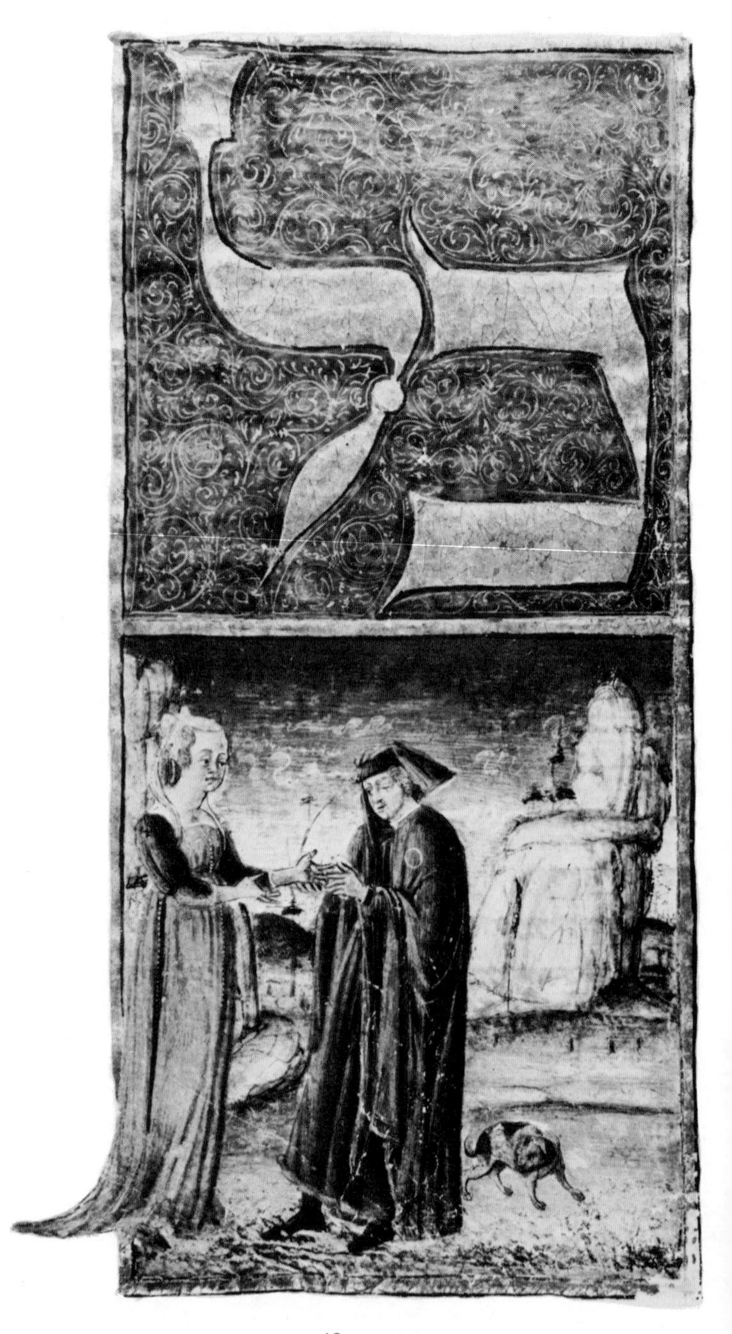

Opposite: *illuminated miniature from a handbook of Jewish laws. Padua, Italy, 1477.*

British Museum's *Mishne Torah*, dating back to 1472, the Hispanic Society Bible of the late fifteenth century and the Bibliothèque National Portuguese Bible. A magnificent example of an elaborately decorated Hebrew manuscript is the Lisbon Bible of 1483.

The Spanish school of Hebrew manuscript illumination, which flourished in the thirteenth and fourteenth centuries, produced some notable Hagadot. Among the finest examples are the fourteenth-century Sarajevo, Kaufmann and Golden Hagadot, all of which have been reproduced in facsimile editions in recent years. What distinguishes most Spanish Hagadot are the many full-page illustrations of Biblical scenes preceding, and unrelated to, the text.

In the Hagadah now ensconced in the Yugoslavia National Museum, Sarajevo, no fewer than sixty-nine miniatures, mostly of Biblical scenes, fill thirty-four pages preceding the text. These begin with the Creation and end with Moses's final address and his blessing to Joshua. The Sarajevo Hagadah miniatures bear a striking resemblance to the Latin Bible manuscript illuminations produced at that time in Spain. However, the illuminator's scrupulous abstention from anthropomorphic representations of God, and his obvious intimate acquaintance with Jewish Midrashic sources and certain Jewish customs and traditions indicate that he was a Jew, perhaps even the manuscript's scribe.

The Kaufmann Hagadah is also prefaced by Biblical miniatures, but with fewer illuminations (only fourteen full-page miniatures) distributed throughout the book. Here too the artist's knowledge of Midrashic lore indicates he was probably a Jew.

One of the most beautiful illuminated manuscripts of the medieval period, and undoubtedly the most elegant of all Hagadot, is the Golden Hagadah, so named because of the burnished gold background of its miniatures. The Golden Hagadah is prefaced by fourteen full-page illuminations, including Biblical scenes from Exodus and depictions of customs relating to Passover preparations. The different illuminators of the Hagadah reflect a strong French Gothic influence in their styles. Although the miniatures show an awareness of Midrashic teachings, the inclusion of such a purely Christian element as the halo around an angel appearing before Moses at the Burning Bush would tend to indicate that the artists were not working in the Jewish tradition and might not have been Jewish.

Figurative art abounds in the illuminated Hebrew manuscripts of South Germany from the medieval period. Here we find the unique practice of substituting the heads of birds and animals for those of humans, or the animal-like distortion of facial elements, with extraordinary results. While the iconoclastic tendencies prevalent in local Christian illumination may have had some influence on the customs, it probably had more to do with the existence of a contemporary *Halachic* decision by a leading area rabbinic sage regarding depictions of human beings on religious Jewish books. Apparently, substituting the heads of birds or animals for human heads was considered an acceptable means of not violating a prohibition against complete depictions of human beings. While the evidence of such a *Halachic Responsum* is lacking, such a ruling could well have come from the spiritual leader of thirteenth-century German Jewry, Rabbi Meir of Rothenburg (1215–1293). It is known that he disapproved of the illustration of Hebrew prayer books because they distract the reader from prayer, but he did not otherwise prohibit such artistic endeavours.

A characteristic example of fourteenth-century German Hebrew illuminated manuscripts is the *Mahzor Lipsia*. Containing prayers for the festivals of the Jewish year, it is lavishly illustrated with full page and marginal illustrations. The manuscript features illustrations and initial words depicting the Purim story from the book of Esther in a continuous narrative style. Passover scenes show the way that *matza* (wafer-like unleavened bread) was prepared in the fourteenth century. There is also a chase scene with Moses shown parting the waters of the Red Sea and the pursuing Egyptians depicted as medieval knights in armour. *Rosh Hashana* scenes include the sound-

Opposite: *illuminated page from a Hebrew legal treatise, featuring a bride and wedding musicians. Italy, 15th century.*

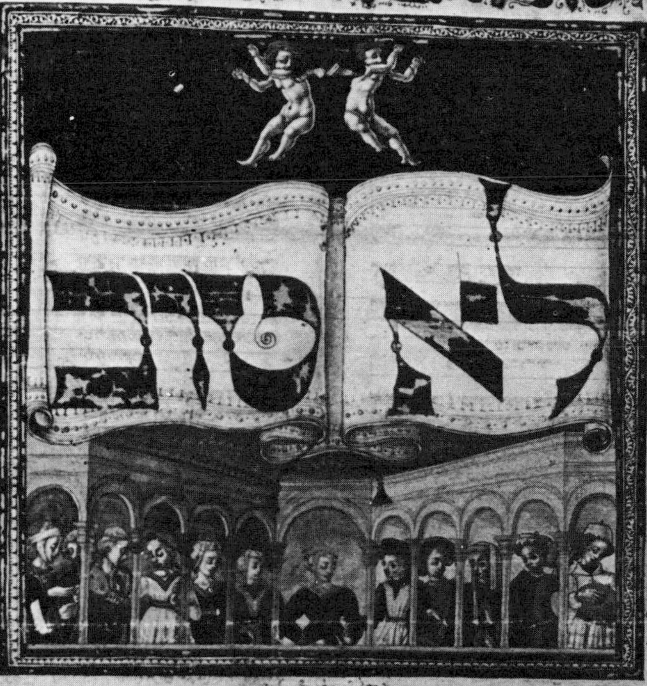

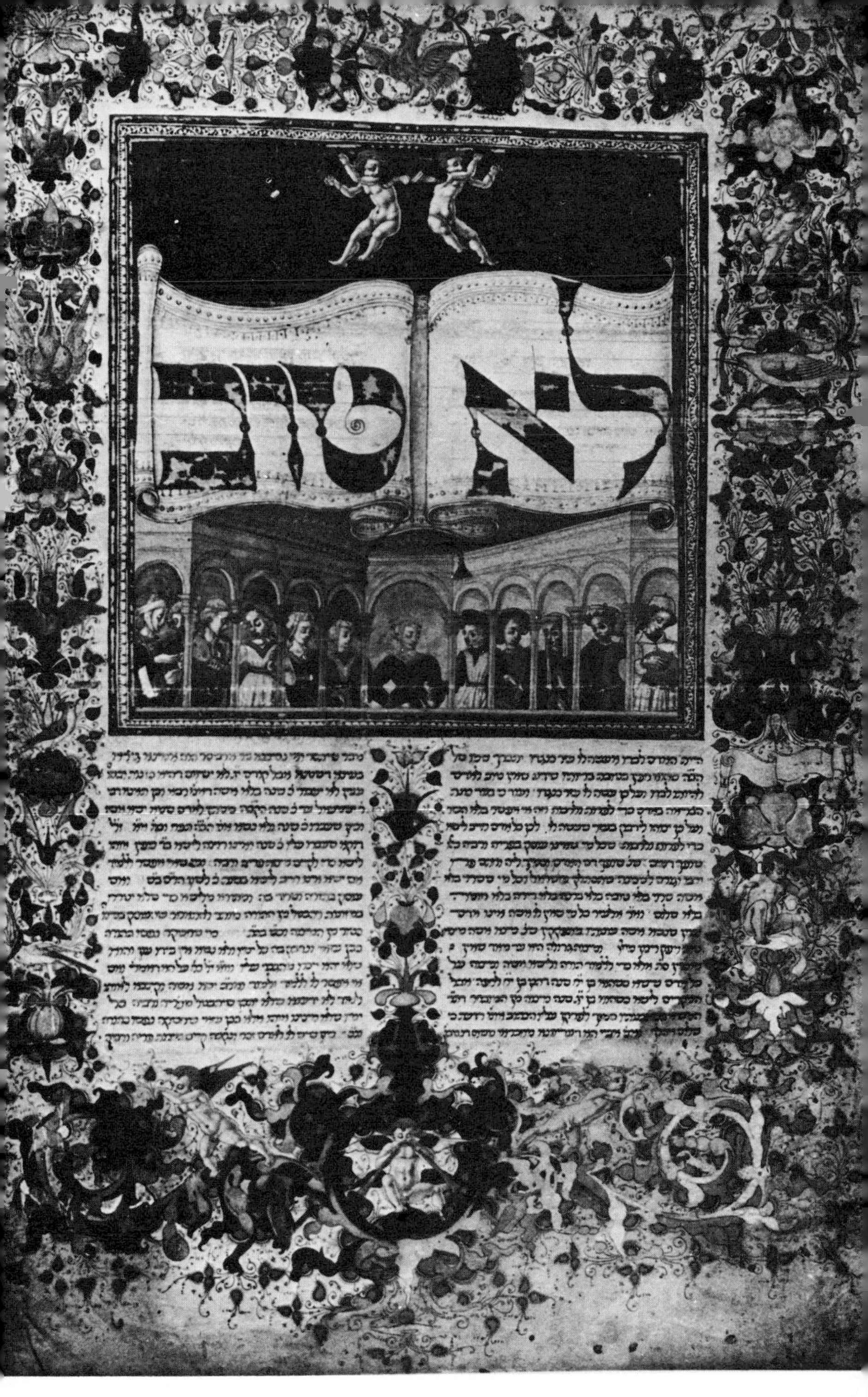

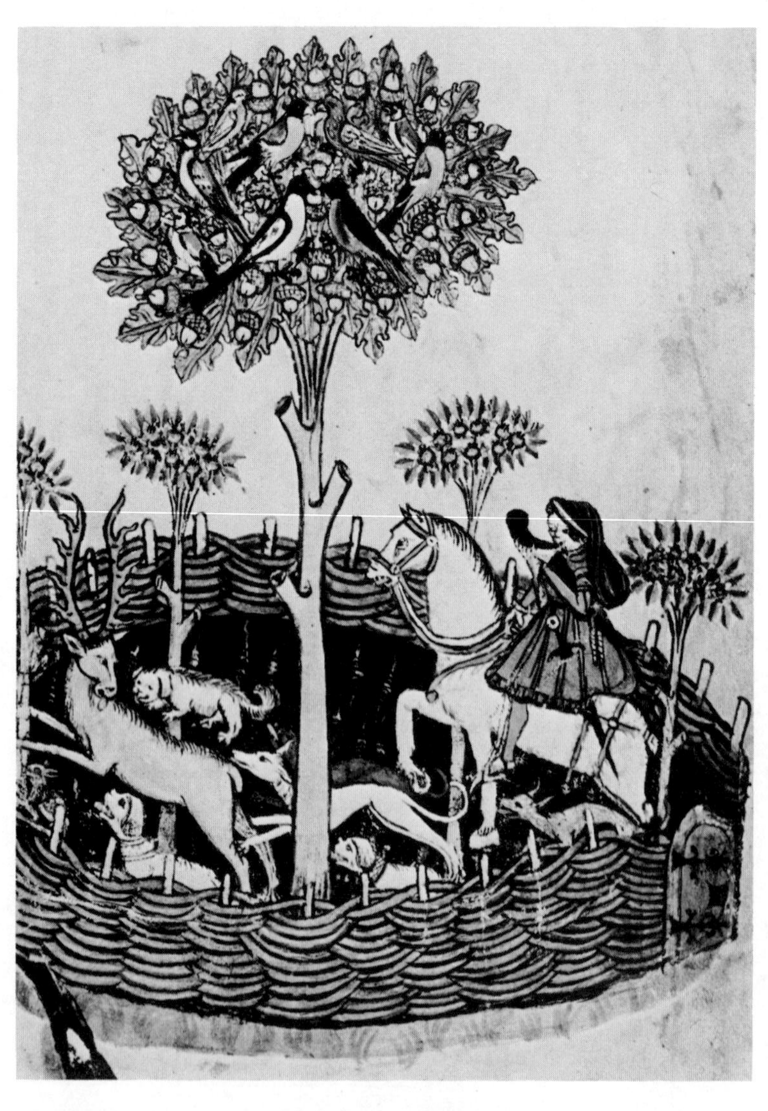

Illuminated page from the Darmstadt Hagadah, showing a stag hunt. Germany, 15th century.

ing of the shofar and the Binding of Isaac, as well as the ceremony of casting bread upon the water. The borders of a number of the illuminated pages are done in the form of gothic architectural arches. All the human figures have bird beaks, and the Jews are dressed in bell-shaped '*Judenhut*', the compulsory headgear for German Jews of the period.

Other outstanding German illuminated festival prayer books are the Tripartite, Worms and Laud *Mahzorim*. Illuminated manuscript Bibles of note include the Regensburg Pentateuch, the Shocken Bible and the Duke of Sussex Pentateuch.

Medieval South Germany is famous for its illuminated Hagadot, with some of the outstanding ones being the Nuremberg, the Bird's Head, Erna Michael, Cincinnati, Washington, Yahuda and Darmstadt Hagadot. These frequently have scenes of a hare or a stag hunt, which is particularly puzzling because they do not relate to any textural reference, and Jewish law prohibits the hunting or the killing of animals for pleasure. However, their inclusion can be explained by the fact that the sequence of blessings recited at the Passover *Seder*, when Passover eve coincides with the termination of the Sabbath, forms the initials of '*Yaknehaz*', for which the similar sounding '*Yag den Haz*' (chase the hare) is an easily recognisable mnemonic. This apparently jarring intrusion into the illumination of German Hagadot actually is also a poignant reminder of Jewish history, with the hunter representing Israel's enemies and the hare or stag, the Jewish people. Sometimes the hare or stag would be shown approaching a water source, symbolising the much-sought haven – the land of Israel.

Although Jewish residence in Italy goes back to the Second Temple period, well before the Christian era, the earliest known Italian Hebrew illuminated manuscripts date back only to the thirteenth century. A number of Northern Italian centres were particularly associated with medieval Hebrew manuscript illumination, notably Rome, Florence, Mantua, Pisa and Ferrara. Among the Hebrew books illuminated in Italy were the *Mishne Torah* and the *Guide to the Perplexed* by Maimonides. There is also a Hebrew translation of the medical treatise by the philosopher-physician Avicenna (988–1037) which was beautifully illuminated.

Other books on Jewish law illuminated in Italy include the Jerusalem *Mishne Torah*, the Vatican *Arbah Turim* and the Vercelli *Tur*

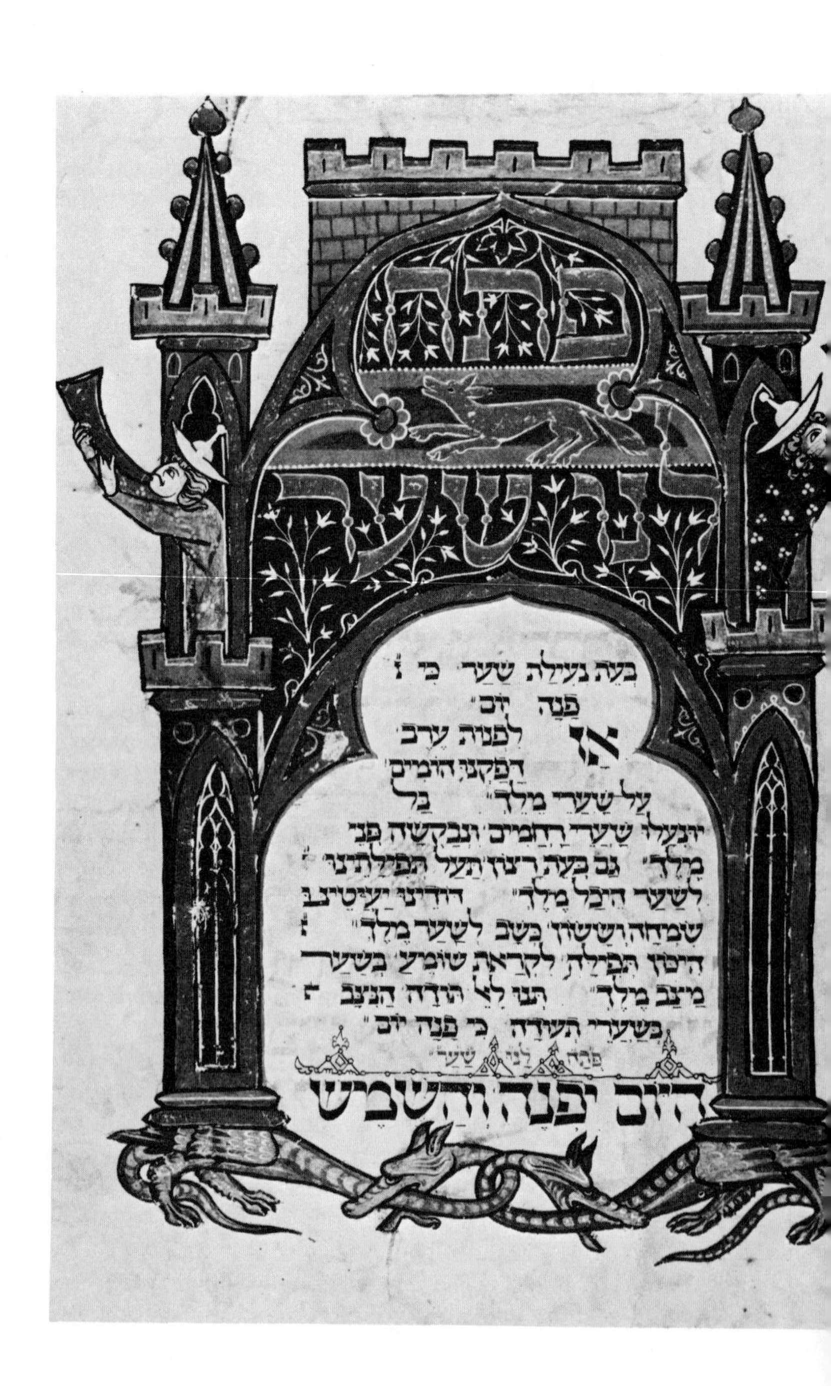
פתח לנו שער
היום יפנה והשמש

Even Ezer. The Paris Bibliothèque National Bible, the Aberdeen Bible and the Bishop Bedell Bible in Cambridge are fine examples of the sumptuousness of Italian Hebrew Biblical manuscript illumination. A magnificent copy of a book of diverse prayers is the illuminated Rothschild Miscellany in the Israel Museum in Jerusalem.

A number of the medieval Hebrew illuminated manuscripts were signed, thus identifying their artists and more accurately the date of the manuscripts. One of the illuminators of Hebrew books in Germany was Meir of Heidelberg, who in the early fifteenth century produced the Darmstadt *Hagadah* masterpiece. His son, Meir Jaffe of Ulm, also an artistic bookbinder, is noted for his beautiful Cincinnati Hagadah. Nathan ben Simon Halevi of Cologne, who produced a *Mishne Torah* in 1295–1296, was also an excellent illuminator.

The magnificent Spanish Farhi Bible was written and decorated between 1366 and 1382 by the noteworthy scribe–illuminator Elisha ben Abraham Crescas. The best known of all is the fifteenth-century scribe–illuminator Joel ben Simon, sometimes called Feibush (Phoebus) Ashkenazi of Germany and Italy, because of the many manuscripts signed by him or attributed to him or his workshop. No fewer than eleven extant manuscripts carry his signature, while at least three others have been attributed to him.

Such was the popularity of the art of manuscript illumination that there was even a book on the subject (*Libro de como se facem*, composed by a Portuguese Jew, Abraham ben Judah ibn Hayim) written in Portuguese in Hebrew script for the would-be Hebrew scribe–illuminator.

Opposite: *illuminated page from the Mahzor Lipsia. Germany, 15th century.*

6 The Art of the Hebrew Printed Book

The invention of the art of printing in Mainz, Germany, by Johannes Gutenberg of Strasbourg in about 1450–54 has a bearing on the history of the Jews of that period. As the Jews were prohibited from most forms of enterprise in the Middle Ages, and since Canonical law forbade Christians from taking interest on loans, Jews resorted to finance for their livelihood, serving both prince and pope as

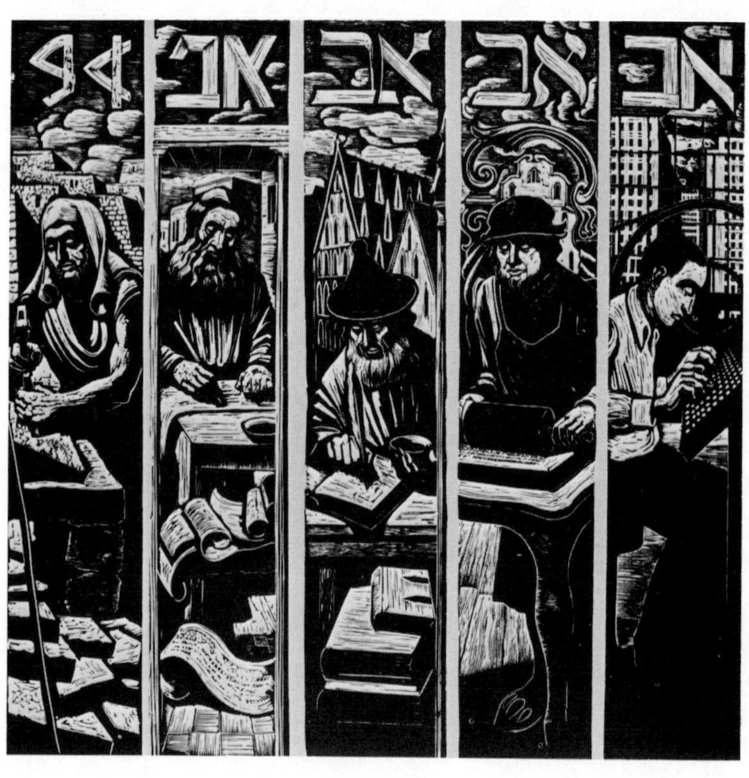

bankers and tax collectors, unenviable occupations in those times. In order to prevent profits thus earned from remaining in Jewish hands, the church or feudal princes would arrange periodically, by direct or indirect means, the confiscation of all moneys from the Jews to enrich their own coffers. When Gutenberg needed money to develop his new invention he applied to Andrea Dmitzehan, his former associate in Strasbourg, who negotiated a loan from the Jews, and to John Fust, another associate who arranged a loan from the Jews and gave these moneys to Gutenberg.

Gutenberg's invention of a process of printing with movable type had a particularly strong impact on the Jews. While the Jewish masses had always been occupied in learning and the transmission of knowledge from generation to generation, only the well-to-do could afford the handwritten manuscripts. Scholars, teachers and students laboured under the greatest difficulty; that is, the Talmud alone consists of twenty huge tomes, and few complete sets were available for study. But with Gutenberg's invention, Hebrew typefaces were designed, and beginning in 1475 Hebrew books began coming off the presses in large numbers, proving a blessing for Jews and an incalculable boon to their spiritual and intellectual life. The printing press also had an important side effect since Jewish literature could now be more secure against total destruction by the agents of fanaticism and ignorance.

Since the early printed book was merely a copy of the handwritten manuscript, the manuscript form was long retained in the early stage of the printing of Hebrew books, with space left at the beginning for initial words to be hand-illuminated by artists, and the colophons made up of lines in gradually diminishing size to fill in the last page.

The early Jewish printer considered his a 'holy' craft, and did his work with painstaking and loving care. The productions of the early Hebrew printing presses had style and vitality and were printed on quality paper with good ink. Broad spacing with wide margins and artistic Hebrew letters were utilised. A decorative effect was achieved

Opposite: *the development of Hebrew printing. Woodcut by Jakob Steinhardt (1887–1968).*

in the printed books of the late fifteenth and early sixteenth century by broad bands of decorative borders which imitated the work of manuscript illuminators, and by elaborate initial letters and words, especially in the opening pages of sections and chapters.

The first illustrated Hebrew book produced by a printing press was *Mashal Hakadmoni*, a book of fables bearing a number of woodcut blocks, which was published in Brescia in 1491. A favourite type of work for early Hebrew illustrators was that of *Minhagim* (customs) and handbooks which contained occasional prayers. In Prague in 1514, a *Birkat Hamazon* (grace after meals) book was illustrated with woodcuts. In 1593 and 1601 two *Minhagim* books lavishly illustrated with depictions of many events in the Jewish year were produced in Italy.

But the vintage year for the early illustrated Hebrew book was 1526, when the Prague Hagadah was published. Its magnificent woodcut borders and illustrations, which were a blend of Italian Renaissance and German Gothic style – perhaps best termed 'German Renaissance' – made it one of the truly superb achievements of the printing press during the first century and a half following its invention. Featuring splendid, bold borders, beautiful medieval German lettering modelled after the finest scribal manuscript lettering of the period, handsome ornamental initial-letters and words, and sixty woodcuts, the Prague Hagadah is indeed a beautiful book. It is understandable that it created a stimulus and served as the prototype for all subsequent illustrated editions of the printed Hagadah. The Prague Hagadah had a woodcut of the Messiah entering Jerusalem, a scene which had appeared in a number of manuscript Hagadot. Other editions of the Hagadah were subsequently published in Prague over the next century.

In 1550, a similar, but much more Italianate, Hagadah was produced in Mantua. In 1609 a Hagadah was published in Venice with many woodcut illustrations which were destined to influence subsequent editions in Venice, Leghorn and elsewhere for *'Sephardi'* and Italian Jews.

Opposite: *the Prague Hagadah, 1526.*

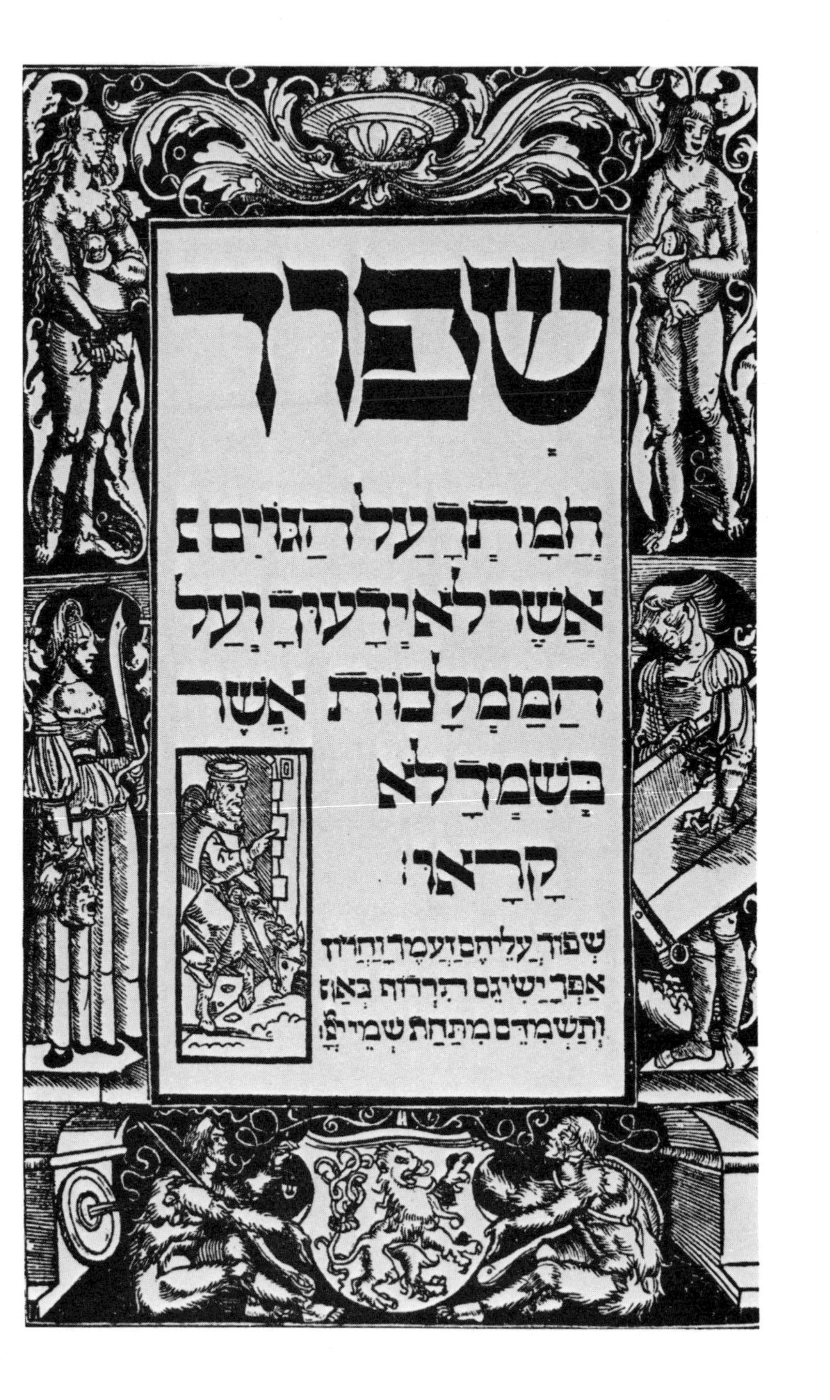

שפוך

חמתך על הגוים

אשר לא ידעוך ועל

הממלכות אשר

בשמך לא

קראו

שפוך עליהם זעמך וחרון

אפך ישיגם תרדוף באף

ותשמידם מתחת שמי ה׳

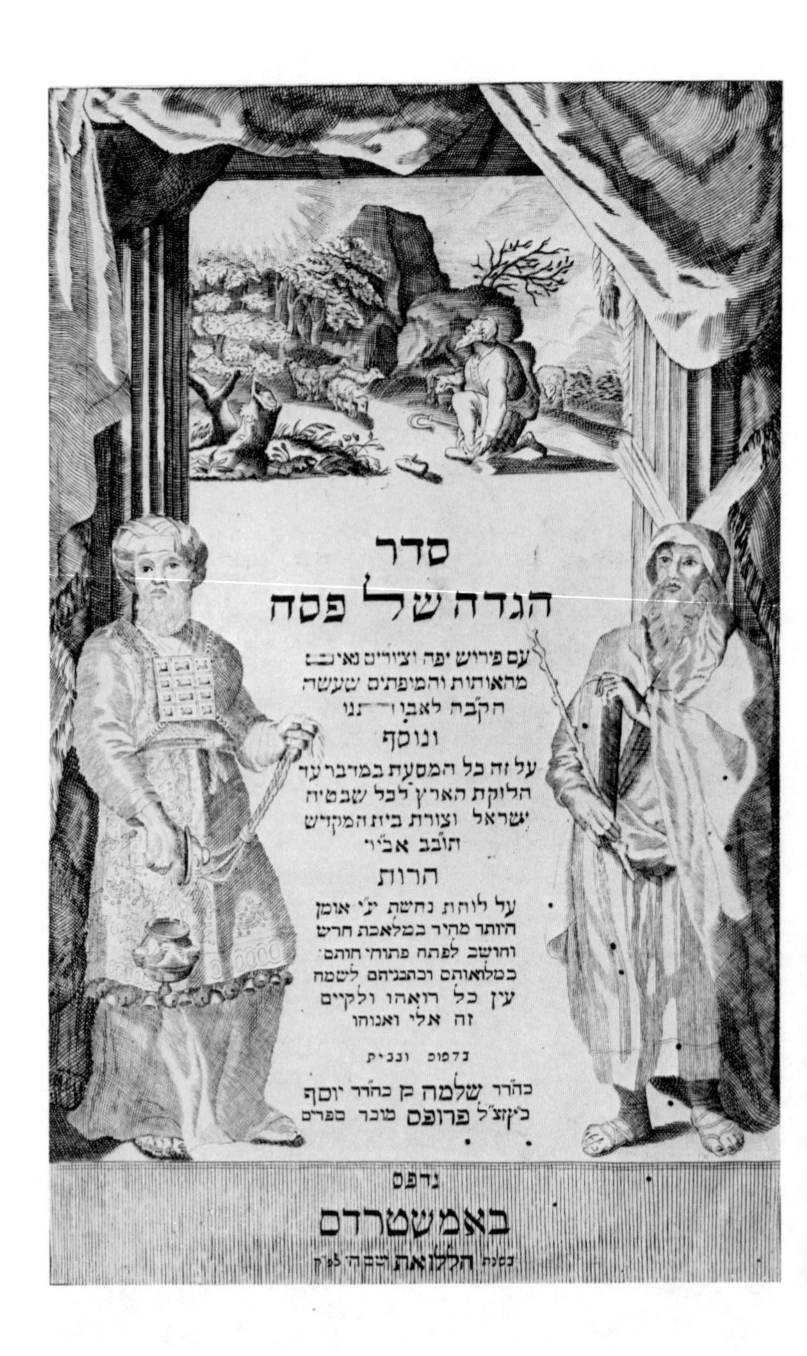

סדר
הגדה של פסח

עם פירוש יפה וציורים נאים
מהאותות והמופתים שעשה
הקב״ה לאבותינו

ונוסף

על זה כל המסעת במדבר עד
הלוקת הארץ לכל שבטיה
ישראל וצורת בית המקדש
תובב אב״י

הרות

על לוחות נחשת ע״י אומן
היותר מהיר במלאכת חרש
וחושב לפתח פתוחי חותם:
כמלואותם וכתבניהם לשמח
עין כל רואהו ולקיים
זה אלי ואנוהו

נדפס ונבנית

כה״רר שלמה בן כה״רר יוסף
כ״ץ זצ״ל פרופס מוכר ספרים

נדפס

באמשטרדם

בשנת הללואת שבח ה׳ לפ״ק

Following the Prague Hagadah, the most significant achievement in the art of the Hebrew printed book took place more than a century and a half later, in 1695, with the publication of the Amsterdam Hagadah. Unlike earlier styles, the Amsterdam Hagadah contained copper-plate engravings. These were done by the proselyte Jew Abraham bar Yaakov and, as a major innovation, featured a large fold-out copper-engraved map of Israel showing the travels of the Israelites from Egypt to the Promised Land. Profusely illustrated, the Hagadah, especially the improved 1712 edition, was destined to become the most influential and most copied of all Passover Hagadot throughout the Jewish world up to the present day. In the eighteenth century even Hebrew manuscript illuminators vied with one another to produce more faithful or more interesting copies of the Amsterdam Hagadah, their illustrations and their formats all based on the original printed edition.

Opposite: *title page of the Amsterdam Hagadah, 1712.*

Part Two
Jewish Ceremonial Art

7 The Sabbath in Jewish Art

Central to an understanding of Judaism is an awareness that the *mitzvot* (the six hundred and thirteen Biblically ordained commandments) are designed to help man achieve a measure of godliness. As a guide to a total way of life they serve to sanctify man's every act and infuse them with spiritual meaning, thus elevating man and aiding him to become an ethical, moral, totally God-directed individual.

A basic premise behind the performance of virtually all mitzvot is the concept of *hiddur mitzva* ('the enchantment of the command') which is expressed in the adornment of the implements used in performing God's commands. 'This is my God and I shall glorify (literally *adorn*) Him', sings Moses (*Exodus XV:2*). The Talmudic sages interpreted this phrase as meaning to make and use especially beautiful objects in the performance of the mitzvot (*Bab. Talmud, Shabbat, CIII:b.*) In essence, this is the spirit of Jewish ceremonial art.

The commandment most frequently mentioned in the Bible refers to the keeping of the Sabbath, and is so fundamental a concept in Jewish life that it takes precedence over the entire system of Jewish law. The concept of a day of spiritual rest each week when physical labour is forbidden is now considered one of Judaism's greatest gifts to civilisation, and has long since been adopted by most of the civilised world. But it was not always thus, for the ancient Greeks and Romans who could not fathom the far-reaching social and humanitarian significance of the Sabbath, derided the concept as a sign of Jewish indolence. But for the Jew the Sabbath meant a liberation from the mundane and consecration of the sacred, a '... perpetual covenant throughout their generations', linking the Jewish people in an eternal bond of faith with God, whose symbolic cessation of Divine creativity after six days is commemorated every Seventh Day by the Jew as a supreme act of faith in the Creator. An abstract

Paper-cut mizrach tablet depicting stags, eagles and lions (flanking a Torah Ark) and a seven-branched menorah. Eastern Europe, c.1800.

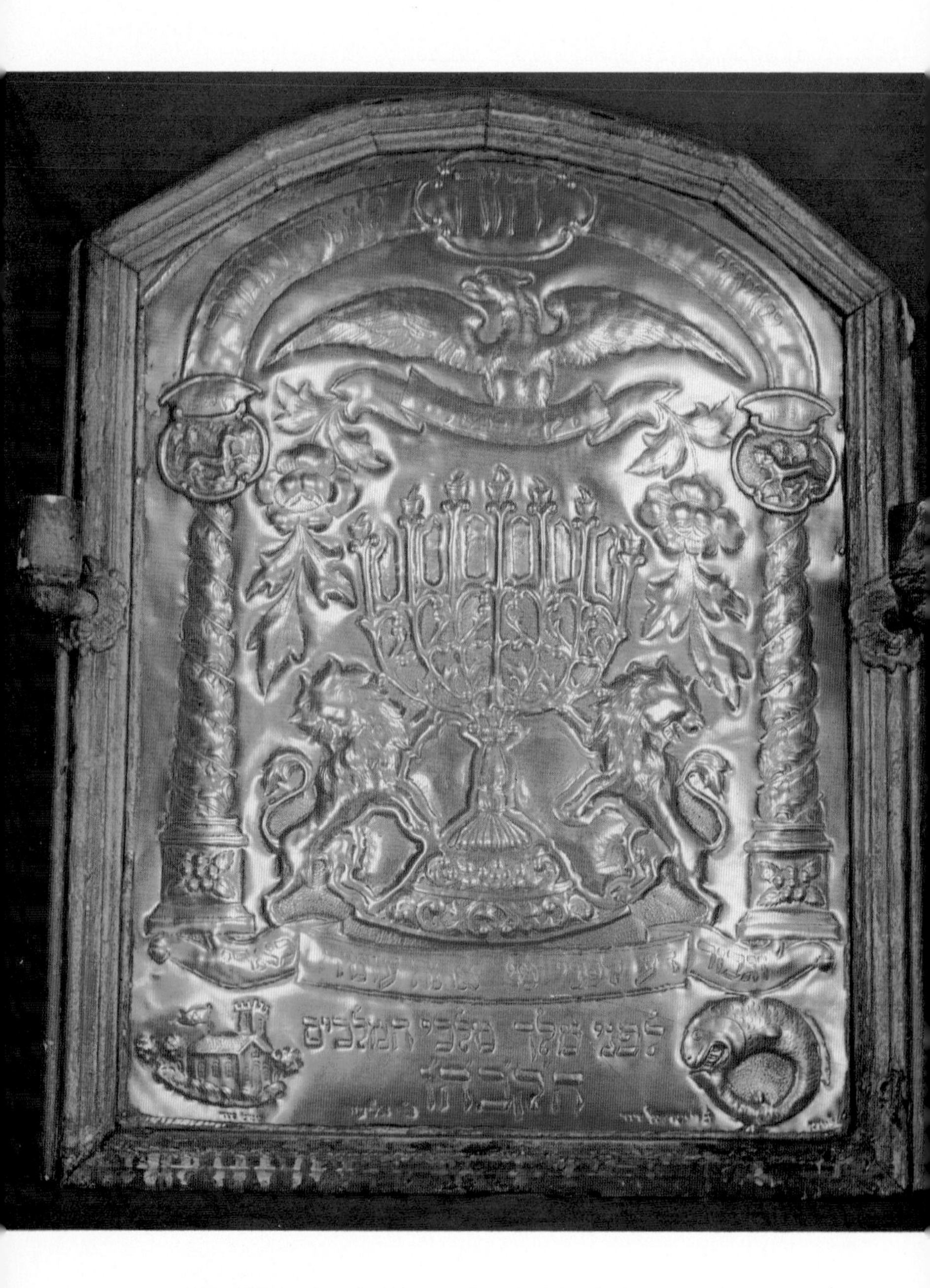

Brass Shiviti mizrach tablet. The four Jewish folk animals (the lion, the stag, the leopard and the eagle) are depicted with a seven-branched menorah and the great fish, Leviathan, which will be eaten by the righteous in the world to come. Eastern Europe, c.1800.

Opposite: mizrach tablet, in the form of a Persian rug, which was hung on the Jerusalem-oriented wall of the home. It depicts Moses and Aaron. Kashan, Persia, 1839-40.

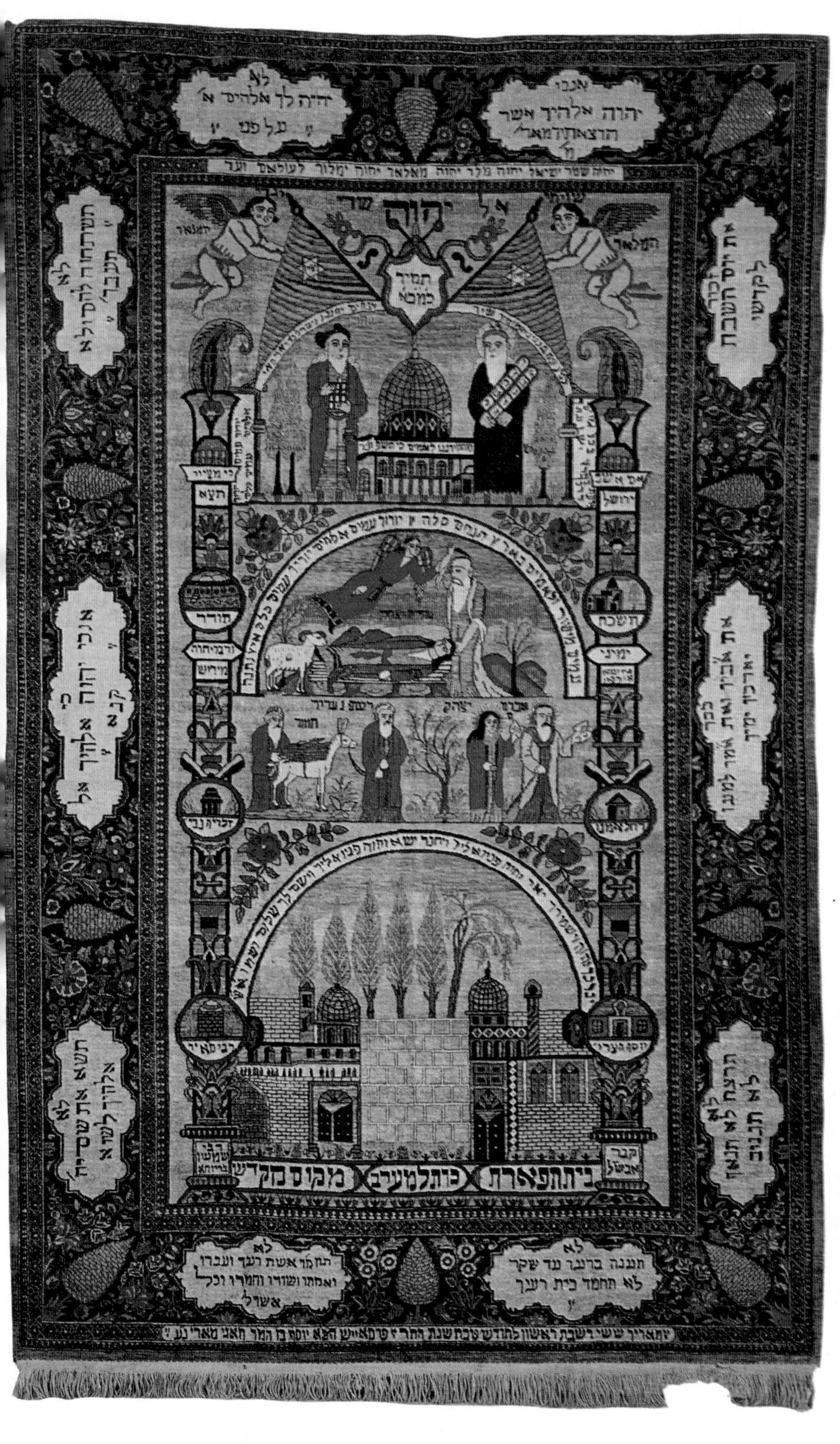

לא
היה לך אלהים א׳
על פני
אנכי
יהוה אלהיך אשר
יהוה שמר ישראל יהוה מלך יהוה מלאך יהוה ימלוך לעולם ועד
יהוה שדי
אל
תמיד
בית תפארת
כותל מערב
מקום הקדש
קבר
אבשל
שמשון
לא
תחמד אשת רעך ועבדו
ואמתו ושורו וחמרו וכל
אשר ל
לא
תענה ברעך עד שקר
לא תחמד בית רעך

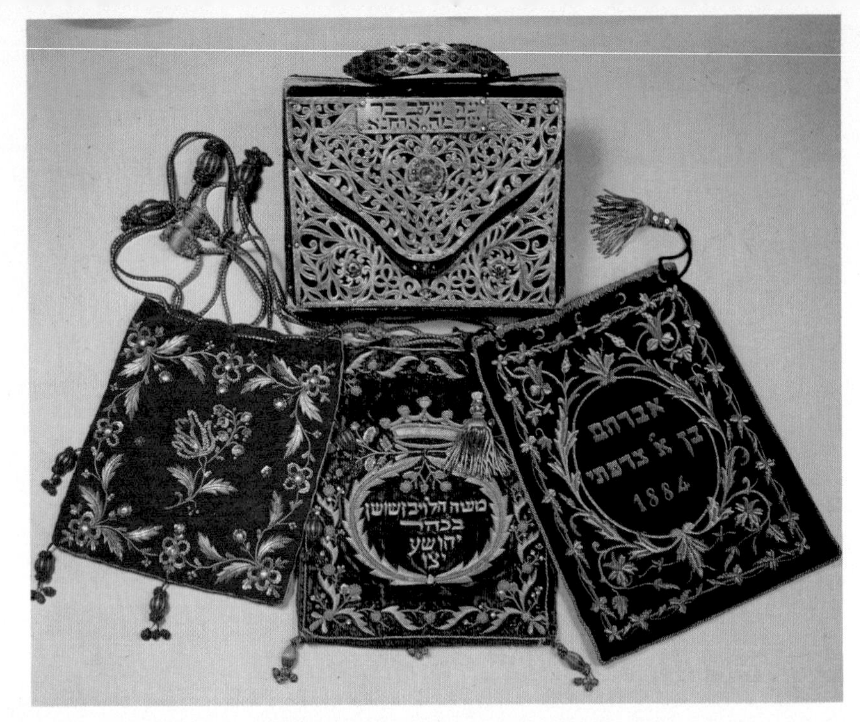

Embroidered Tallit and T'Fillin containers. Gibraltar and Morocco, 19th century.

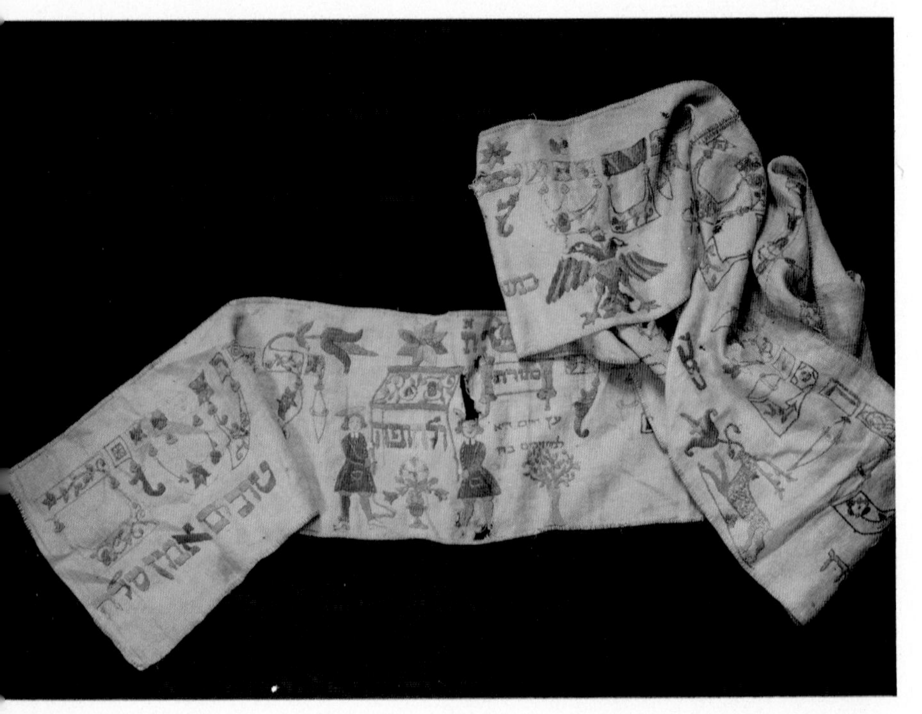

Embroidered Torah binder. Germany, 18th century.

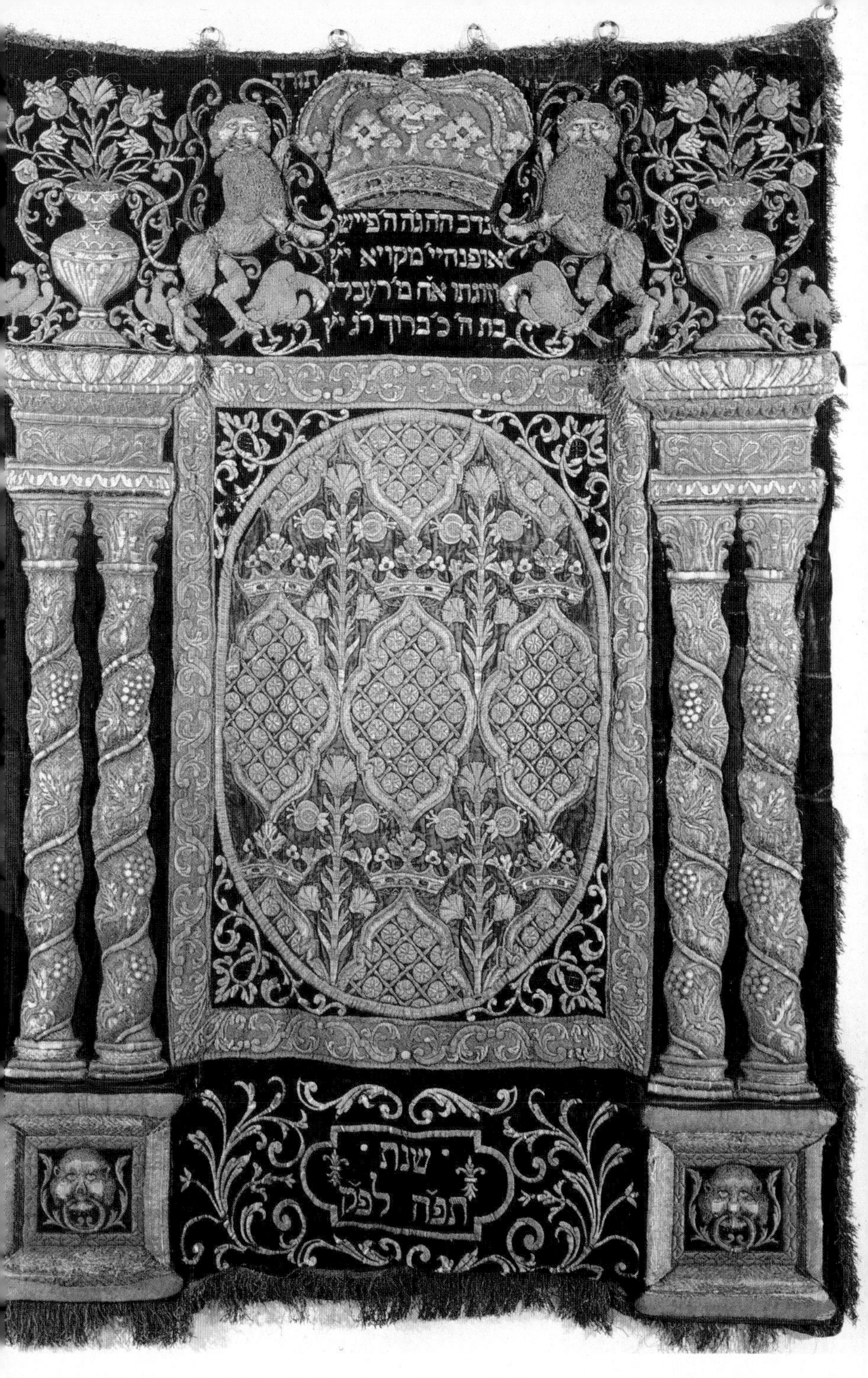

Embroidered Torah Ark curtain featuring architectural columns, representing those in the Jerusalem Temple and lions of Judah rampant supporting a 'Crown of Torah'. Germany, 1725.

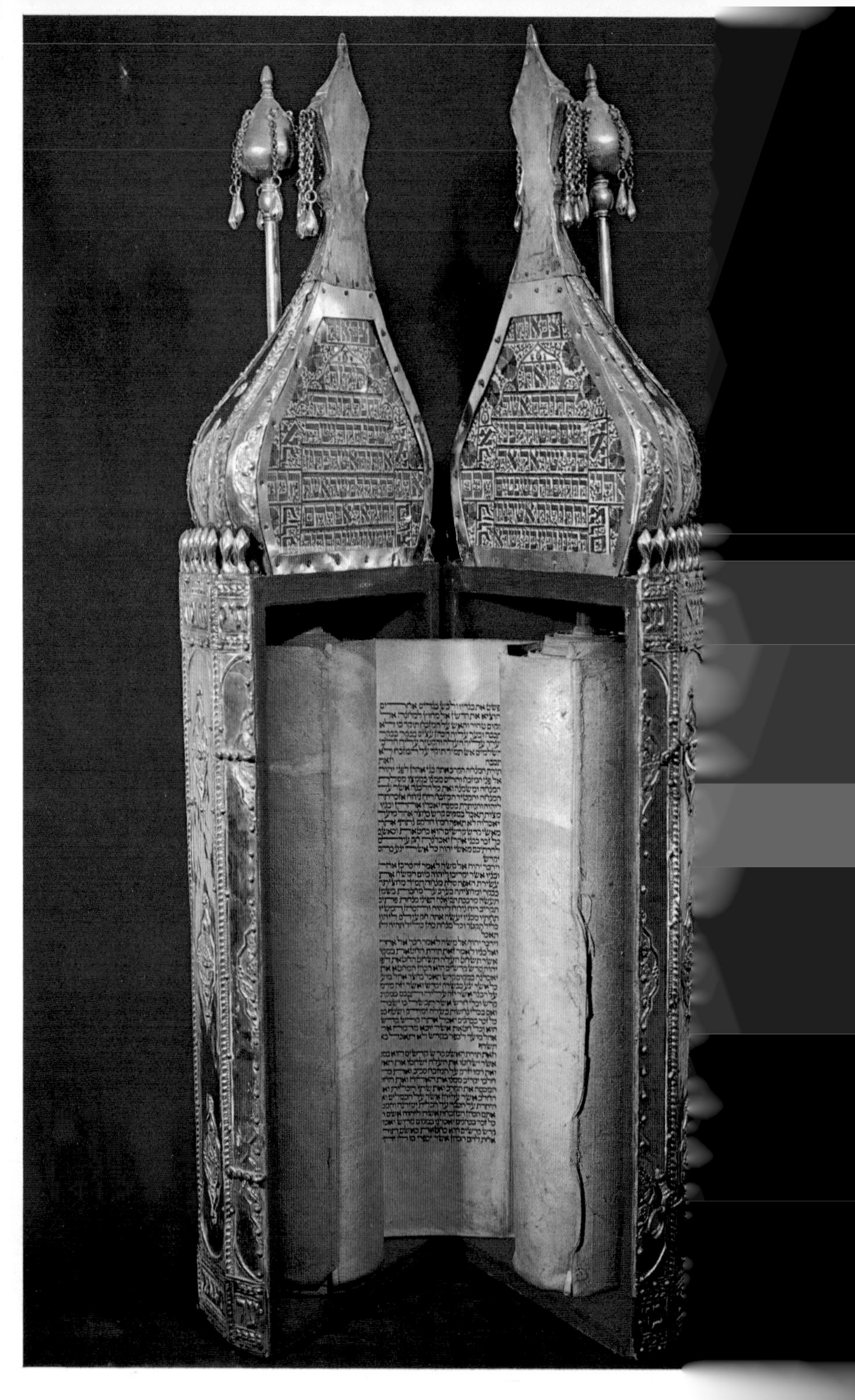

Silver gilt Torah case open to show Torah. Baghdad, c.1850.

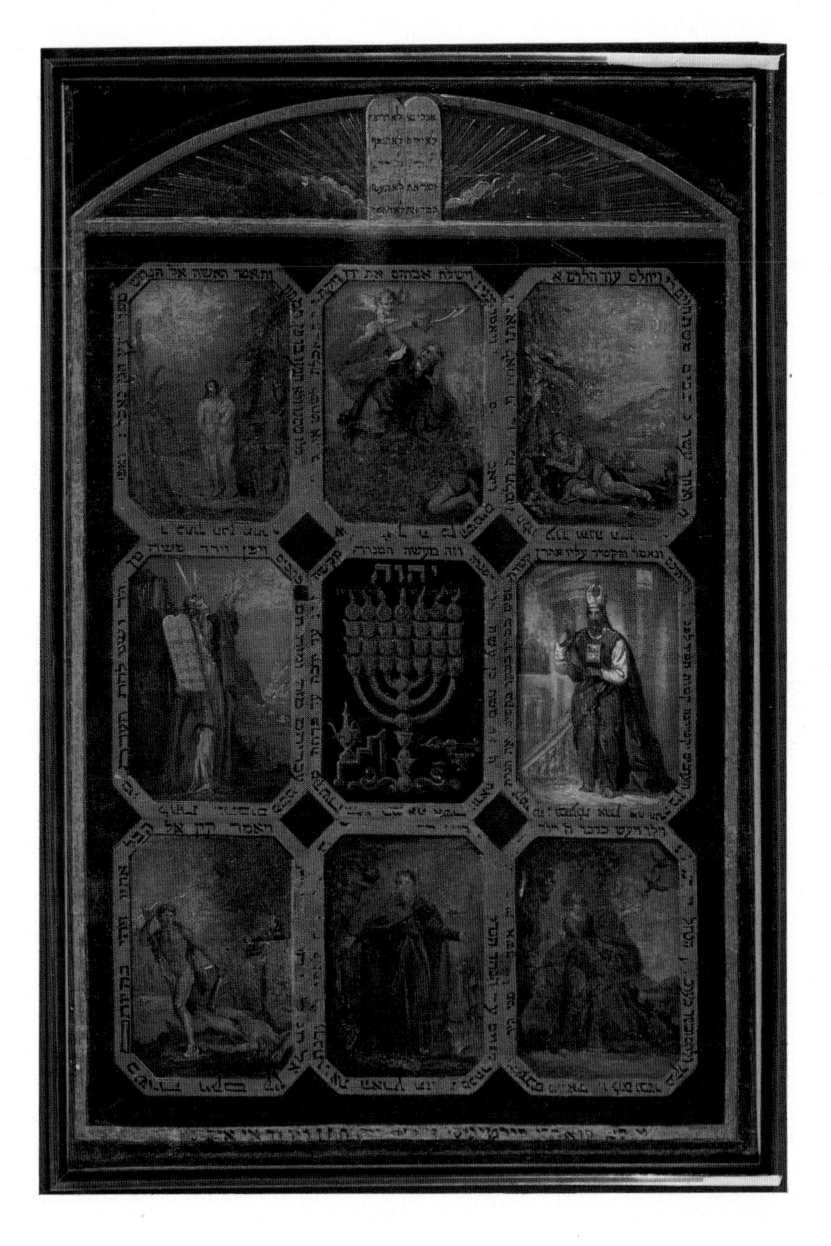

Mizrach tablet, an oil painting on canvas. Biblical scenes from the lives of Adam and Eve, Cain and Abel, Abraham and Isaac, Jacob, Joseph, Moses and Aaron are depicted. In the centre are the ritual implements of the temple. Italy, c.1700.

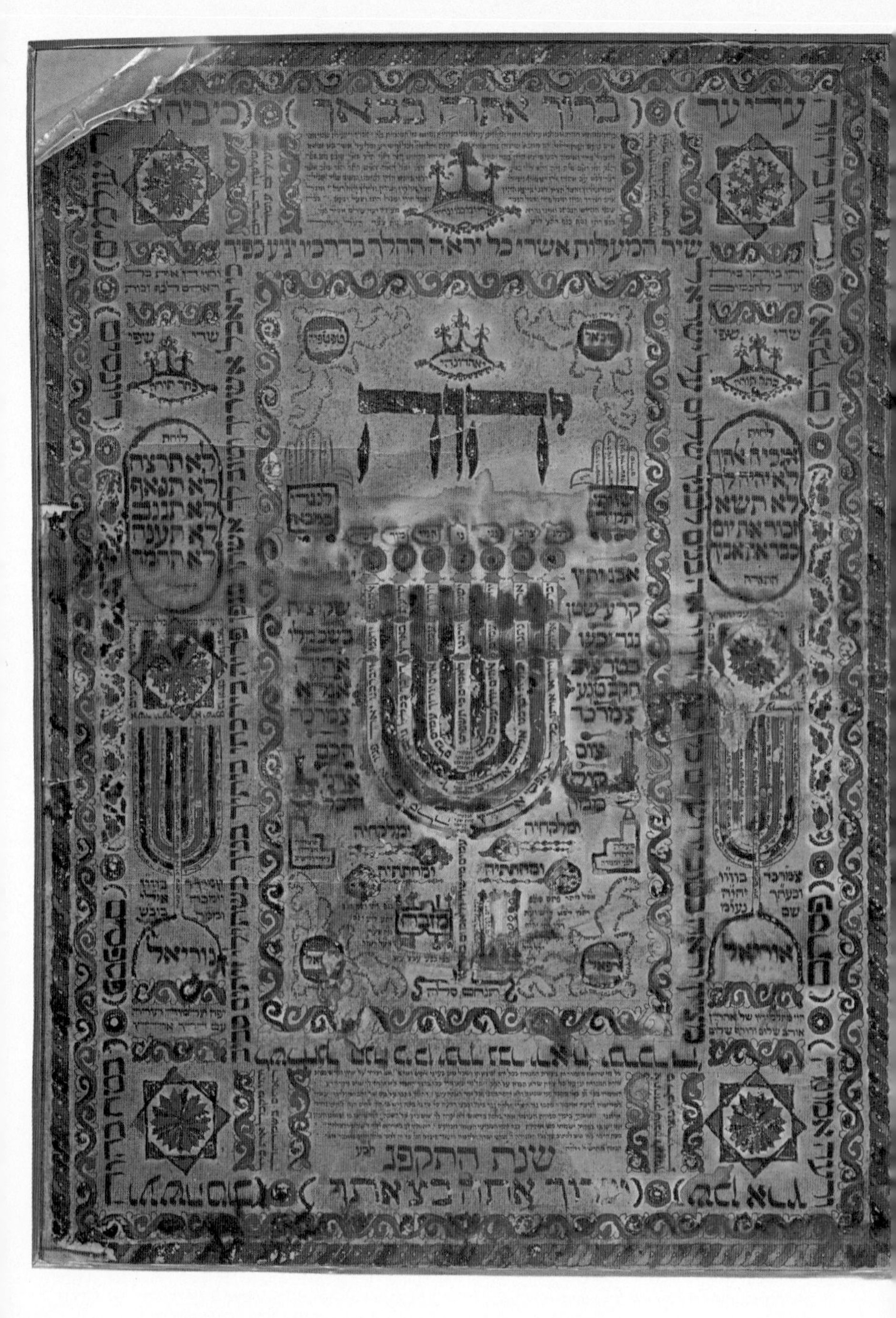

Illuminated mizrach tablet on paper featuring Hebrew micrography, with three seven-branched menorahs and depictions of the ritual implements of the Jerusalem Temple. Gibraltar, 1823.

measure of time was thus hallowed and converted into a day of peace of mind and soul and spiritual contentment. Through study of the Torah and meditation, and discourse with the family, the Jew has found that the Sabbath offered an opportunity for moral regeneration and enabled him to withstand the degradation and persecution he so often faced in the outside world.

The Jewish woman has the honour of ushering in the holy day by kindling the Sabbath lights before sunset on Friday afternoon.

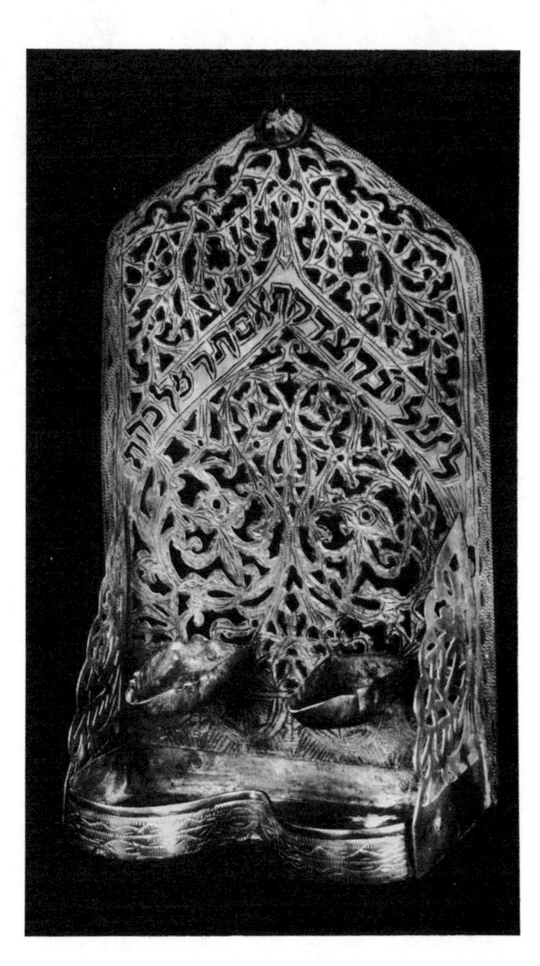

Silver Sabbath lamp. Morocco, 19th century.

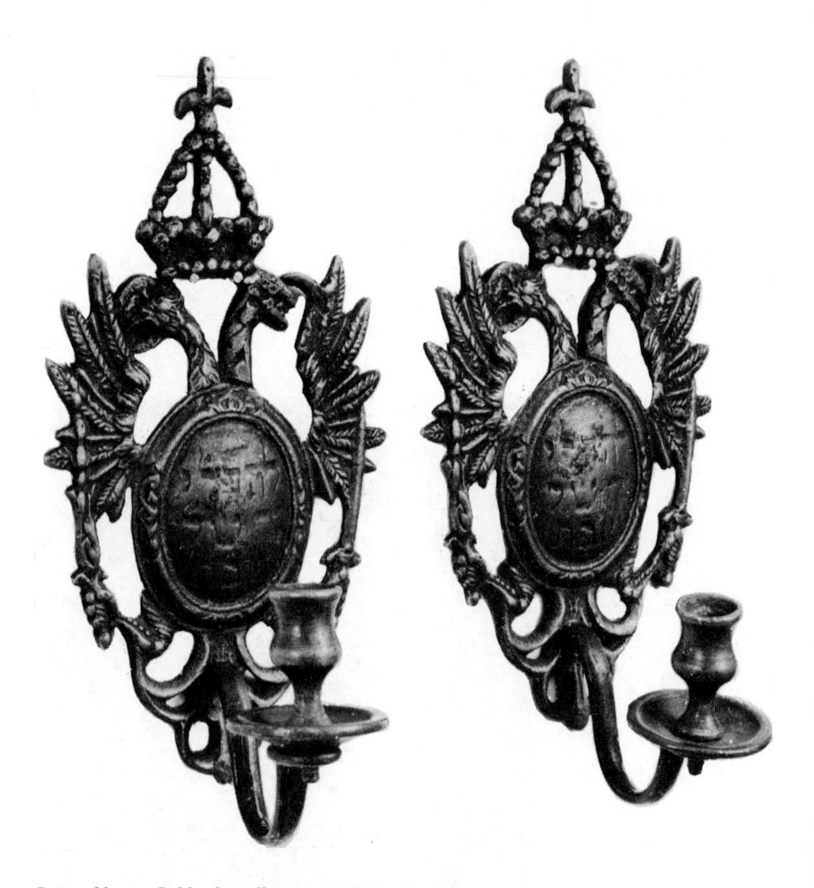

Pair of brass Sabbath wall sconces. Poland, 17th century.

Just as the confusion, turmoil and darkness described at the opening of Genesis were swept away by the words 'Let there be light' when God is described as 'dividing the light from the darkness', so does the Jewish woman symbolically separate this day from the other six days of the week by lighting the Sabbath lamp at the beginning of the Sabbath and her husband the special *Havdala* candle at the end of the Sabbath.

Light and Fire in Jewish Ritual

Ancient peoples, awed by the power of fire to destroy and to give light and heat, worshipped fire. It was a rare nation in ancient times that did not have its fire gods and sun gods. Among Israel's neighbours, this awe of fire was expressed by the worship of idols which represented the fearsome god Moloch, and which had fires burning inside them into which children were thrown as sacrifices.

Although light and fire play an important role in Judaism and indeed the concept of sacred light permeates Judaism, they were never objects of worship. But God, the 'Creator of the heavenly lights' is blessed each day for providing the heavenly orbs which give light to man and thus reflect praise on their creator. This prayer also praises the Sabbath as a day of light and delight, and God 'Who forms light and ... darkness ... Each day God opens the windows of heaven's vault and brings the sun ... the moon ... In His love He gives light to the entire world and to those who dwell in it ... Illuminating orbs He has made for our good, justice and knowledge alone gave them form, kindling within them both power and strength, loftily ruling the courses of space, manifesting lustre and splendour ablaze, nature throughout is aglow with their flame. On rising and setting ... they ... perform the will of their Maker ... and give glory and praise to His name, ... Praise be God Who on the seventh day rested from.... Creation ... In his holiness He granted to Israel His people the heritage of rest on the holy Sabbath day ... Be You blessed ... for the glory of the work of Your hands and for the luminaries which provide the light of Your creation, which sing everlastingly of Your praise ... a Lord of wonder, who in His goodness ever reviews each and every day the work of Creation, as it is said: "To Him who made the great lights of heaven ... may You cause a new light to shine forth upon Zion, and may we all be worthy of sharing soon in that light ..."'

In associating light with creation and the Sabbath day of rest, the prayer provides an important reason for the kindling of lights at the beginning of the Sabbath and for the Havdala candle at its termination. They constitute man's way of thanking God on His day of rest for the gift of the Sabbath and for the life-giving light formed during the six days of Creation. The prayer's latter part appears to relate to a mystical *Midrashic* (traditional body of non-Talmudic Biblical commentary and lore) interpretation which links Jewish observance of the command to kindle the Sabbath lights with an eschatological blessing for the world-to-come: 'If you properly observe the command relating to the Sabbath lights, I will cause the lights of Zion to provide light for you, and I shall no longer make it necessary for you to see by the light of the sun, for by My own splendour will I provide light for you. As it is said: "And the sun shall be no more your light by day, neither for brightness shall the moon give light to you, but the Lord shall be to you an everlasting light." And why should all of this come about? Because of the lights which they kindle for the Sabbath.'

Fire itself is a very significant element in the Bible. According to a well-known *Midrash*, at the very dawn of monotheism, when Abraham smashed the idols of his father, Terah, to dramatise the impotence of the man-made objects universally worshipped by mankind at the time, he was thrown into a fiery furnace and walked out unscathed. This was to be repeated later in the Bible, when Hanania, Mishael and Azaria emerged from a furnace similarly unaffected. It was a pillar of fire which served as a visible form of God's omnipresence, guiding the Israelites at night through the wilderness until their arrival in the Promised Land. At Revelation when the Jews received the Torah at Mount Sinai, the climactic moment of Jewish history and the most powerful, transcendental Jewish religious experience, God is described descending upon Sinai in fire. Indeed, in the *Midrash* the Torah itself is said to have been made of white fire, the engraved letters of black fire – fire mixed with fire, hewn out of fire and given from the midst of fire.

Fire was used in the Temple altar to consume sacrificial offerings and was kept continually burning, and 'strange fire', that is, fire newly kindled or taken from profane places, was not permitted. The sacred fire in the First Temple in Jerusalem (but not that of the Second Temple) is said to have been of divine origin. Fire was considered an agent of the Divine Will, and linked to this is the conception of God Himself as a consuming fire. It was thus as an inexhaustible burning bush that God appeared to the shepherd Moses. God also appeared in the form of fire to the prophets Ezekiel and Daniel.

The Menorah – Symbol of Judaism

One can readily understand, therefore, the significance of the seven-branched lampstand in the Temple called the menorah. Historically it is the most important Jewish symbol and the Jewish artistic emblem and ornamental device most frequently found in ancient times. It was so extensively used in antiquity that the menorah became the single, immediately identifiable emblem of Judaism throughout the ancient world. Originally, the menorah was made of pure gold for the Tabernacle in the desert and filled with pure olive oil. It was kindled by Aaron the High Priest and was to burn from morning to evening. Such was its importance that the Midrash relates that God revealed to Moses and Bezalel, the craftsman, a fiery menorah of various colours, complete in all its details to ensure that it would be created precisely to specification.

The menorah appears as a Jewish symbol in the remains of synagogues throughout ancient Israel and elsewhere. Throughout the lands of Jewish habitation – in Israel, Egypt, Ephesus, Carthagena, Sicily and the Roman provinces in the Danube basin – the menorah was the prime artistic symbol of Jewish religious life in the home and in the synagogue. It is found extensively in Jewish funerary art and on Jewish gold glasses, coins, seals and amulets. It is presumably the Temple menorah that is depicted on the triumphal Arch of Titus in Rome, being carried by Jewish prisoners exiled from Israel following the Roman victory over the Jews in 70 BC. Its actual whereabouts became a matter of legend, and gave rise to a good deal of theorising and speculation.

Traditionally, the menorah is regarded as a representation of the tree of knowledge that stood in the Garden of Eden. Its central location in the Temple sanctuary, in front of the Ark of the Covenant which contained the Tablets of the Law, underlined its symbolic representation of the Jewish ideal – spiritual and intellectual understanding of the Torah. This is emphasised by a Biblical passage referring to *ner* and *or*, the Hebrew words for lamp and light (both of which can be found in the word menorah) which declares: 'For the mitzvah (the Torah command) is a lamp and the Torah is light' (*Proverbs VI: 23*). The Hebrew words *ner* and *or* served as metaphors for life as well as spiritual light, enlightenment and insight. Conversely, 'extinguishing the lamp' is used in the Scriptures as an indication of misfortune, and the cessation of life or happiness. This leads to the conclusion that the menorah also represents another basic Jewish religious symbol, the Tree of Life, an appellation given

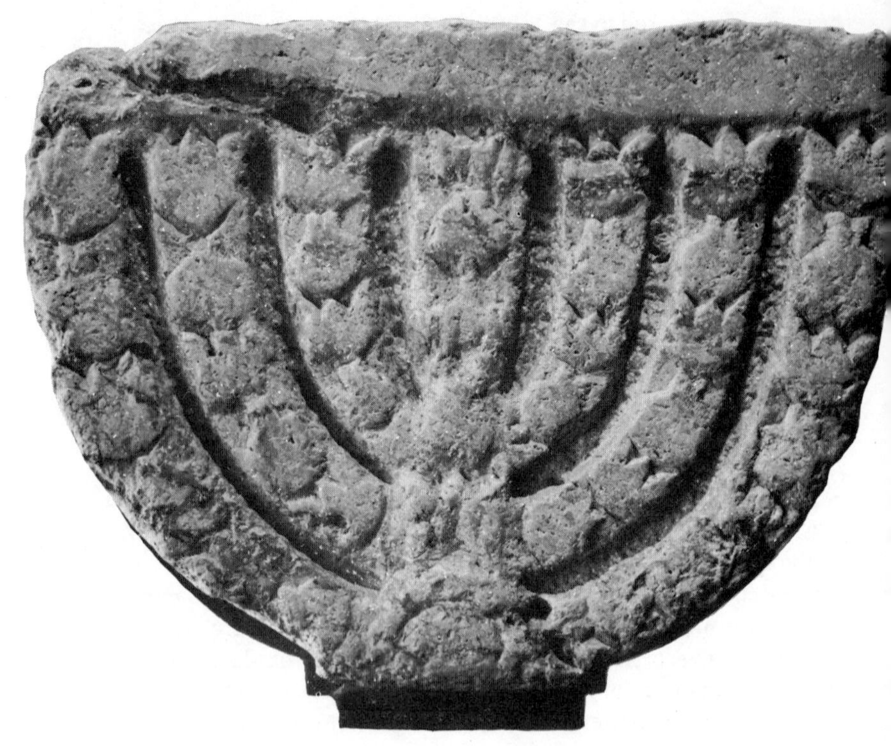

Stone seven-branched menorah, dating from the 2nd century, discovered near Tiberias.

in the Bible to the Torah itself. The symbolic importance of the menorah as a figurative Tree of Light can be seen by comparing it with another Tree of Light, the Burning Bush through which God Himself first addressed Moses. The menorah lights are thus symbolic of the light emanating from God and his gift to the Jew – the Torah.

The menorah as a symbolic representation of God's light serving as the protection of Israel can be derived from the Biblical passage: 'For see, darkness covers the earth and deep darkness the nations, but God radiates over Israel and His glory shines about them, and nations walk by His light and kings by the rays of His dawn' (*Isaiah LX: 2*).

Some also saw the menorah as the 'Candlestick of the Redemption,' an apocalyptic symbol of the future Messianic redemption of

Israel. Philo and Josephus, the one a Jewish philosopher, and the other a Jewish historian, both stressed the important role of the menorah during the classical period. Both endowed the seven-branched lamp with cosmic significance, representing heaven or, more specifically, the planetary system, with the central light representing the sun and the branches on either side, the planets to which the sun gives light.

A Talmudic view is that the three lights on each side of the menorah faced the central light – a view reflected in many ancient artistic depictions of the menorah – and the central light faced the *Shechina* (the Holy Spirit). It would appear, therefore, that the philosopher, the historian and the sages all see the menorah as reflecting God's light on the universe. It is little wonder, then, that the kindling of the 'menorah in the home' (the Sabbath lamp) became the central ritual for the inauguration of the Sabbath, for in this simple ceremony the primary symbolic elements of Judaism are concentrated.

Kindling the Sabbath Lamp

The Sabbath lamp also represents *shalom bayit*, the peace of the home. The sages taught that where there is light, there is peace. The glow of the Sabbath lights in the Jewish home on Sabbath eve served to remind each member of the family that the sacred day had arrived and must be observed with reverence, care and love.

As an old and important ritual, Jewish women usually wore special attire to kindle the Sabbath lights. In parts of Eastern Europe, the mistress of the household wore a *Shterntichel* (Yiddish: a covering of the forehead) decorated with pearls, which resembled a tiara, symbolic of a queen's headdress. On occasions, one of the pearls in the Shterntichel would be missing, a poignant reminder that even the joy of the Sabbath is incomplete since the destruction of the Temple and the exile of the Jewish people from their homeland. Many women of Hungary donned a special white apron which they wore throughout the Sabbath, in contrast to the plain workaday apron. In the Yemen, some women put on their gold-coloured wedding dresses and set festive silver and gold-trimmed *gargoush* bonnets upon their heads.

The lighting of the Sabbath candles became so intimately associated with the holy day and with the Jewish woman that artists, seeking a scene to typify the Sabbath frequently depicted a woman kindling the lights. In Eastern Europe, tombstones of women were sometimes carved with a pair of candlesticks, at times showing a woman's hands hovering over them in the position of blessing.

Before approaching the Sabbath lamp, it became customary for the woman of the house to drop a few coins in an alms box for the benefit of the poor and the scholars of the Holy Land. The most popular charity box among both Sephardi and Ashkenazi Jewish women bore the name of Rabbi Meir Baal Hanes (Rabbi Meir 'the Miracle Worker' was a second-century Talmudic sage.) '*Meir*' is the Hebrew word for 'enlighten' and institutions named after Rabbi Meir were the favourite beneficiaries at candle-lighting time. Then, in a quiet and impressive ceremony, the Sabbath lights are kindled while the children stand at their mother's side. She covers her eyes to prevent herself from looking at the lights until after the blessing, recites the required words to sanctify the holy day, murmurs a silent prayer for the happiness and well-being of her family, and with a final '*Shabbat Shalom*' (peaceful Sabbath) or 'Good Shabbes', welcomes the Sabbath.

Two lights were set as the minimum for every Jewish household. These represent the two versions of the Fourth Commandment in the Bible; the one in *Exodus XX*, beginning with *Zachor* (Remember) the Sabbath day, the other in *Deuteronomy V* where it is given as 'Shamor' (observe) the Sabbath day. (Although Jewish tradition has it that both words were communicated by God simultaneously, each stressed a particular aspect to the commandment.) According to another interpretation, the two Sabbath lights symbolise husband and wife.

The use of candlesticks and candelabra, although prevalent throughout the world today, is a relatively recent custom. While we do not know exactly what the earliest Sabbath lamps looked like, the original Sabbath lamps may have been similar to the small clay and ceramic oil lamps in use for centuries throughout the Mediterranean area. These lamps were small, generally flattened, hollow vessels, usually circular or pear-shaped, with an opening at the top for the insertion of the oil and a spout-like opening at the front for the wick. Such lamps, if made for the Sabbath, may have had two openings for wicks, and may well have been decorated with Jewish symbols, such as the seven-branched menorah. Similar lamps were indeed made for and used by Jews in the early centuries AD.

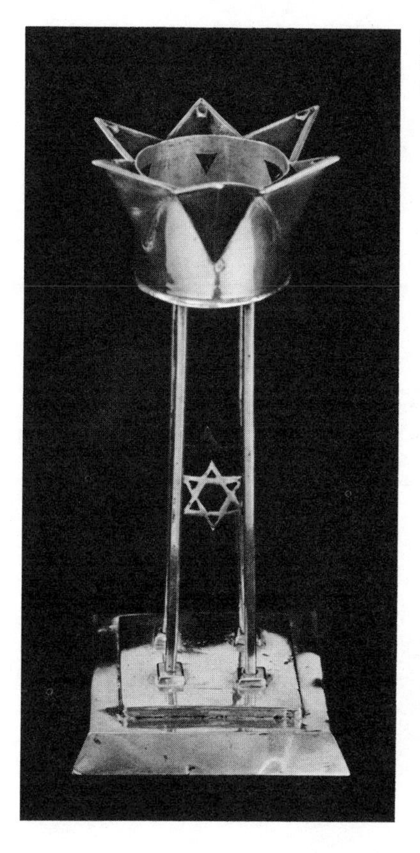

Silver Sabbath lamp in the form of a Star of David. Probably from Baghdad, 18th century.

Indeed, both Jewish and non-Jewish artisans devoted considerable attention to making Sabbath lamps. Because of the injunction to have 'beautiful light' to sanctify the Sabbath, much effort and expense was expended to acquire attractive implements with which to fulfil properly and 'enhance' the command to kindle the Sabbath lights. Whether rich or poor, every Jewish family had a special Sabbath lamp or candlesticks which were usually used for kindling the Sabbath or festival lights.

The most common type of European Sabbath lamp had six, seven, eight or ten radial spouts for floating wicks, forming a tray which jutted out from a central trunk. Used primarily in Central Europe

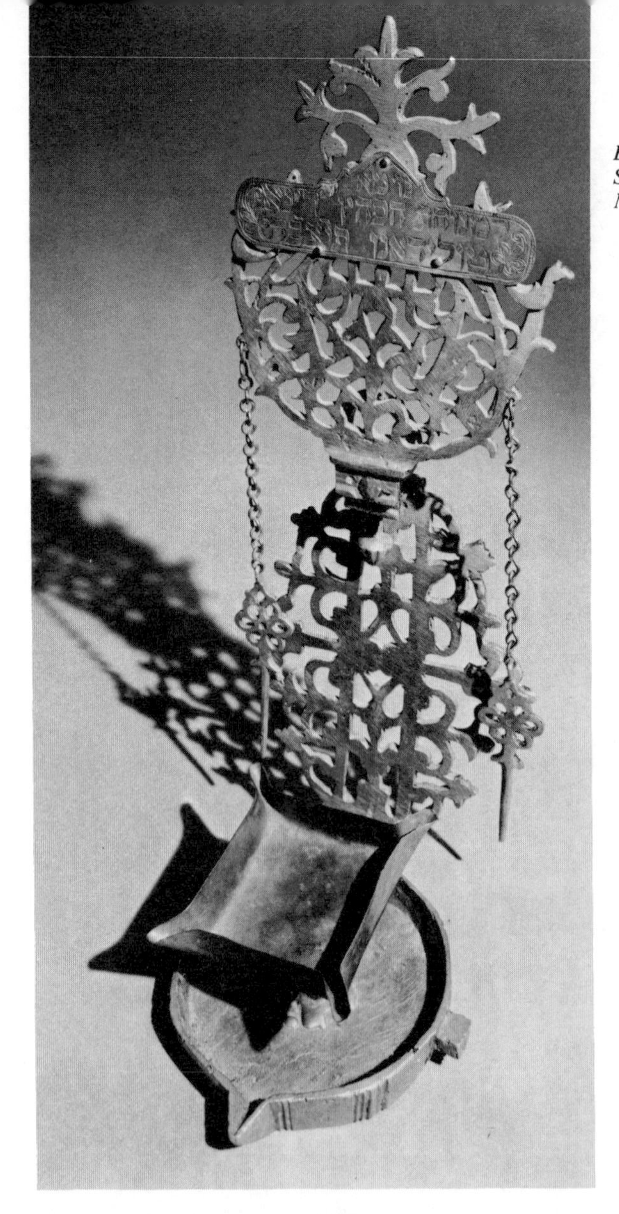

Brass and silver Sabbath lamp. Morocco, c. 1800.

and Holland, it was commonly known as a '*Judenstern*' – Jewish star. These were usually made of brass or copper, but sometimes of silver or pewter, with a drip-cup for oil suspended under the lamp. During the week the lamp hung high, suspended from, and close to, the ceiling, usually above the dining room table. Often there was an adjustable saw-shaped ratchet to raise or lower the lamp, and on Friday afternoon the lamp was lowered, giving rise to the expression, '*Lamp herunter, sorg hinaug*' (the lamp descends and worry disappears).

It is difficult to give a precise date for the hanging Sabbath lamp since the oldest existing examples go back only some three centuries. Copper engravings and woodcuts dating from the sixteenth and seventeenth centuries depict Jewish women lighting Sabbath oil lamps. Hand-written illuminated Passover Hagadot and other decorated Jewish religious manuscripts of medieval origin bear similar illustrations. A sixteenth-century German goldsmith's book, *The Master Book of the Goldsmiths*, published in Frankfurt refers to a Sabbath lamp which was made in 1540, and calls it a '*Judenstern*'. One Frankfurt-am-Main goldsmith, Valentin Schueler, working in the second half of the seventeenth century, produced several notable silver Sabbath lamps, each bearing Jewish ceremonial art objects associated with the Sabbath and the festivals of the Jewish year, and other decorative motifs. Johann Adam Boller is another seventeenth-century Frankfurt-am-Main master who produced at least one notable silver Sabbath lamp. In Italy, depictions of well-known Biblical figures were used to decorate the Sabbath lamp.

A possible prototype, or at least contemporary, of the early hanging Sabbath lamp is said to be a bronze lamp dating back to the twelfth century, now located at the Cathedral of Erfurt, Germany. The star-shaped lamp surrounds a tall, cylindrical trunk, decorated with Biblical scenes. Although all of the scenes come from the Old Testament, the lamp has been identified by one authority as being Christian, on the grounds that Jews would not have 'tolerated such representations in an age when the Biblical prohibition of images was heeded with the utmost severity'. But the examples of imagery in Jewish religious art are numerous and almost commonplace in medieval Germany, and Jewish Sabbath lamps are illustrated in a number of medieval German Jewish illuminated manuscripts. There are also examples of later Sabbath lamps bearing depictions of Old Testament scenes. One may therefore conclude that the hanging lamp in the Cathedral of Erfurt may indeed be the oldest existing Sabbath lamp (possibly representing the spoils of a medieval German pogrom against a Jewish community) and thus also one of the earliest objects of Jewish ceremonial art extant.

Beautiful silver and brass Sabbath lamps were made in Frankfurt and Hamburg in the eighteenth century. In the early nineteenth century, in England, the noted woman silversmith, Hester Bateman, designed a lovely silver Sabbath lamp. Almost a century earlier, in London, the Sephardi Jewish silversmith Abraham Lopez de Oliveyra is said to have created distinctive silver Sabbath lamps.

Candlesticks made expressly for Jewish ritual use are very rare, as most households used ordinary silver or brass candlesticks. There are, however, a number of types with Jewish symbols or inscriptions which were crafted specially for the Sabbath and festival lights. Notable among these was the 'Crackow Lamp', a brass candlestick, usually with three candle-holders resting on a single shaft, upon which were set twin lions or stags, frequently surmounted by a double-headed Russian or Polish eagle and sometimes bearing an inscription in Hebrew from the benedictions over the Sabbath lights such as 'to kindle the light of the Sabbath'. Common in Poland in the seventeenth, eighteenth and nineteenth centuries, they were named after the city in which the lamp was first created. Also in use in Poland during this period was a distinctive type of Sabbath wall sconce in the form of twin stags or eagles supporting candle-holders.

Among the most beautiful and distinctive types of all Jewish candlesticks are the silver, sometimes gilded, pairs which were made in Germany in the eighteenth and nineteenth centuries. Twin upright lions stand on bell-shaped bases, each carrying in his forelegs a flower stem terminating in a candle-holder. The monumental lions are intended as victorious Lions of Judah, and on top of the bases and at the feet of each of the lions are the prone figures of a lizard, a crawfish and a fly. The bases are divided into compartments with alternating ornamentations of floral motifs and Biblical scenes. On one candlestick are scenes of Jacob's dream, the shepherd Moses at the Burning Bush, and Samson defeating the lion. On the other are the Binding of Isaac, the Judgment of Solomon, and a woman in contemporary dress kindling the Sabbath candles. The lizard, the crawfish and the fly symbolise three of the four elements; the fourth, fire, is represented by the candlesticks themselves.

In Southern Morocco, a tall, heavy-cast circular candlestick was likely to be used. In Northern Morocco, where many descendants of Spanish and Portuguese Jewish exiles lived, an oil lamp made of pierced silver, often containing arabesque *mihrabs* (typical of a design found in general art in the area) was used. In Spanish-speaking Morocco, Sabbath oil lamps were sometimes suspended from the wall. These were made of brass and had decorative bird figures at the top. Also occasionally in use in this area was a tiered hanging Sabbath lamp similar to that used by Sephardi Jews in Holland.

The Tunisian Sabbath lamp, called a *'Kandil'*, was a wick dipped in a glass of oil, suspended on a wooden plaque which was overlaid with silver or brass. In much of the Middle East, oil lamps were preferred over candlesticks. The most attractive of these were made of silver and were small enough to be placed on a special stand. The Sabbath lamps of Kurdistan consisted of simple wicks dipped in large, oil-filled vases of earthenware or glass.

In Jerusalem, it was the custom for centuries to use a special hanging oil lamp. Designed simply in the form of a large, circular, brass wheel, it carried seven or twelve small glass vessels, often covered, filled with olive oil. Above is a smaller 'wheel' with three, five or seven small rings, surmounted by a large brass dome from which supporting chains were suspended. When a large number of European Jews arrived in the Holy Land they introduced their custom of lighting candles for the Sabbath. Many established Jerusalem families adopted the new method, but did not abandon the old one, and would usher in the Sabbath with both candles and oil lamps.

While oil lamps predominate for Sabbath use throughout most of Jewish history, there are some indications that candlesticks were also used during certain earlier periods. An illuminated Italian prayer book dating back to about 1500 depicts a Sabbath candlestick with two candles.

The Fruit of the Vine

Wine is an indispensable element in many Jewish rituals. It is present at the Sabbath and festival eve meals and the Sabbath and festival luncheon feasts the following day. It is used also in the marriage and circumcision ceremonies. On many occasions the Bible emphasises that the fruit of the vine is considered worthy of special attention, and singles out for praise the quality of the wine of the Holy Land as a noble drink considered worthy to be consumed with a special benediction when sanctifying the Sabbaths and festivals and key ritual occasions in the life cycle of the Jew. Occupying a special

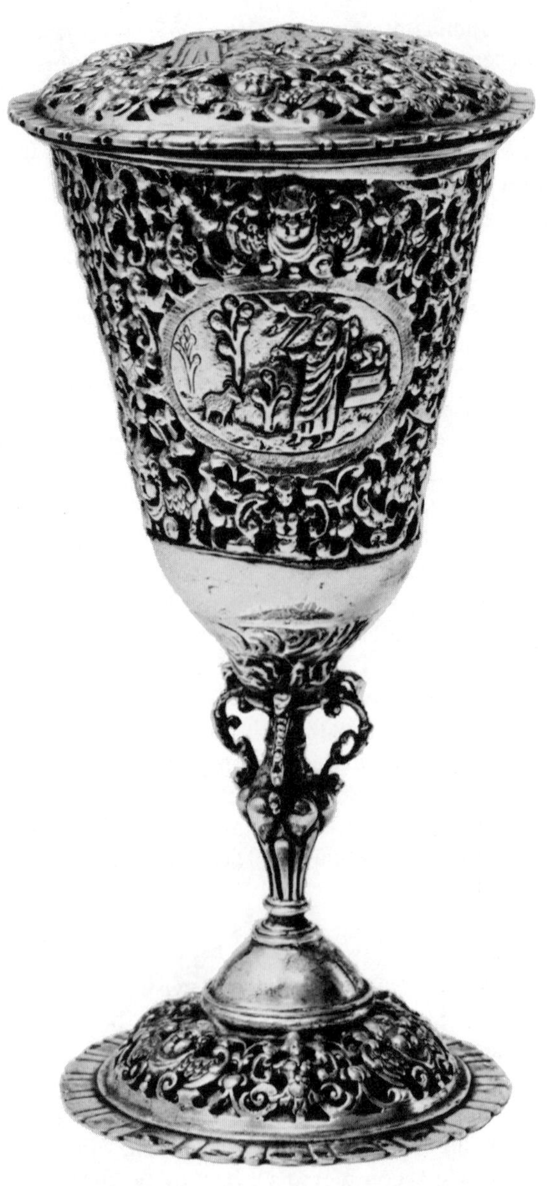

Covered silver Kiddush goblet, with cartouches of Biblical scenes. Holland, 18th century.

place in the Jewish ritual, Jews were warned to drink wine only in moderation and not to excess.

Wine is depicted frequently in ancient Jewish art, and is represented by a variety of symbols: the vine, the grape cluster, the wine cup, a wine jar, a basket of grapes, vineyard scenes and the wine press. Grape clusters as expressly Jewish symbols also appeared on ancient coins, beginning with those of Herod Archelaus (4 BC–6 AD). Wine symbols appeared as Jewish symbols on coins minted by the Romans, and during the Bar Kochba revolt (132–135 AD) Jewish coins themselves invariably carried some references to wine. As a decorative element in Jewish art, wine representations appeared in the Temple in Jerusalem and on the remains of ancient synagogues throughout the Middle East, from Hamam Lif in Tunisia to Dura Europos in Syria.

Kiddush means 'sanctification' and designates the formal ritual performed by the head of the household over a cup of wine upon his return from the Sabbath eve synagogue service and which precedes the festive Sabbath eve feast. In this way the Sabbath is formally proclaimed in the Jewish home and the home life of the Jew is consecrated. For Kiddush, the master of the house usually stands, the Kiddush beaker in his right hand. The Kiddush benediction itself emphasises both the religious and the national significance of the Sabbath. It includes the portion of the Bible describing God's day of rest underlining the belief that the universe is the product of God's work, not chance, and includes references to Israel's redemption from Egypt and to God as the Redeemer. The father is then seated and he and all those at the table drink from the cup.

Old Jewish wine decanters are rare today, but there is no doubt that special decanters were employed for the Kiddush wine even in antiquity, since wine was frequently used in ancient times for idol-worship, and such contaminated wine was expressly prohibited for Jewish use. Most Kiddush wine decanters used during the past several centuries were ordinary wine bottles usually of glass, silver or brass, that have been 'Judaised' at times merely by hanging small silver plates about their necks bearing appropriate Hebrew inscriptions. A few decanters were distinguished by decorations of Hebrew inscriptions or appropriate symbols.

The Kiddush ceremony is an ancient ritual, dating back to around the third or fourth century BC, and the Kiddush cup is, therefore, one of the oldest Jewish ritual objects. The 'Jewish gold glasses' (see also Chapter 4) dating from the third or fourth centuries found in areas where Jews lived throughout the ancient world, and of which only fourteen have been discovered, may well have been fragments of early Kiddush goblets. The bases were adorned with

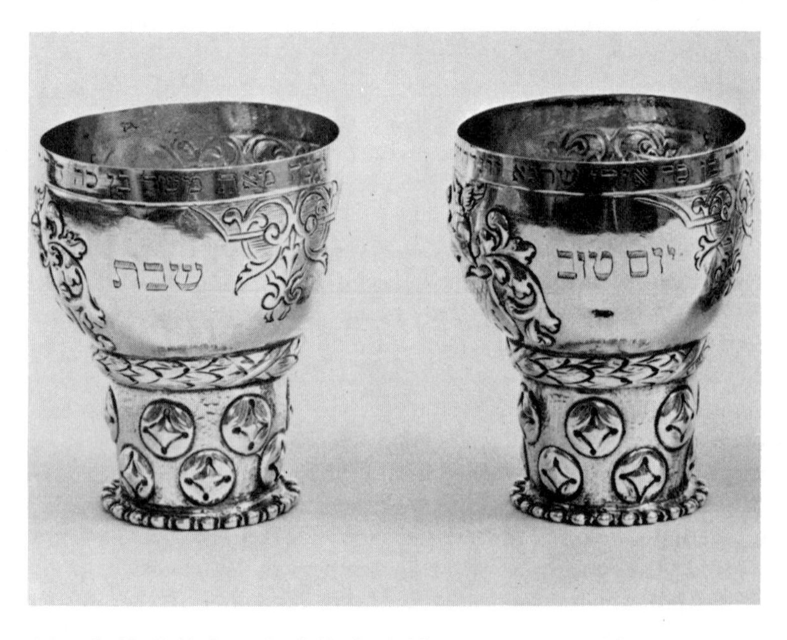

Silver double Kiddush cup for Sabbaths and festivals. Germany, 19th century.

images or scenes fashioned in goldleaf, and mounted between two layers of glass fused together. They featured Jewish symbols such as the menorah, the Torah Ark, and the shofar, and sometimes bore inscriptions in Latin or Greek which freely translated read: 'Take the sanctified drink and live'. One of the fragments depicts a banquet table on which there is a fish ready for eating, and this has been taken to represent the festive Sabbath eve meal, substantiating the hypothesis that the ancient glass fragments are part of Kiddush cups.

Kiddush cups in use in recent centuries were, for the most part, ordinary wine goblets which were sanctified merely by their ritual use. A Hebrew inscription differentiated them from ordinary cups. However, there is a genre of Kiddush beakers which was created especially for the Jewish ritual. A few such glass Kiddush beakers have been preserved and occasionally even a gold beaker will appear; but the vast majority of these were made of silver.

Elaborate inscriptions bearing portions of the Kiddush benediction, or even the entire Kiddush appear on some. Others proclaim they are 'in honour of the holy Sabbath'. Some contain the Biblical command to 'observe the Sabbath day to sanctify it', and some (for the festivals), the Biblical quotation: 'These are the appointed festival seasons of the Lord, the hallowed assemblies . . .' or 'And Moses declared to the children of Israel the appointed festival seasons of the Lord; both of which make up parts of the Kiddush benediction for festivals. Among this group is a type of stemmed silver cup of six, seven or eight sides, resting on an inverted quartisphere dome, made by non-Jewish German silversmiths, mainly in Augsburg and Nuremberg, in the eighteenth and nineteenth centuries.

Another wine cup developed in Germany was a cylindrical vessel which rested on three balled feet, and this type too was co-opted for Kiddush, often by the addition of an appropriately engraved inscription, such as 'Holy Sabbath'. In Germany and Central Europe Kiddush cups are sometimes found with distinctive pictorial depictions on the sides, sometimes beautifully executed. They were of Biblical scenes or scenes associated with the Sabbath or festivals, indicating they were created especially for Jewish ceremonial use.

In eighteenth-century Russia a cylindrical cup with repoussé work around the sides was often used, sometimes featuring a large eagle, and often bearing a Hebrew inscription. In the nineteenth century large numbers of silver wine cups were made in Russia which were decorated in ajouré with scenes of Russian houses, and these too were co-opted for Kiddush. Sometimes scenes of the Holy Land would be engraved. In nineteenth-century Palestine a Kiddush cup made of brownstone and bearing Holy Land scenes was used; and a similar cup, made of silver, featuring Holy Land scenes was crafted in late nineteenth-century Safed.

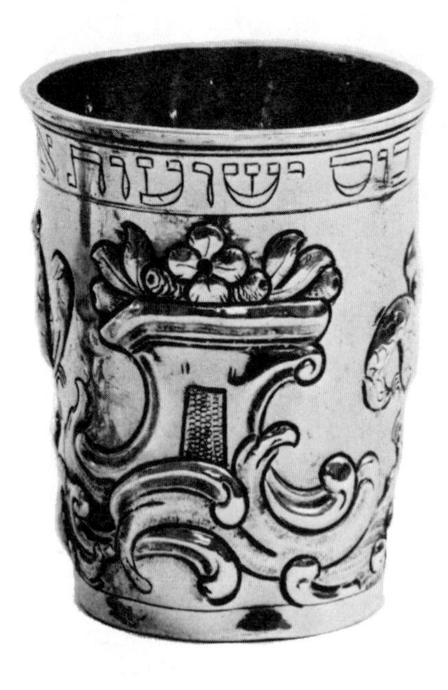

Silver Kiddush cup. Russia, 1774.

In Persia the silver Kiddush cup and tray resembled the contemporary low Western coffee cup and tray, and was distinguished by a Hebrew inscription around the rim. In Iraq, the Kiddush cup was a cylindrical vessel broadening at the top, surmounted with a matching cover featuring a bird finial, and containing a matching tray. Italian Kiddush cups were tall and elaborate, with long stems and large circular bases, and closely resembled the chalices of the Catholic church. In fact, Italian Jews term the cup, '*Calice Da Kiddush*'. These often have their own covers.

After Kiddush comes the ritual washing of the hands. The ceremony, a symbolic purification, precedes the partaking of bread at every meal and is related to the ceremonial handwashing in the Temple prior to the priestly service. The Jewish home is called a 'little sanctuary', and is compared to the Temple, and the dining table likened to a sacrificial altar. For the handwashing, a special vessel evolved, called the *Laver*, generally of copper or silver, tall and cylindrical, with twin handles extending from one side.

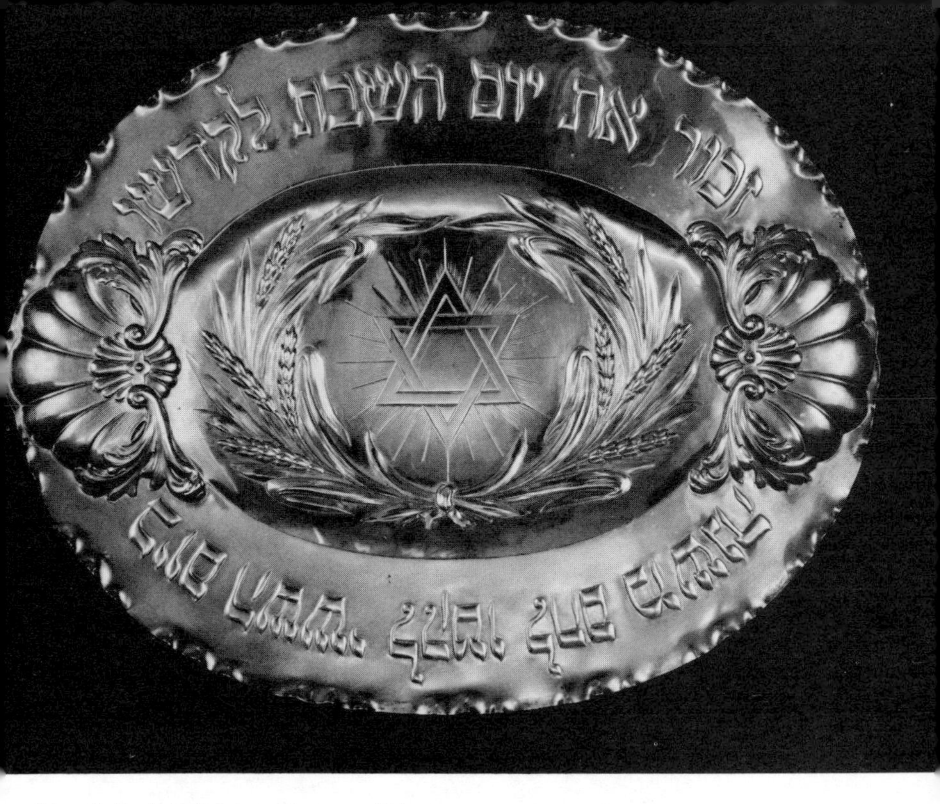

Silver Sabbath Hallah tray. Germany, 19th century.

The Sabbath bread is also special: the two braided *Hallah* loaves are set out to provide the first morsels at the festival banquets of Sabbath eve and Sabbath day and of the festival feasts. They commemorate the double portions of *manna* gathered by the Israelites who prepared for the Sabbath in the wilderness on their way to the Promised Land. Placed prominently on the table, the Hallah loaves are traditionally covered with a special cloth reminiscent of the coating of dew on the desert manna. Usually embroidered, often by the woman of the house, Hallah covers are frequently colourful works of folk art, often fringed and inscribed with the Jewish benediction over bread, and sometimes decorated with depictions of ritual objects and foods associated with the Sabbath and festivals.

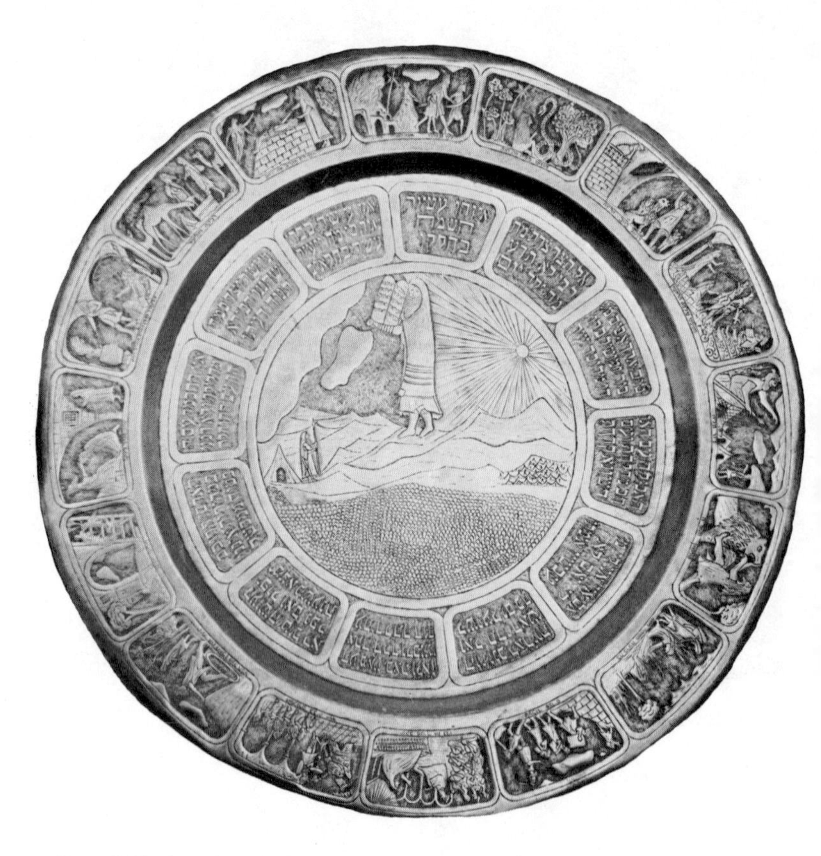

Brass Sabbath and Festival tray. The centre shows Moses with the Tablets at Sinai. Around the rim are depicted sixteen scenes from the Bible. Tripoli, Lebanon, 1849–50.

Another custom is to place the Sabbath loaves on a special *Hallah tray* in memory of the blanket of dew *under* the manna. The tray is generally made of silver or brass, and hammered in repoussé to depict one or two Hallah loaves at the centre. Around the rim the blessing for bread would be inscribed, or the quotation 'Eat your bread with joy.'

The tray is often accompanied by a *Hallah knife*, inscribed with the Hebrew words *Shabbat Kodesh* (Holy Sabbath), identifying it for Sabbath use. Sometimes Sabbath scenes decorate the handle. At times the handle, of silver or mother-of-pearl, allows the blade to fold into it to assure that when not in use the Sabbath table is not marred by an open blade.

Sometimes special Sabbath Tablecloths were used, especially in Persia and Bokhara, which were embroidered with Biblical verses related to the Sabbath, and at times with scenes of the Holy Land.

Before grace is said after the meal, the hands are rinsed, and in Europe a special *Mayim Aharonim* ('the final waters') laver developed for this purpose.

Havdala

The Sabbath is formally ended each Saturday with a special ceremony called *Havdala* ('separation'). A cup of wine is filled to overflowing to symbolise the hope that the new week will be brimful of

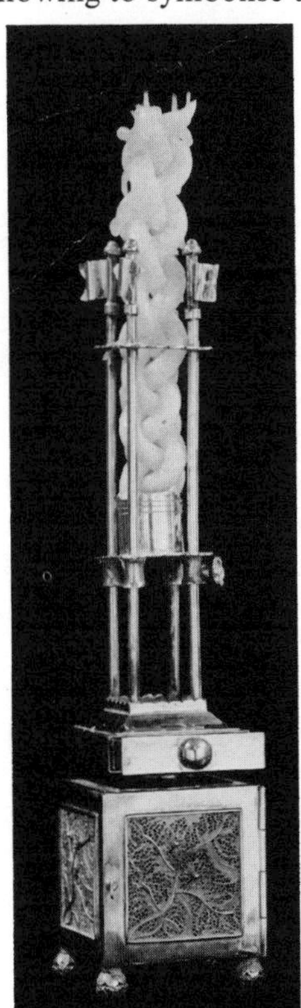

Left: *silver filigree combination Havdala Candle-holder with spice container and drawer. Germany 19th century.*

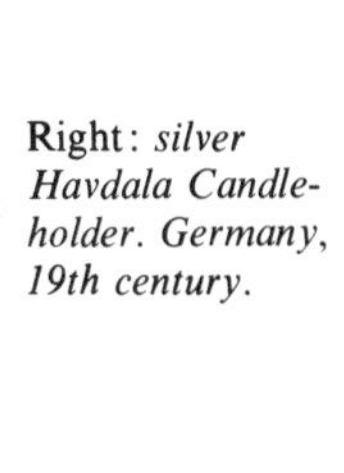

Right: *silver Havdala Candle-holder. Germany, 19th century.*

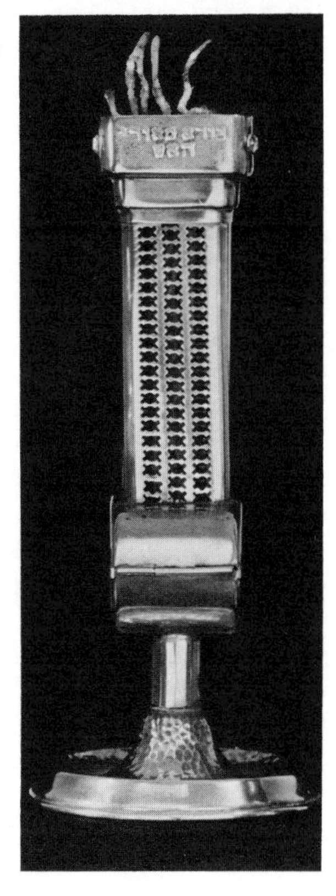

joyous living, and marks the division between the holy and the profane – in the words of the Havdala benediction – between Sabbath bliss and the weekly cycle of creativity.

The *Havdala cup* was most likely an ordinary silver Kiddush cup co-opted for the past-Sabbath ceremony. Occasionally, however, a special cup was used, perhaps carrying words from the Havdala service: 'I lift up the cup of salvation.' References to the prophet Elijah to whom special hymns are sung at the conclusion of the Sabbath, are also to be found on these cups.

Another item for this ceremony is the *Havdala candle*, a braided taper kept lit throughout the service to signify the pleasure derived from the renewed permission to kindle fire – something forbidden to Jews during the preceding twenty-five hours. Lighting this taper also commemorates God's gift of fire at the conclusion of Creation Week as well as man's assumption of mastery over nature when, according to Jewish legend, God gave Adam two stones which he rubbed together to produce fire.

Although the Havdala candle is usually held by a young member of the family, in central Europe a special holder was devised. This was generally made of silver or brass, and often had movable sockets so that it could be raised and lowered depending on the remaining length of the taper. Sometimes it contained a special drawer for spices.

The *Spice Container* is the third, indispensable partner in the Havdala ceremony. Since the Sabbath, with its special food, its joy and rest and quiet all providing man with spiritual strength, is a source of invigoration and consecration, the pleasure of smelling aromatic spices was considered something of a compensation for the natural let-down at its end. The special container for the post-Sabbath spices is possibly as old as the Havdala ceremony itself, though its earliest recorded use dates back only to the twelfth century.

The spice container, a specifically and characteristically Jewish ceremonial object, became very popular and was found in every Ashkenazi Jewish home. Its design was taken up by Jewish craftsmen and folk artists who, with a wealth of imaginative creativity, produced spice boxes of many materials and in a greater variety of forms than exist for any other Jewish ceremonial art object.

By far the favourite shape was that of the medieval gothic tower, topped by turrets and pennants, and at times with a clock in the

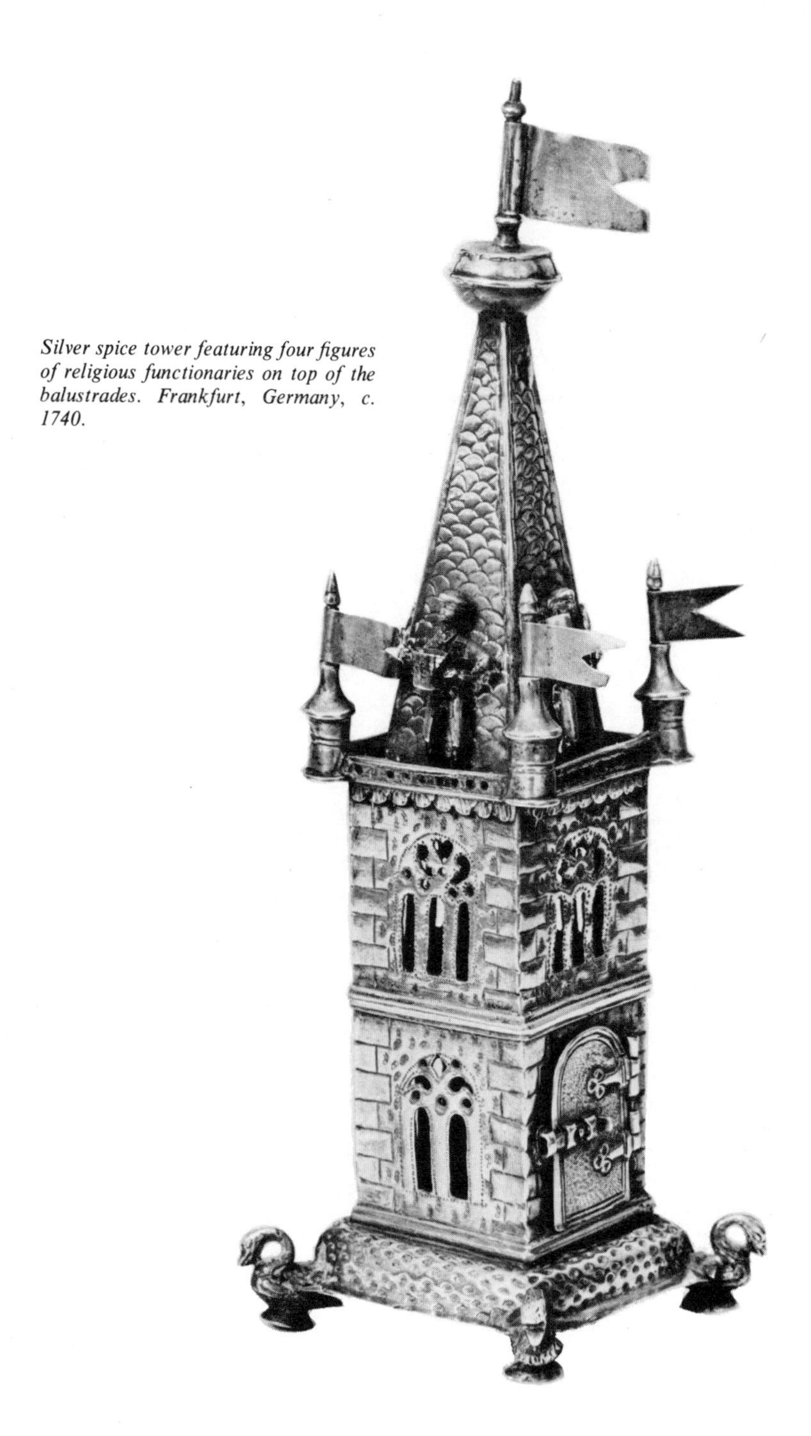

Silver spice tower featuring four figures of religious functionaries on top of the balustrades. Frankfurt, Germany, c. 1740.

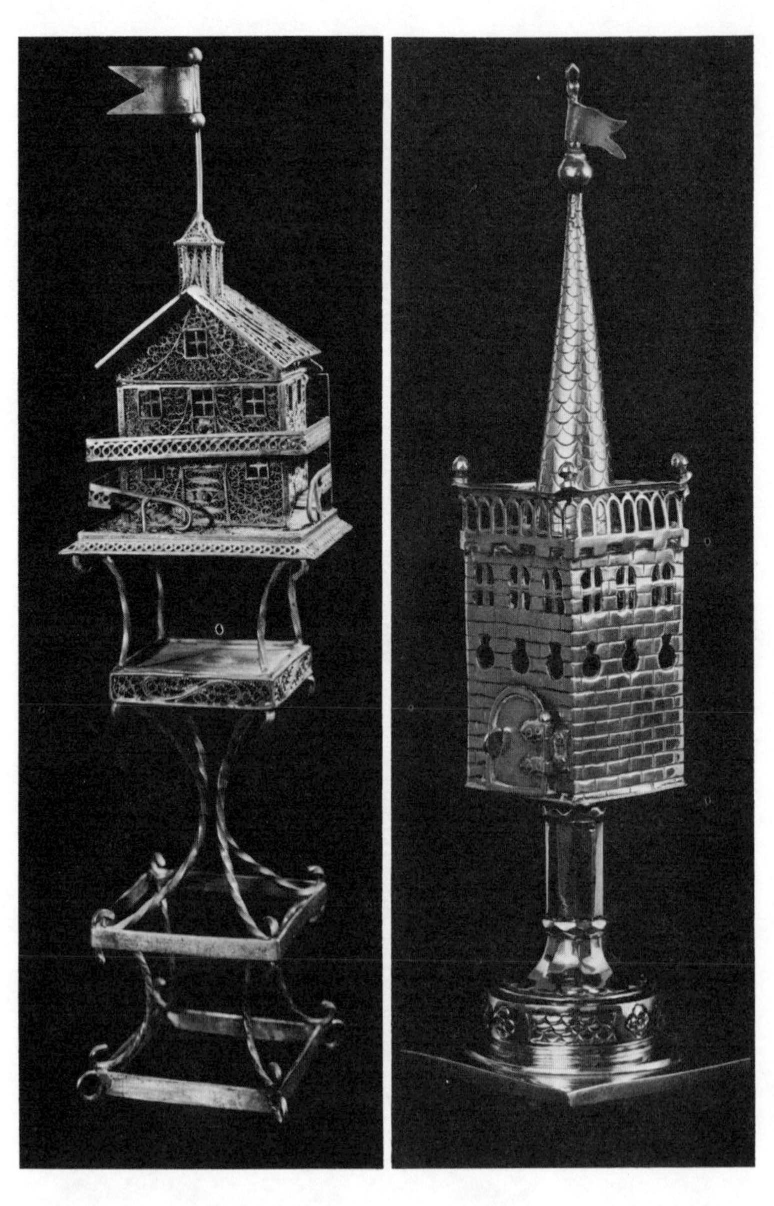

Silver filigree spice tower in the form of a house. Germany, c. 1780.

Silver spice tower. Germany, c. 1750.

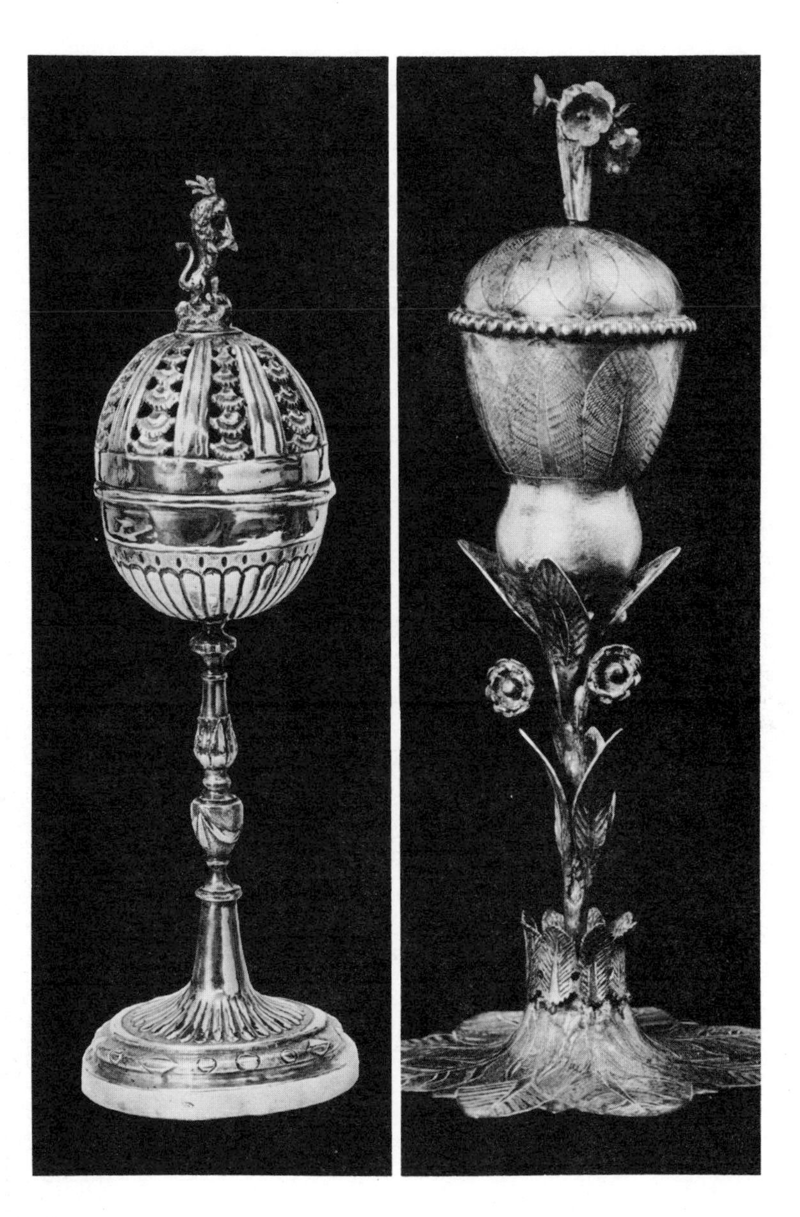

Silver spice container in the form of a fruit. Italy, c. 1800.

Silver spice container in the form of a pear. Eastern Europe, 18th century.

centre. Some towers had figures of guards or even religious functionaries at the four corners, each holding a symbol of his trade: a *shamash* (sexton) with a Kiddush cup, a rabbi with a Bible, a *shohet* (ritual slaughterer) with a knife, and a baker with a Passover *matzah* (wafer).

The tower form itself probably resulted from the fact that spices were a rare and valuable commodity in medieval times and were frequently stored in fortified towers. There is also a Biblical allegorical precedent in the Song of Songs, where Solomon refers to a bunch of spices in distant towers (*Song of Songs, V: 13*). The tower and turret forms for the spice container probably originated in medieval Germany as indicated by records kept by a German silversmith regarding spice containers in the 1530's, and even a sketch by one German silversmith for a spice tower in 1553.

In Poland and elsewhere in Eastern Europe, silver spice containers took the form of flowers, animals, fish, coaches, windmills, houses and even locomotives. Filigree was often used to simplify the inhalation of the aromas. On rare occasions a spice tower would show Jewish symbols or even contain enamel plaques bearing Biblical scenes.

Among the Hassidim of Hungary there arose a custom of creating spice containers out of the lulav, the palm used during the *Sukkot* festival, with the long leaves being braided to form narrow, elongated containers into which the myrtles and willows were placed. Wealthier Jews commissioned silversmiths to duplicate this effect; distinctive braided silver spice containers, averaging fifteen to eighteen inches (38–47 cm) long, were thus created.

The imagination of the designers of this charming group of Jewish ceremonial objects was boundless. One spice container takes the form of a large bird sitting on branches that rest on small lions. One designer fashioned a silver filigree spice tower surmounted by a silver filigree house.

In northern Italy, the spice container often took the shape of a pierced globular vessel surmounted by a lion rampant, sitting on a tall stem on a wide base. In the holy land in the late nineteenth and early twentieth centuries, spice containers were made of olive wood with designs of the Western Wall and other local religious sites carved around the sides.

In Persia, Iraq and India, the silver or brass *Basmia* was developed. This was a bottle with a long, narrow neck and a pierced

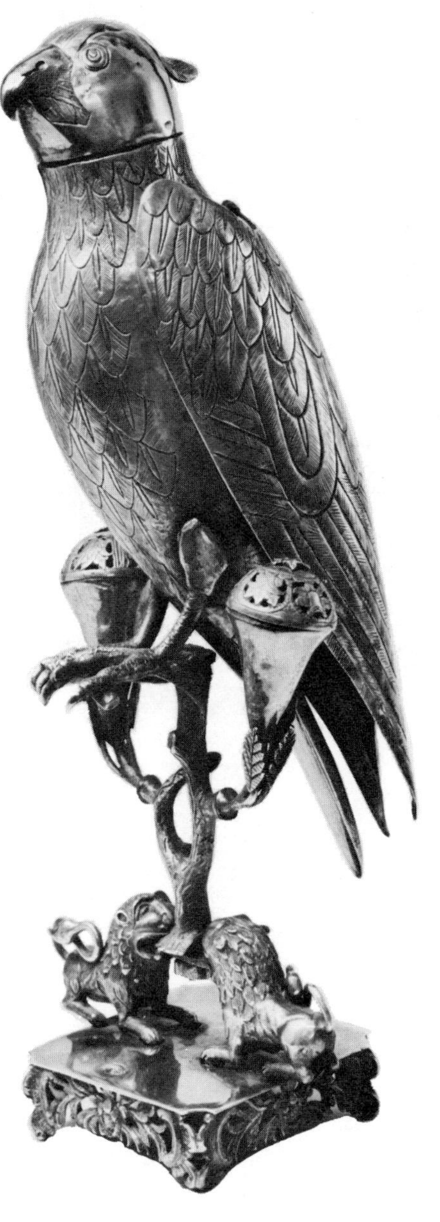

Silver spice container in the form of a large bird resting on a branch bearing pears, and supported by two Lions of Judah. Eastern Europe, 18th century.

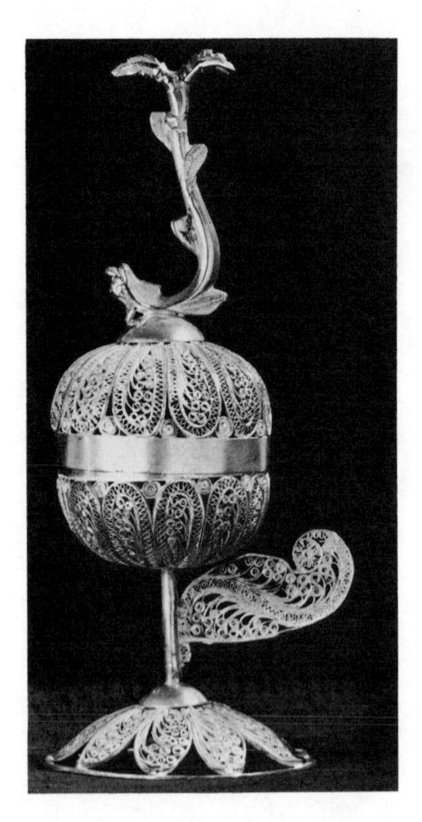

Silver filigree spice container in the form of a fruit surmounted by a dolphin finial. Eastern Europe, 18th century.

cap that was filled with aromatic liquid spices. Unlike the custom in most of the Ashkenazi world, where the Havdala was mainly a home ritual, the practice in these countries was to recite the Havdala in the synagogue after the Sabbath evening service and for the Shamash to sprinkle rose-water from the Basmia on the congregation. The Basmia was also used in this way during the Sabbath and festival days and on such occasions as the circumcision ceremony.

The Havdala service is concluded by drinking from the wine and then pouring some of it on the Havdala tray. The candle is extinguished by dipping it into the wine, indicating that it was lighted only in fulfilment of the ritual. Fingers are then dipped in the wine on the tray, denoting love for Judaism's ceremonials and command,

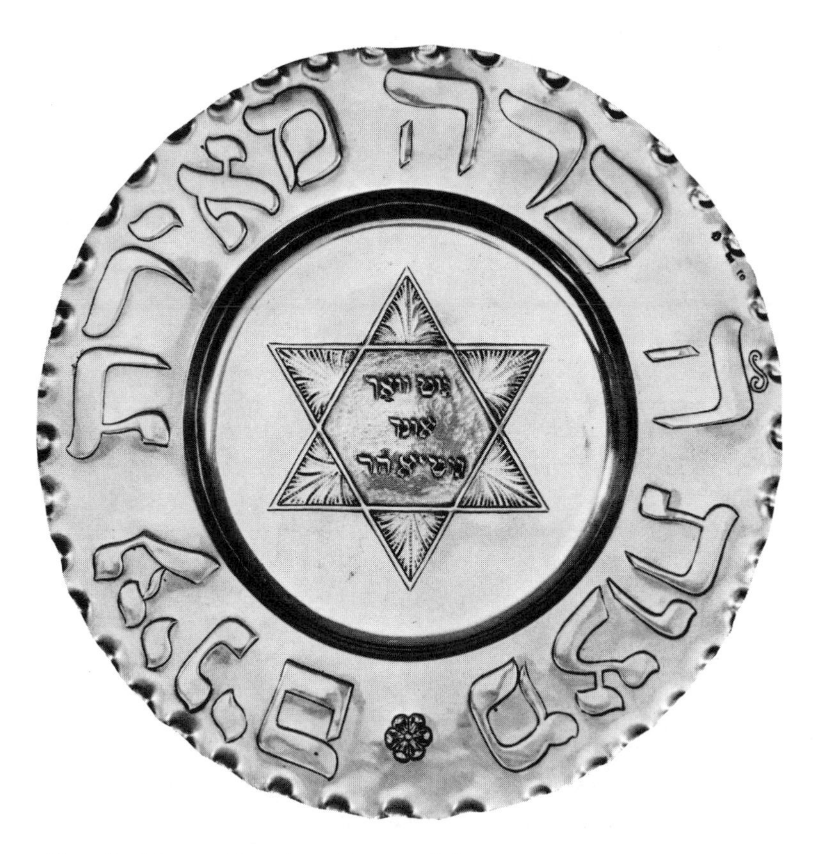

Silver Havdala tray. Nuremberg, Germany, 18th century.

and placed on the eyes, with the reciter quoting from Psalms: 'The commandment of the Lord is clear, enlightening the eyes' (*Psalms XIX*).

The Havdala tray, usually made of porcelain, silver, brass or pewter, often carried the same quotation around its rim. At its centre, at times inside a large Star of David, another inscription read: *Gut Voch* (Yiddish, 'Good Week').

8 Jerusalem and the Jewish Home

Jerusalem has been the soul of the Jewish people for nearly three thousand years. Since the tenth century BC when David made the city his capital and for the nearly two thousand years of Jewish exile, Jerusalem has served as the focal point for the Jewish people, wherever they have lived. In his Psalms, David exclaims 'If I forget thee O Jerusalem may my right hand lose its cunning' (*Psalms CXXXVII: 5*), and thrice daily the observant Jew turns to Jerusalem in prayer and beseeches God to rebuild Jerusalem. A similar prayer is recited upon concluding every meal. Both the Yom Kippur day of fasting and the Passover Seder feast end with the cry 'Next Year in Jerusalem,' and many of the joyous occasions in the life of the Jew are ritually interrupted with an act designed to remind him that no joy can be complete so long as Jerusalem is not rebuilt in accordance with David's exhortations to 'place Jerusalem above my chiefest joys' (*Psalms, CXXXVII: 6*).

When building a new home the Jew is enjoined to leave unfinished an area about half-a-yard (47 cm) square as a reminder of Jerusalem. And in the home, on the Jerusalem-oriented wall, he is instructed to hang a significant mnemonic device – the *Mizrach*. 'Mizrach' means 'east' and the Mizrach tablet served to orient Western Jews when praying, and as a constant reminder of the destruction of Jerusalem. Because it was prominently in view at all times, the Mizrach developed into a decorative wall ornament upon which the attention of the Jewish artist was lavished. Sometimes it was a block of wood with an ornate carving of the word 'Mizrach', or it could have been a tablet of metal engraved or hammered with scenes of Jerusalem or the remaining Western Wall of the Temple.

Often the Mizrach was colourfully executed on paper or parchment by a scribe-illuminator. Sometimes the artist used the art of the paper-cut or parchment-cut, placing the cut-out against a background colour. To the word 'Mizrach', sometimes the quotation from Psalms was added: 'From the rising of the sun in the East (Mizrach) until the setting thereof the name of God is to be praised.' Since the Mizrach was at times used for the '*Shiviti*', a tablet which stood facing the precentor in the synagogue, it would include the quotation from Psalms '*Shiviti*': 'I have placed the Lord always before me', and at times 'Know before Whom you stand, before the King of all Kings, the Holy One Blessed be He.' Both phrases are intended to emphasise the sanctity of the Jewish home.

Another example of Jewish decorative art in the home is the *Mezuzah*. A small piece of parchment bearing hand-written Biblical verses, it emphasises the Jewish love for God and the acceptance of His commands. The verses are headed by the phrase: 'Hear O Israel, the Lord our God is One.' Jews are commanded in the Torah to affix the Mezuzah to the entrance doorpost and to that of all inner doors of the home. In Jerusalem, the parchment was inserted into a carved out hollow of the doorpost, but elsewhere the parchment was placed in a special Mezuzah container, and attached to the doorpost. Usually of silver, brass or wood, it is often attractively decorated with scenes of the Holy Land.

9 The Art of the Synagogue

Within the synagogue, the central sacred position was reserved for the Torah, the first five books of the Bible. The Torah itself had to be starkly simple. It was to be hand-written with a quill in plain black ink by a trained Hebrew scribe employing traditional, unpunctuated Hebrew letters, on parchment or leather originating from ritually clean animals. The leather strips were then sewn together by tendons and the scroll was wound around tall wooden staves.

The importance of the Torah scroll, however, has always been enhanced by its elaborate outer appearance, for the commandment of *Hiddur Mitzvah* is specifically associated in the Talmud with the adornment of the Torah Scroll. Sumptuously adorned on Sabbaths and festivals, each Torah would be dressed in colourful silks and brocades, would have a silver breastplate and a Torah sceptre hanging over it, and would be surmounted by a regal crown of silver or a pair of tall silver finials with bells. All these artistic accessories were designed to draw attention to the majesty of the Torah and to give it a regal splendour.

Torah scrolls would often be wrapped in a strip of linen about six inches (15 cm) wide and several yards or metres long and which was painted or embroidered and called a *wimple* by German Jews. In Germany and central Europe the wimple was made from the swaddling cloth used in circumcision ceremonies. Carefully cleaned, the cloth would be cut into four strips which were sewn end to end, upon which was stitched the infant's name and birthday, as well as the wish that he grows up to study the Torah, be married and perform good deeds throughout his lifetime. The Hebrew lettering would usually be executed in classical medieval German style. The different elements of the inscription would engender appropriate decoration with folk-art motifs. After the child was weaned, he was ceremoniously carried into the synagogue for the presentation of his wimple to the synagogue.

The Torah was covered with a sheath of coloured velvet or silk brocade, a *Torah Mantle*. Richly embroidered, often with gold, the

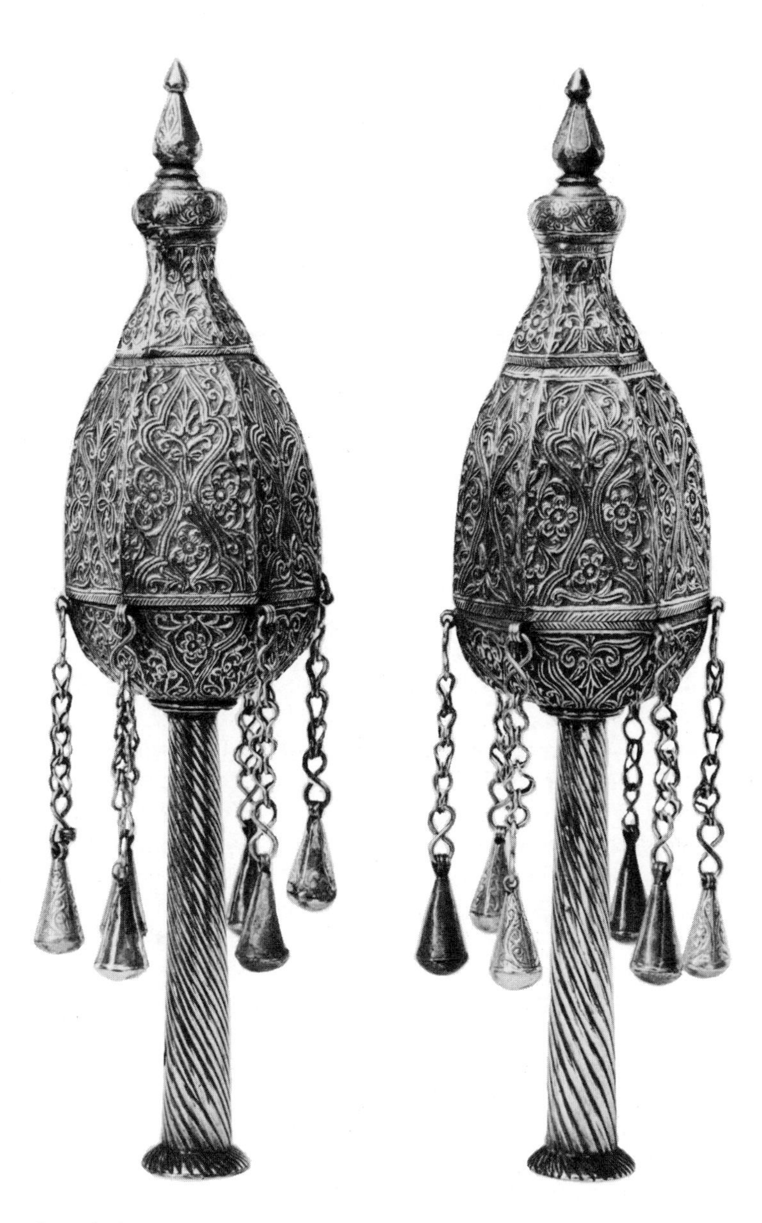

Pair of silver Rimonim. Morocco, 18th century.

Torah Mantle in Europe would frequently carry inscriptions and decorations featuring appropriate Jewish symbols, such as the Tablet of the Law and the Lions of Judah. In Italy and North Africa, the finest of fabrics would be used for Torah Mantles. These were elaborately embroidered, but for the most part inscriptions were eschewed. The Torah staves were sometimes decorated with carvings or appliqués.

The most imposing of all Torah ornaments was the silver Torah crown which surmounted the scroll. It is possible that this was prompted by the Mishnaic tractate *Chapters of the Fathers* (*IV: 17*), where the sages speak of three crowns: one of royalty, one of priesthood, and a crown of Torah, and adds that the 'crown of a good name exceeds them all'. While the reference may have been to actual crowns of Torah, since the two other crowns referred to actually existed, no crowns or other silver ornaments associated with the Torah scroll are to be seen in the various depictions of open Torah arks where Torah scrolls are displayed in the late classical period.

It is not until about 1000 that there is a reference to what could be a Torah crown in a responsum of the rabbinic sage Hai Gaon (939–1038) of Pumpedita in Babylonia. A property inventory of the Palestinian synagogue in Fostat (old Cairo) dating back to 1186–7 lists: 'Two Torah crowns made of silver and three pairs of *rimonim* (Torah finials) made of silver, and twenty-two Torah covers made of silk, some of them brocaded in gold. In 1204 there is a reference to a Torah crown in a work written by Rabbi Abraham of Lunel and Toledo, Spain. In the Sarajevo *Hagadah*, a fourteenth-century illuminated Spanish manuscript, a depiction of an open Torah Ark reveals a gilt Torah crown placed above a Torah scroll.

Sometimes the Torah crown resembled an actual royal crown, but in many cases they were large, generally crown-like objects, sometimes rising up layer on top of layer, usually bearing bells. In Poland they might be decorated with flowers or silver animals, the favourites being lions, stags, eagles and leopards. This is in accordance with another quotation from *Chapters of the Fathers* (*V:23*) which states that a Jew should always strive to be '... strong as a leopard, light as an eagle, fleet as a stag and heroic as a lion, to perform the will of your Father in Heaven'. In Italy the crowns would frequently have cast silver ornaments representing the ritual objects in the Temple of Jerusalem.

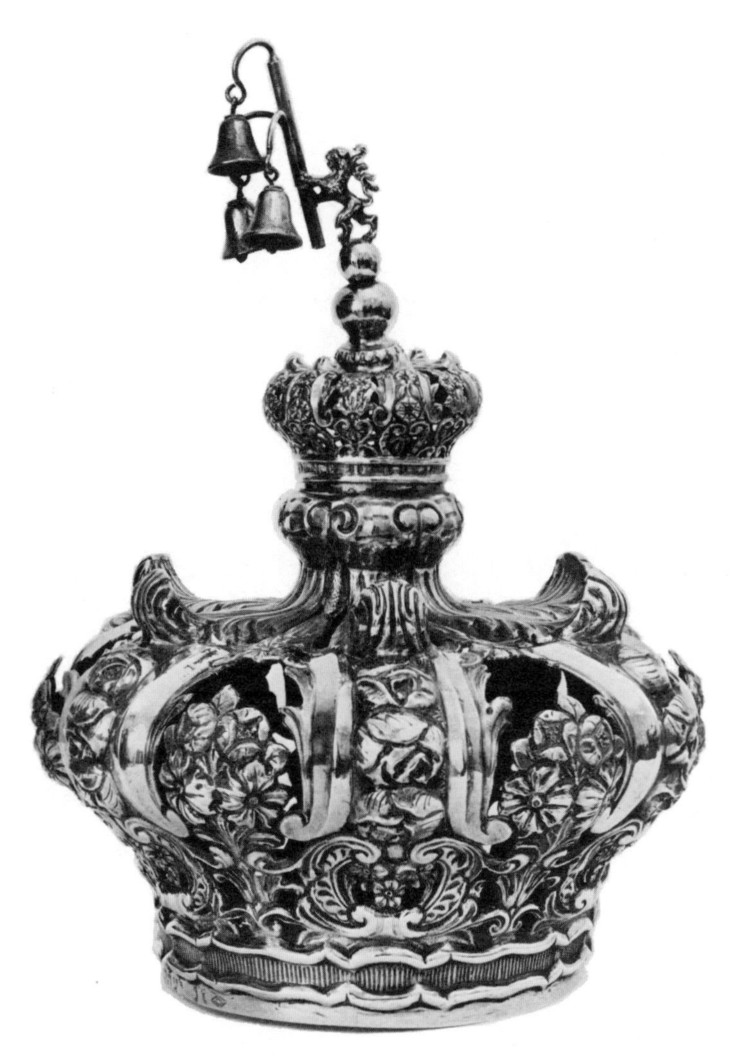

Silver Torah crown. In the form of a large crown surmounted by a smaller one on top of which stands a Lion of Judah holding three bells. Central Europe, c. 1800.

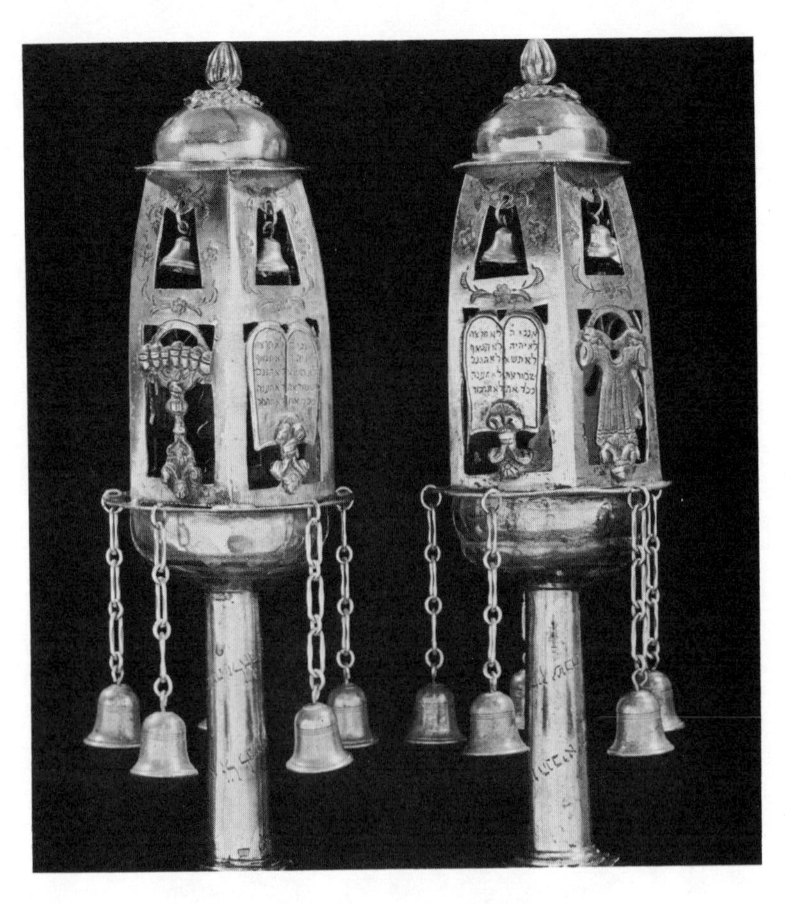

Pair of silver Rimonim, featuring cast and cut-out ritual symbols. Possibly from Southern Europe, 18th century.

Instead of the Torah Crown or in addition, as in Italy, were tall Torah headpieces or finials sitting over the Torah staves called *Rimonim* (pomegranates). The Bible describes the garments of the high priest as being adorned with bells and pomegranates at the bottom, where the sound of the tinkling of the bells informed worshippers in the Temple that the high priest was coming and they

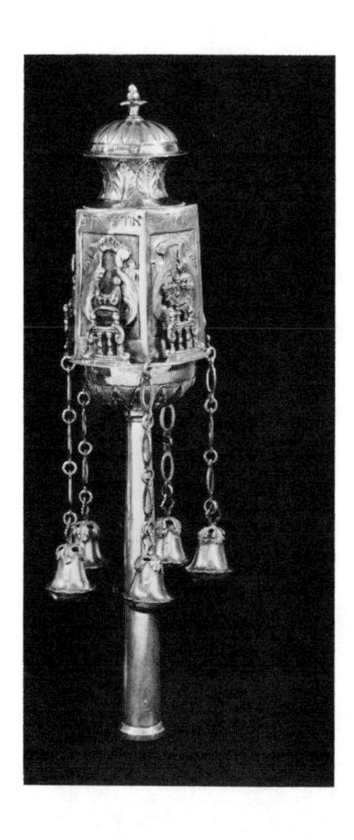

Silver Rimon. Italy, 17th century.

should rise in respect. The Rimonim, which were originally designed to resemble actual pomegranates, and still do in a number of countries, almost always bear many bells, and when the Torah is ceremoniously carried between the Torah Ark and the *Bimah*, the reading desk, the tinkling of the bells from the Rimonim are a signal to the congregation to rise in respect.

The oldest pair of Rimonim known, dating from fifteenth-century Spain, somehow found their way into the possession of the cathedral in Palma de Majorca. Bells are so much a part of most Rimonim that in English the term for the Torah finials is simply 'Bells'. In England, Holland and Germany Rimonim tended to move away from the rounded, bulbous look of pomegranates, took on a somewhat tiered, architectural look, and came to resemble towers.

A notable pair of Rimonim was made in 1799 by Peter, Ann and William Bateman in England. Earlier in the eighteenth century the

Silver Torah-shield. Centred between columns is shown the Binding of Isaac, surmounted by Lions of Judah rampant flanking the Ten Commandments. On top of the columns griffins support a Crown of Torah. Poland, 18th century.

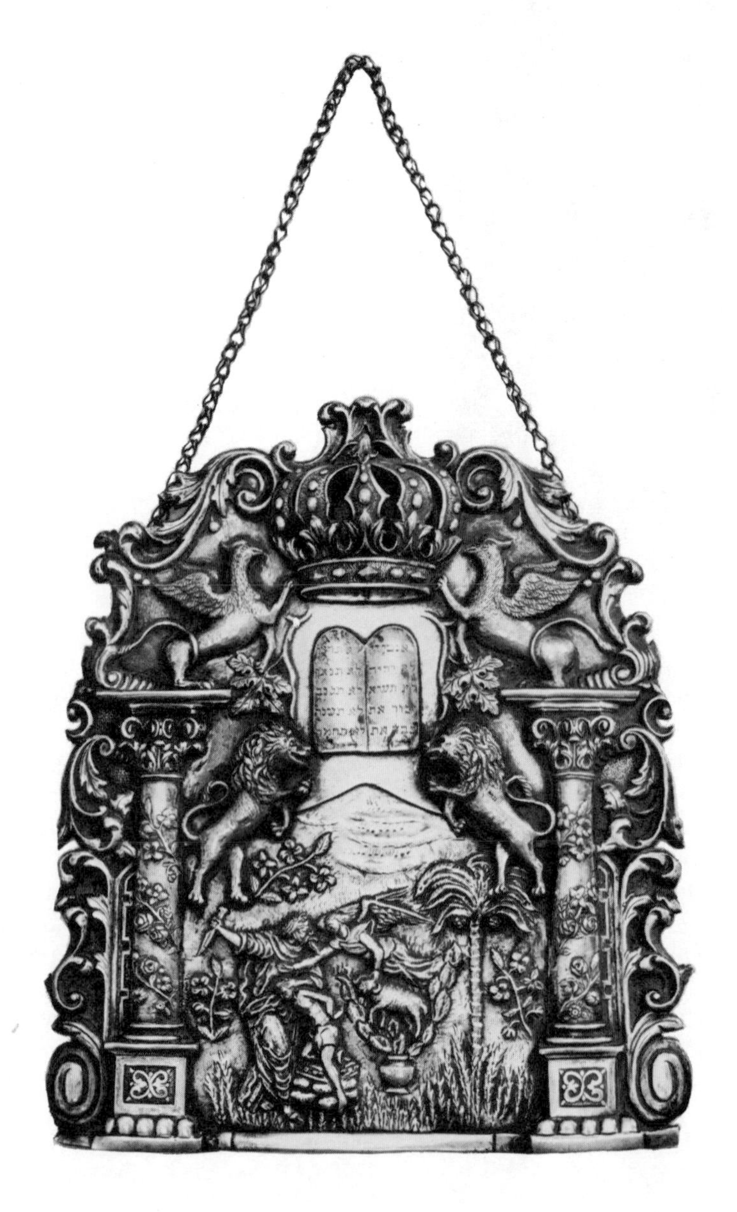

English Sephardi Jewish silversmith Abraham de Oliveyra produced a fine pair. The American colonial period silversmith Meyer Myers is also known for several pairs of fine Rimonim. Rimonim were also made of brass and several extraordinary wooden and gilded pairs were produced in North Africa.

The ornamental Torah-shield or Breastplate hangs by a chain suspended from the Torah staves. The Torah-shield was originally designed to display a small plaque bearing the name of one of the festivals or special Sabbaths of the year. The scrolls in the ark are rolled to specific places where the Torah reading would take place; the plaque made it convenient to identify and to remove from the ark the specific Torah scroll prepared for the reading of the occasion. Gradually the plaque became more elaborate and ornamental and eventually was incorporated as an interchangeable panel within the Torah-shield, which had now become a larger and virtually indispensable Torah ornament.

The Torah-shield was at times made to resemble the breastplate of the High Priest of the Temple, with twelve semi-precious stones to represent the twelve tribes of Israel. The surface was occasionally worked in repoussé with scenes such as the Binding of Isaac or the Revelation at Sinai. Often the twin columns of the Jerusalem Temple, Yachin and Boaz, would decorate its sides, sometimes surmounted with rampant Lions of Judah supporting a Crown of Torah and frequently having bells suspended from the bottom. Figures of Moses and Aaron would sometimes adorn the sides. Most popular was the elaborate baroque style, but at times the breastplate would be a simple square with a plaque on it.

Since the parchment or, in the case of many oriental countries, leather, of the Torah scroll is deemed sacred and thus cannot be touched directly, a ceremonial art object, the Torah Pointer, was created to point to the text and so aid in the reading. Narrow, sceptre-like and usually of silver or gold, it was occasionally set with precious stones: its relatively small dimensions encouraged lavish adornment. Usually a silver or gold chain attached to the Torah Pointer and looped over the Torah staves served as an additional adornment.

The tip of almost all Pointers is fashioned in the form of a small human hand, usually with an outstretched index finger. However, in some oriental countries the Pointer resembled the *Hamsa*, an

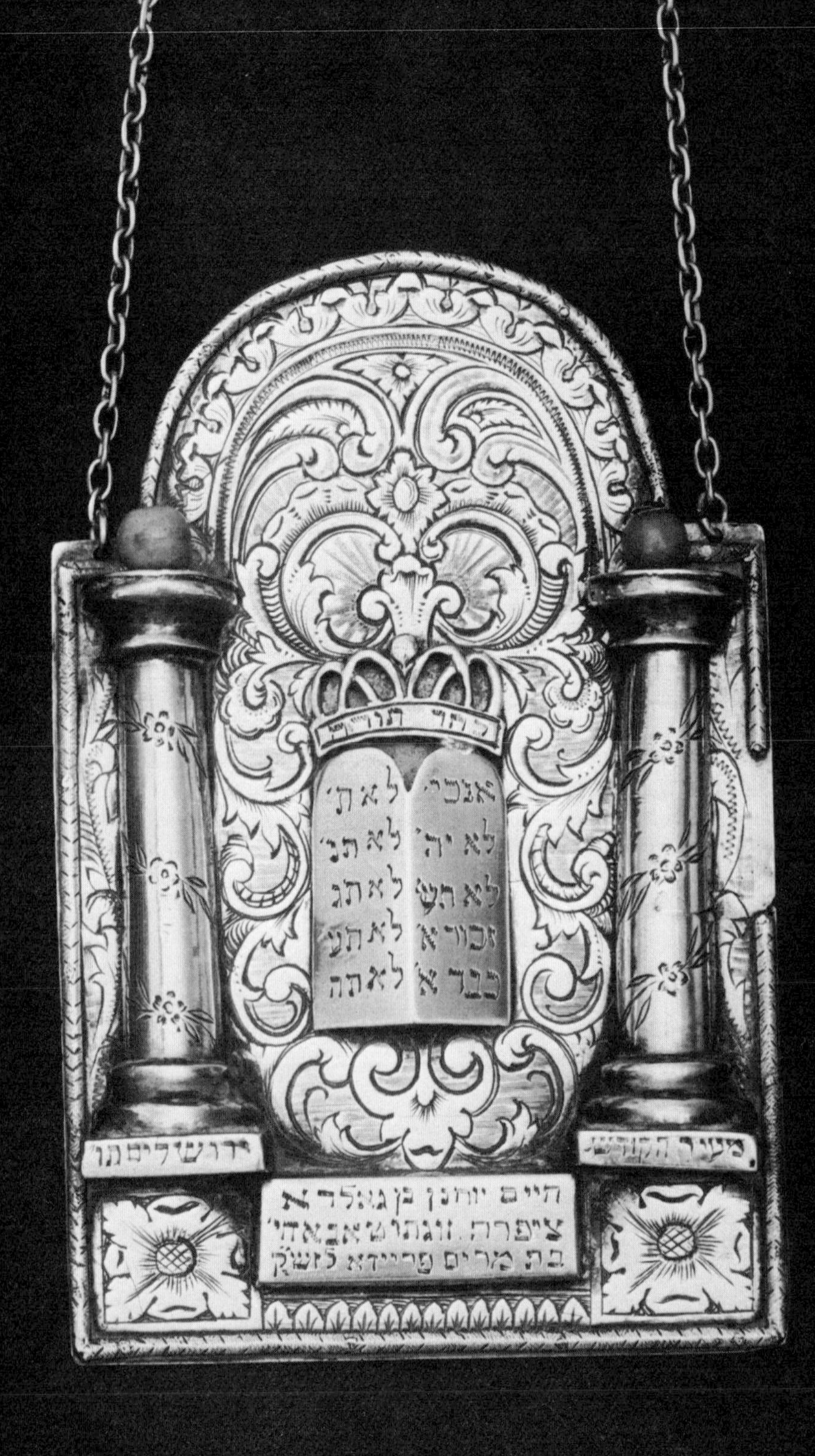

כתר תורה
אנכי
לא יה'
לא תש'
זכור א'
כבד א'
לא ת'
לא תנ'
לא תג
לא תע
לא תח
ירושלים תו
מעיר הקודש
חיים יוחנן בן גאלדא
ציפרה. וזוגתו אבאחי
בת מרים פריידא לזשק

Opposite: *miniature silver Torah-shield. Jerusalem, 19th century.*

Below: *group of five silver Torah Pointers from, left to right, Iraq, Italy, Turkey, Russia and Poland.*

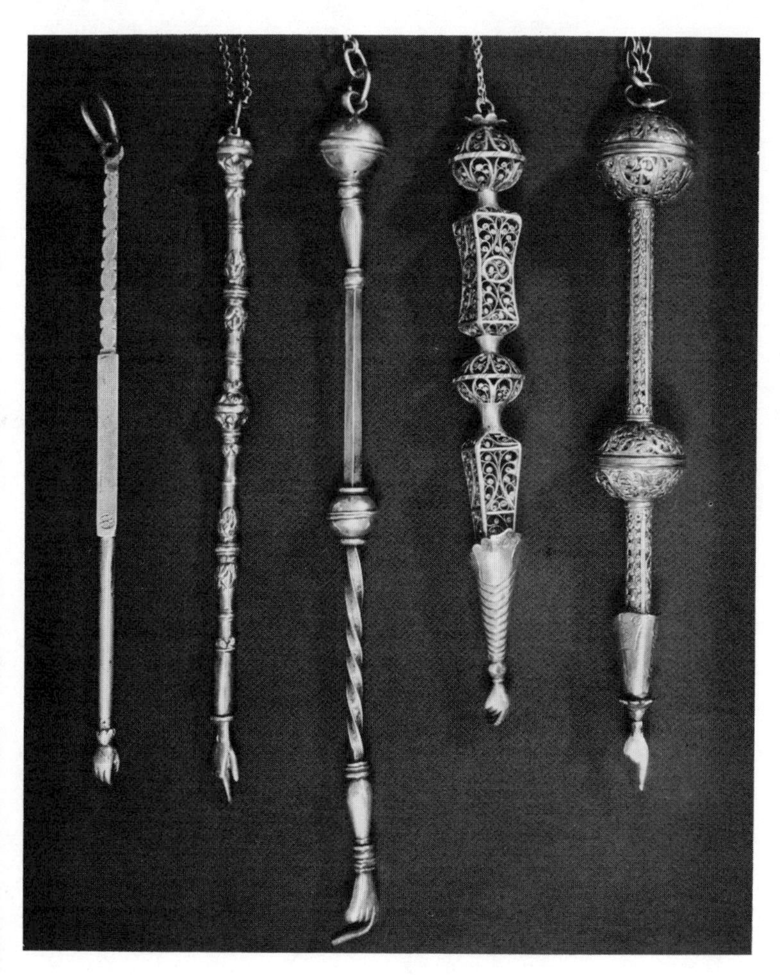

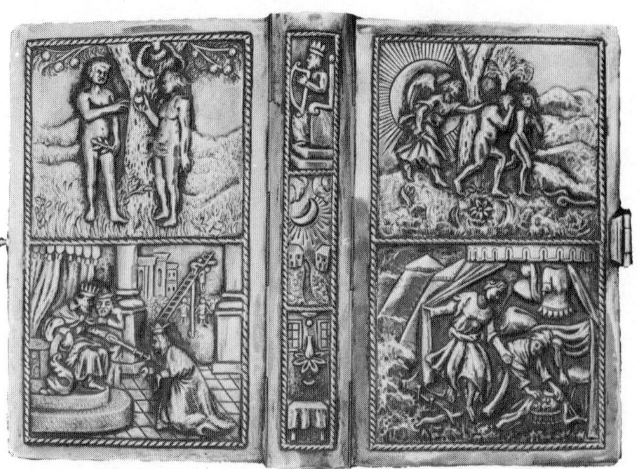

Above: *silver prayer book cover, decorated with Biblical scenes. Amsterdam, 1726.*

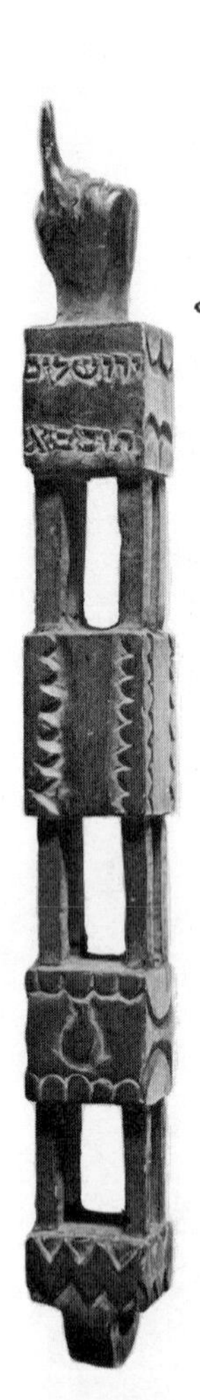

Left: *wooden Torah Pointer. Jerusalem, 19th century.*

open-hand amulet found throughout the Middle East, whereas in Yemen the Pointer simply came to a point. Eastern lands often produced flat Torah Pointers rather than tubular ones.

The influence of the environment is strongly felt in Jewish ritual objects from various parts of the world. All Jewish communities emphasised the Torah's importance by wrapping and decorating the scrolls, but the manner of adornment reflected the craft skills of each particular region. This is quite obvious in the art object called the *Tik* or *Nartik*, a contoured case made of wood, adorned with silver and velvet and with hinges in the rear. The Tik used to cover the Torah in many North African and Asian Jewish communities which rarely employed the soft Torah Mantle sheath.

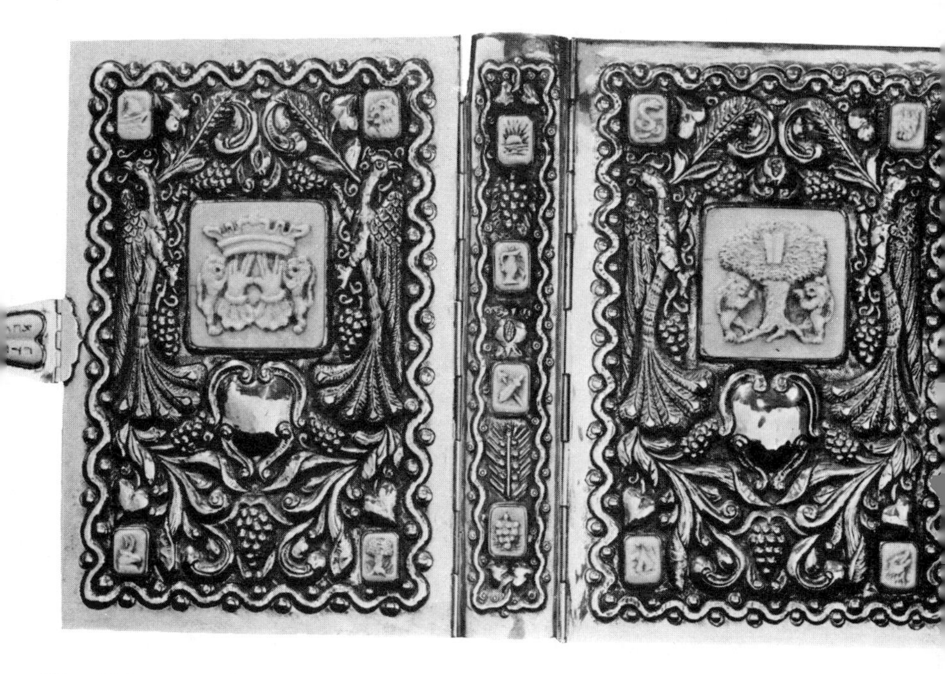

Silver Bible cover, with ivory plates representing Jewish symbols and the twelve tribes. New York, 20th century.

The Tik stands upright on a flat table where it can be opened so that the Torah may be read without removing the scroll. Torah cases, often decorated with a layer of coloured velvet or silver, are imposing examples of Eastern Jewish ceremonial art. Among the most beautiful are those made in Baghdad and India, surmounted by graceful, bulb-shaped cupolas. Generally these bear floral or geometric ornamentations in hammered repoussé bands adorning the exterior, with colourfully painted and decorated plaques of silver or glass inside.

The Torah Ark itself became an important Jewish symbol in ancient times because of its significant role as the abode of the Torah scrolls. It appears in a variety of examples in Ancient Jewish art of

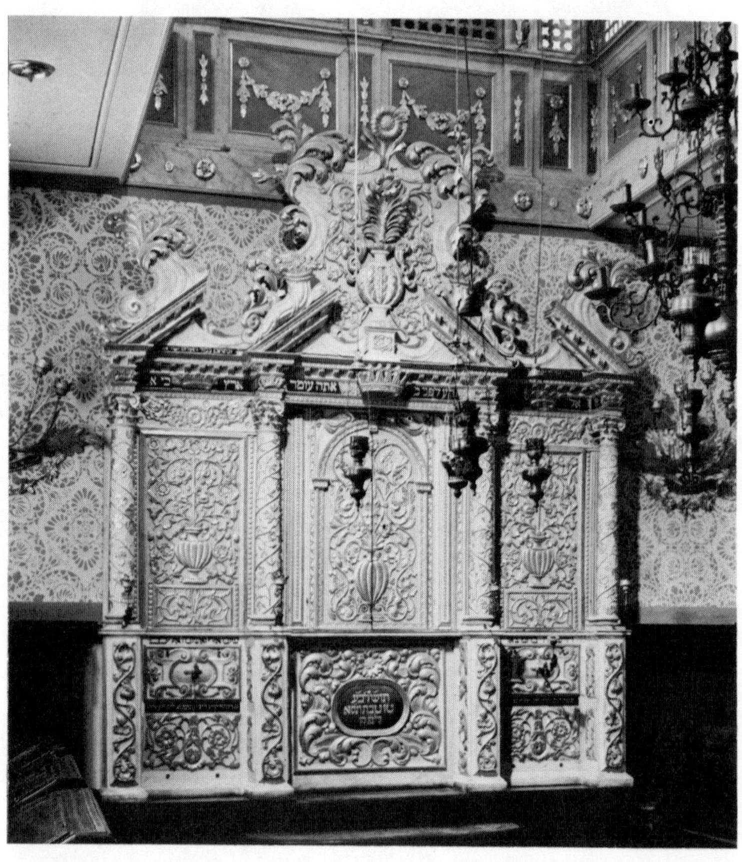

Carved and gilded wooden Torah Ark. Vittorio Veneto (Ceneda), Italy, 1701, now in the Israel Museum, Jerusalem.

the classical period, from synagogue mosaic floors to Jewish gold glasses and to Jewish funerary art. Its sanctity is emphasised by the *Shulhan Aruch*, the Code of Jewish Law, which declares: 'One is obliged to accord great honour to the Torah scroll, and it is a mitzvah to provide it with a special place, to honour that place and to beautify it in an exceptional manner.' Indeed, while it is permissible to sell the synagogue pews or even the Torah reading desk for the purchase of an Ark, Jewish law forbade the sale of a usable Torah Ark even for the purchase of a synagogue.

It is not known when the elaborate ornamentation of Torah Arks began. There is no doubt, however, that by the sixteenth and seventeenth centuries a tradition of artistic craftsmanship centred around the Torah Ark had begun to produce majestic Arks of exceptional beauty. In Italy, Jewish ceremonial art reached its highest level at the end of the Renaissance and during the two centuries following, with beautiful sculptured and gilded wood, brass and silver Torah Arks. Noteworthy examples have been brought to Israel, including the Torah Ark of Conigliano Veneto, dating from 1701, that of Vittorio Veneto (Ceneda), also dating from 1701, and the Torah Ark of the Scuola Grande Italiana of Mantua, dating from 1635. The latter, imposing monumental work is appropriately inscribed 'to exalt the house of the Lord'.

In Eastern Europe as well, considerable attention was lavished on the Torah, but with different results. Often colourfully painted, many of the Torah Arks of Poland and Russia were folkloristic in design, reflecting the nature of the Eastern European Jewish ghetto communities. Floral motifs were frequently used along with depictions of a variety of animals, especially the so-called four Jewish 'folk animals' – the leopard, the eagle, the stag and the lion. Of these the lion predominated because of its association with the Lion of Judah, a prime Jewish symbol. Rampant Twin Lions of Judah appeared frequently at the top of Torah Arks, usually flanking the Tablets of the Law or supporting a Crown of Torah, or sometimes both.

A major appurtenance of the Torah Ark was the *Parochet* or Torah Ark Curtain. In most European synagogues the Parochet hung in front of the Ark, while in Italian and oriental synagogues the curtain hung just inside the doors of the Ark. The custom probably comes from the Bible, which describes a curtain separating the main hall from the *Sanctum Sanctorum* (Holy of Holies) in the

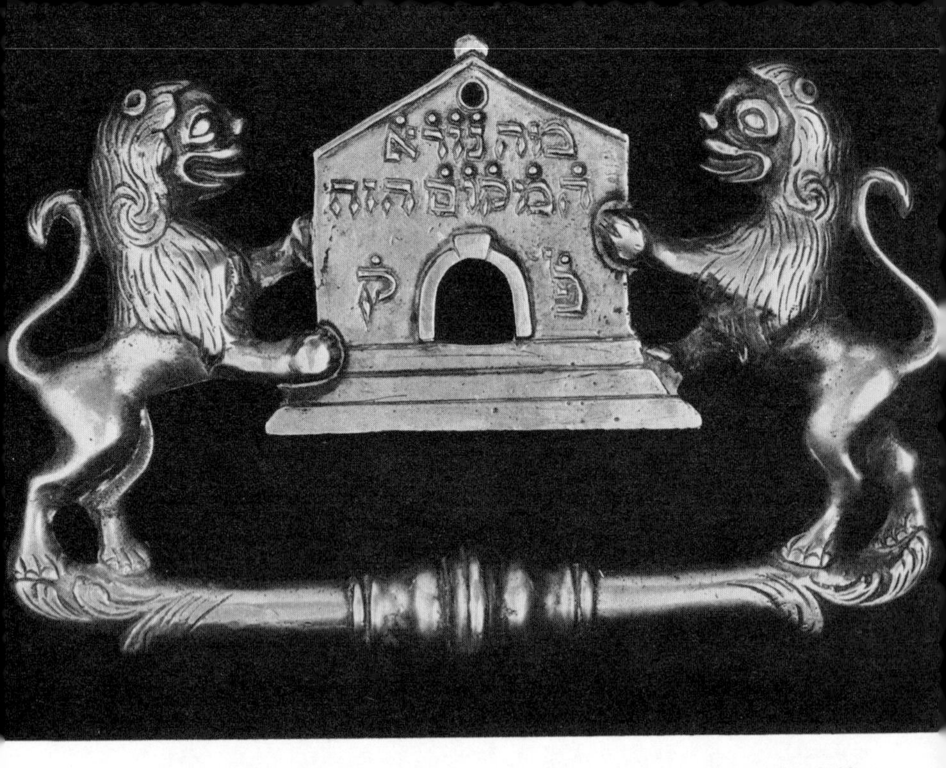

Brass synagogue door knocker in the form of two Lions of Judah rampant holding a house-shaped plate inscribed 'How awesome is this place'. Probably from Prague, 1688.

Tabernacle. The Curtain is made of precious materials such as coloured silk, velvet or velvet brocade, or a combination of different fine cloths, richly embroidered with gold and silver threads. Various Jewish symbols would decorate it, such as the Lions of Judah, the Crown of Torah, the Tablets of the Law and the twin Temple columns.

Often there would be a *caporet* or valance which would complement the Curtain and serve to hide the drawstring used to pull the curtain aside. At times the valance would have a number of protruding sections descending in scallops, on which would be embroidered the menorah and other ritual objects used in the Temple in Jerusalem. Floral patterns predominated in the embroidery on the Parochet.

The centres for making beautiful Torah curtains were Venice, Bohemia and Moravia, and Germany. Since all of the embroiderers of the Torah Ark curtains were Jewish, we can learn much about the development of Jewish embroidery skills. A number of the craftsmen, primarily in the eighteenth century, signed their names to their works. Three Jewish embroiderers of Bavaria, Germany, are especially worthy of note: Gerson Mayer, Elkone of Naumberg and Jacob Koppel Gans. Usually, the Torah Ark Curtains were donated by individuals or groups to the synagogue and they are frequently inscribed and dated.

10 Art for the Jewish Year

The High Holy Days

The *Shofar* is one of the central ceremonial objects in the Jewish tradition. It is sounded in commencement of the ten-day period of reflection and atonement beginning with *Rosh Hashana* (the New Year) and daily during the month preceding Rosh Hashana, and again to mark the end of the ten-day period, *Yom Kippur* (The Day of Atonement). The Shofar, the most ancient wind instrument known to man, is made from the hollowed-out horn of any ritually pure animal except the bull. The ram's horn is most commonly used, probably in association with that existentialist moment in Jewish consciousness, the Binding of Isaac, when the ram was substituted and Abraham's son was spared. While pictorial decorations were forbidden for the Shofar, it could be inscribed. Those bearing Biblical quotations are rare and are highly prized.

The Bible mentions a number of occasions when the Shofar is sounded. It was blown to call attention to important public announcements and national events, to serve as an alarm during battle and as a clarion call to inspire heroism and exceptional effort, to honour the Holy Ark and to express joy, elation and religious exaltation in the service of the Lord. We read that its trumpet-like blasts reduced the walls of Jericho to rubble. It also warned the people of an invasion or of impending natural disasters such as floods or locusts. It was sounded to usher in the Sabbath, to announce the start of festivals and to make known the advent of a feast or of the New Moon. Its solemn tones sounded the dreaded excommunication ban, announced the passage of a funeral cortège and heralded the appointment of a new king.

According to Jewish tradition, the long-awaited coming of the Messiah will be proclaimed by the prophet Elijah sounding his great Shofar of the Redemption. This tradition has been expressed in a number of illustrated Hebrew books and medieval illuminated manuscripts, where the Messiah is shown approaching the walls of Jerusalem on a donkey and sounding the Shofar. Considerably

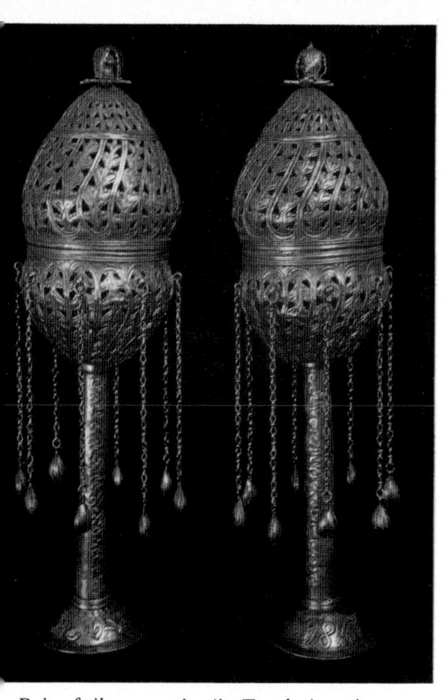

Pair of silver, partly gilt, Torah rimonim. Asia Minor, 1837.

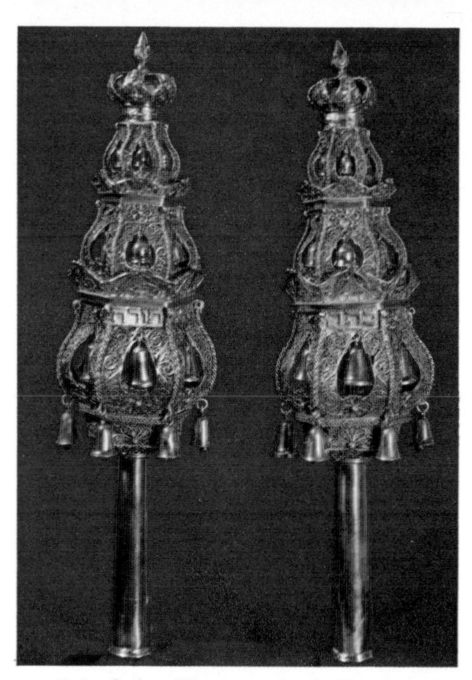

Pair of silver filigree, partly gilt, Torah rimonim. Holland, c.1700.

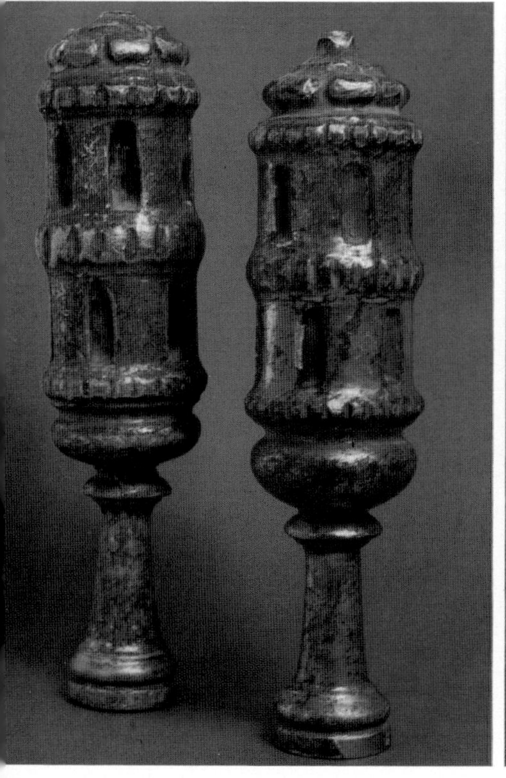

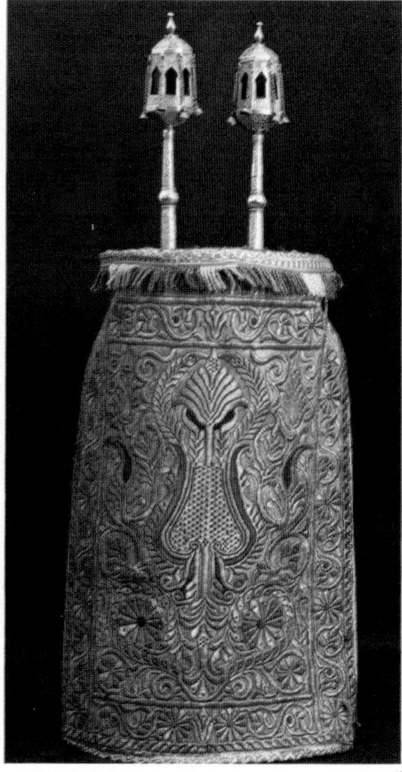

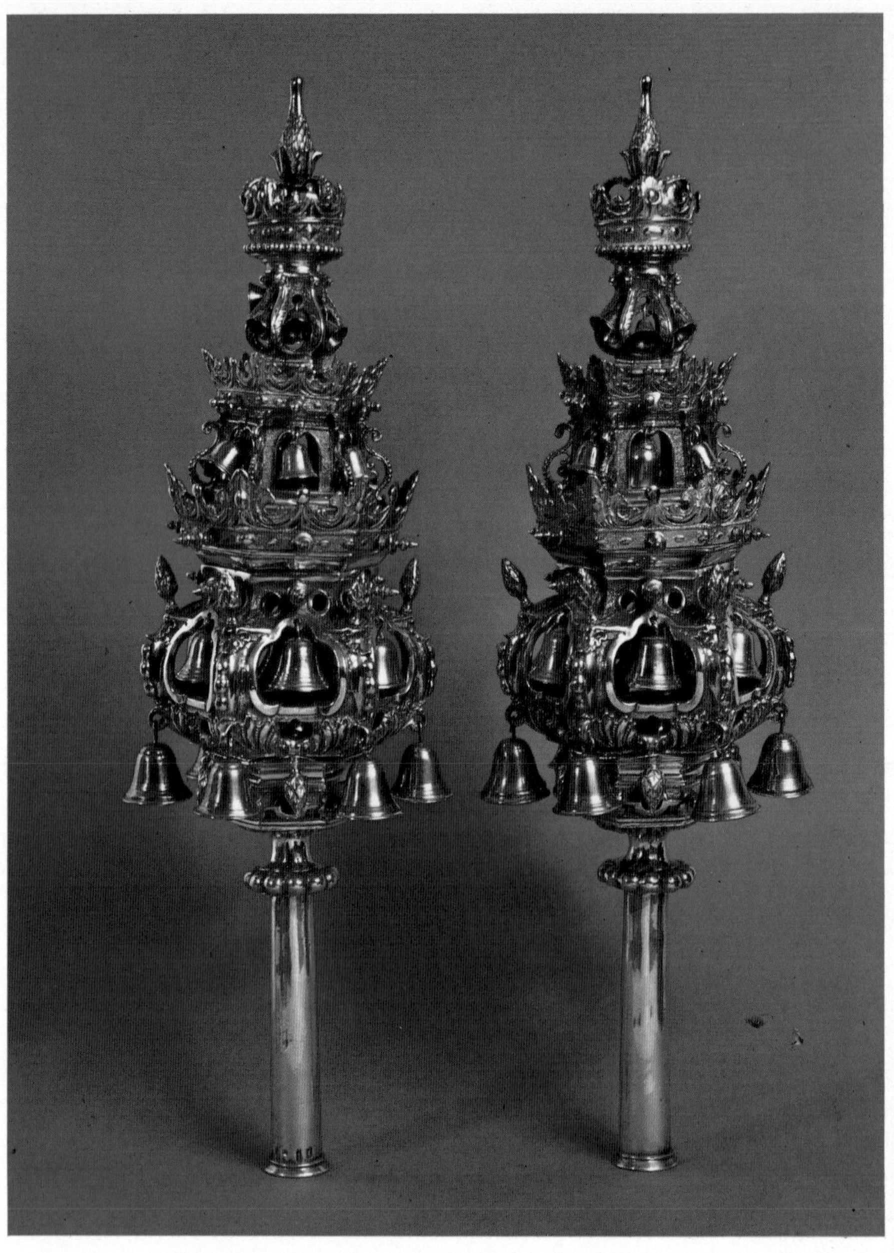

Pair of silver, partly gilt, Torah rimonim in architectural style, surmounted by small crowns. Amsterdam, early 18th century.

Previous page, bottom left: pair of painted wooden Torah rimonim. Tunisia, c.1800.
Bottom right: velvet Torah mantle with gold and silver thread embroidery, Morocco, c.1800. Pair of rimonim (Torah finials) in silver and glass, Morocco, c.1800.

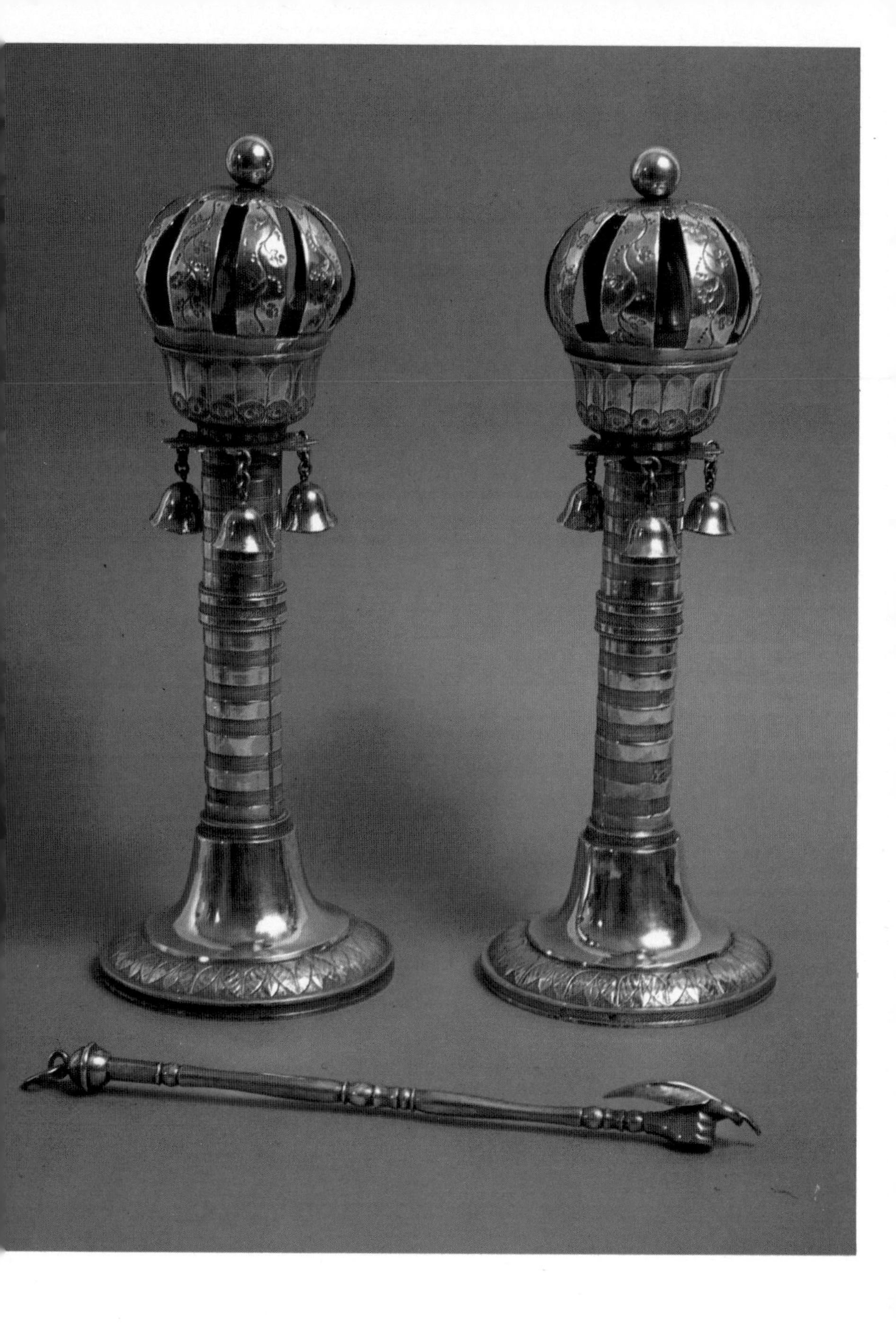

Pair of silver, partly gilt, rimonim. Austria, c.1820. Silver gilt Torah pointer. Germany, 1783.

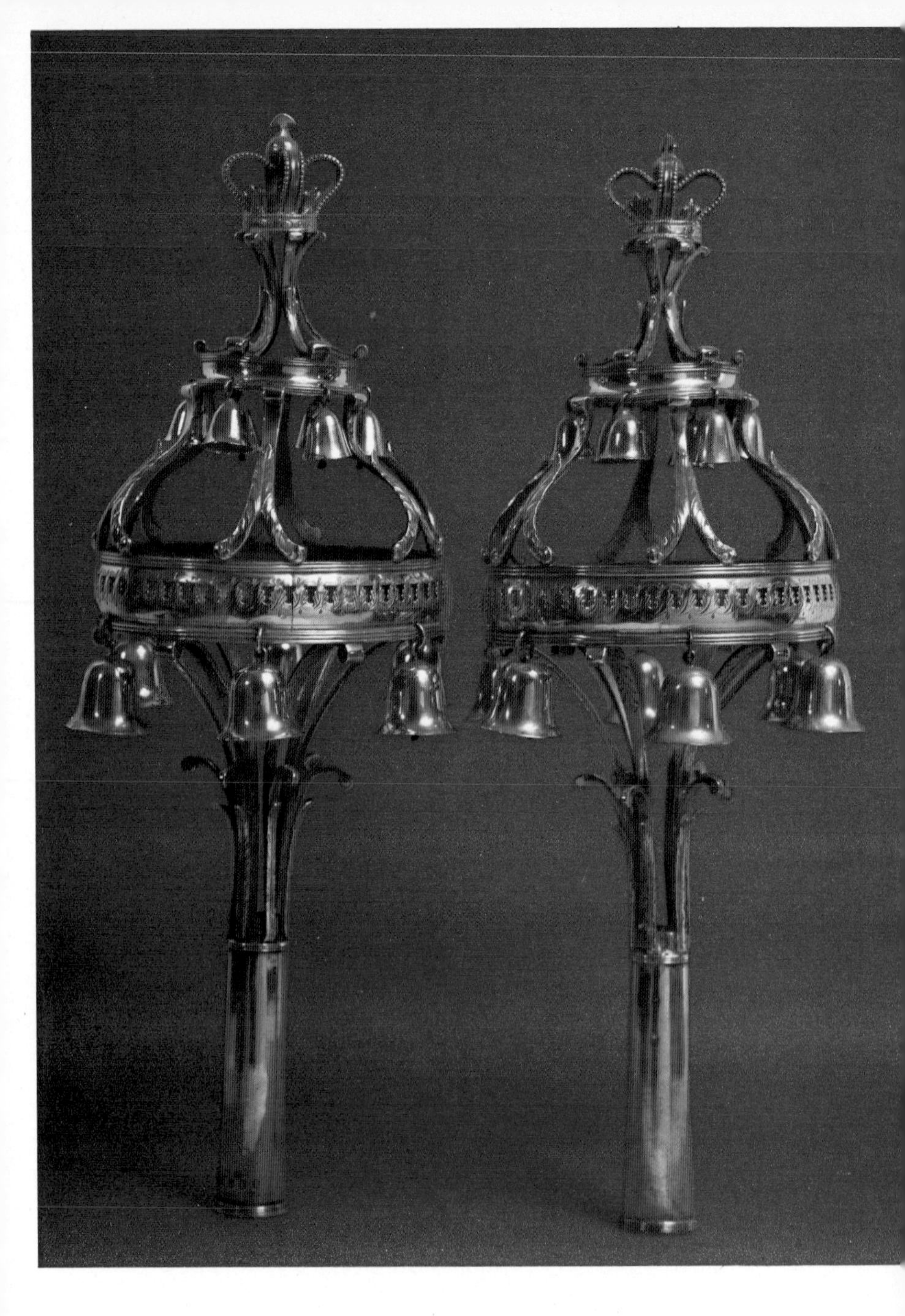

Pair of silver, partly gilt, rimonim, by Peter, Ann and William Bateman. London, 1799.

Opposite: carved, painted and gilded wooden Torah Ark doors decorated with stags, birds and lions couchant holding scrolls proclaiming: 'The Torah of the Lord is perfect'. Poland, c.1800.

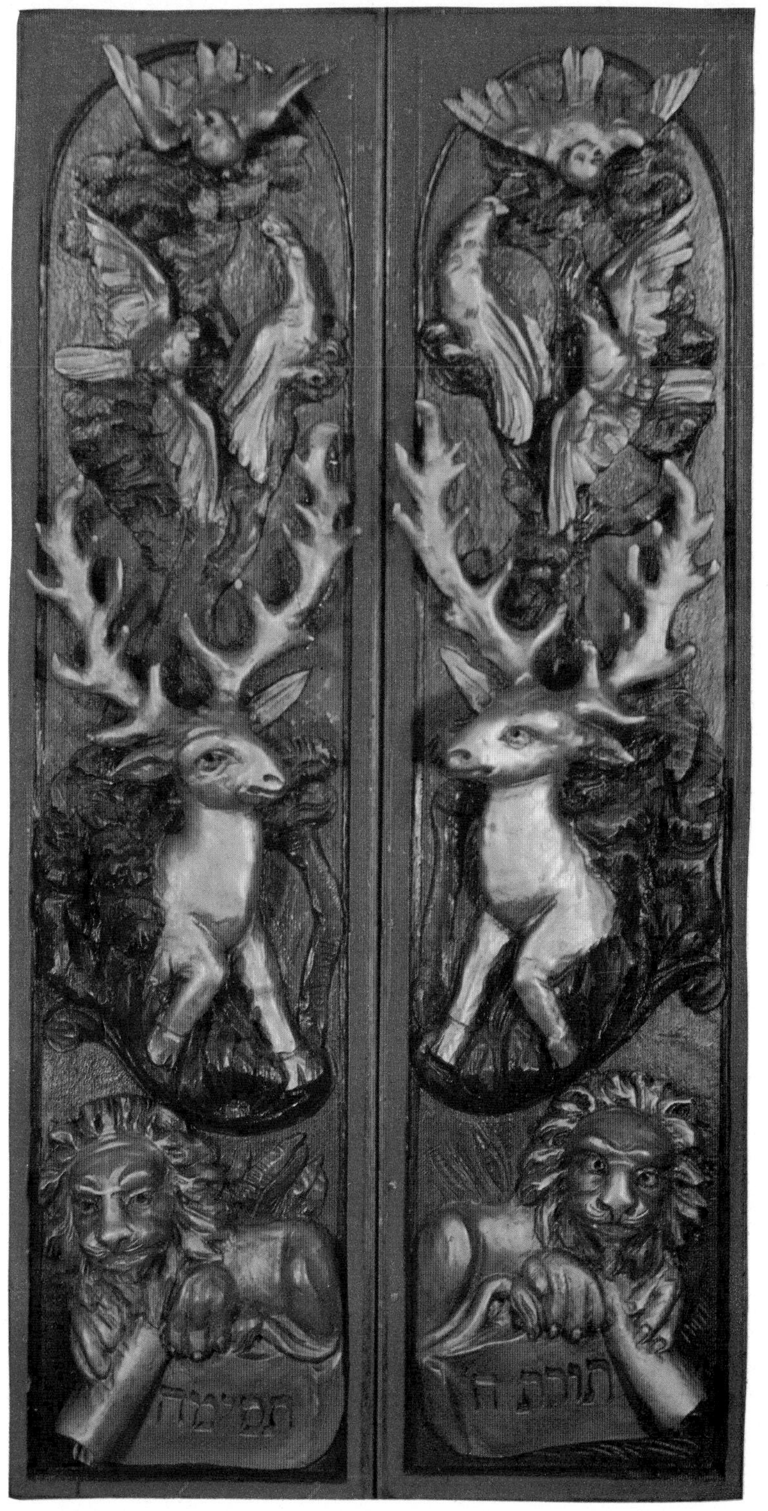
תורת ה'
תמימה

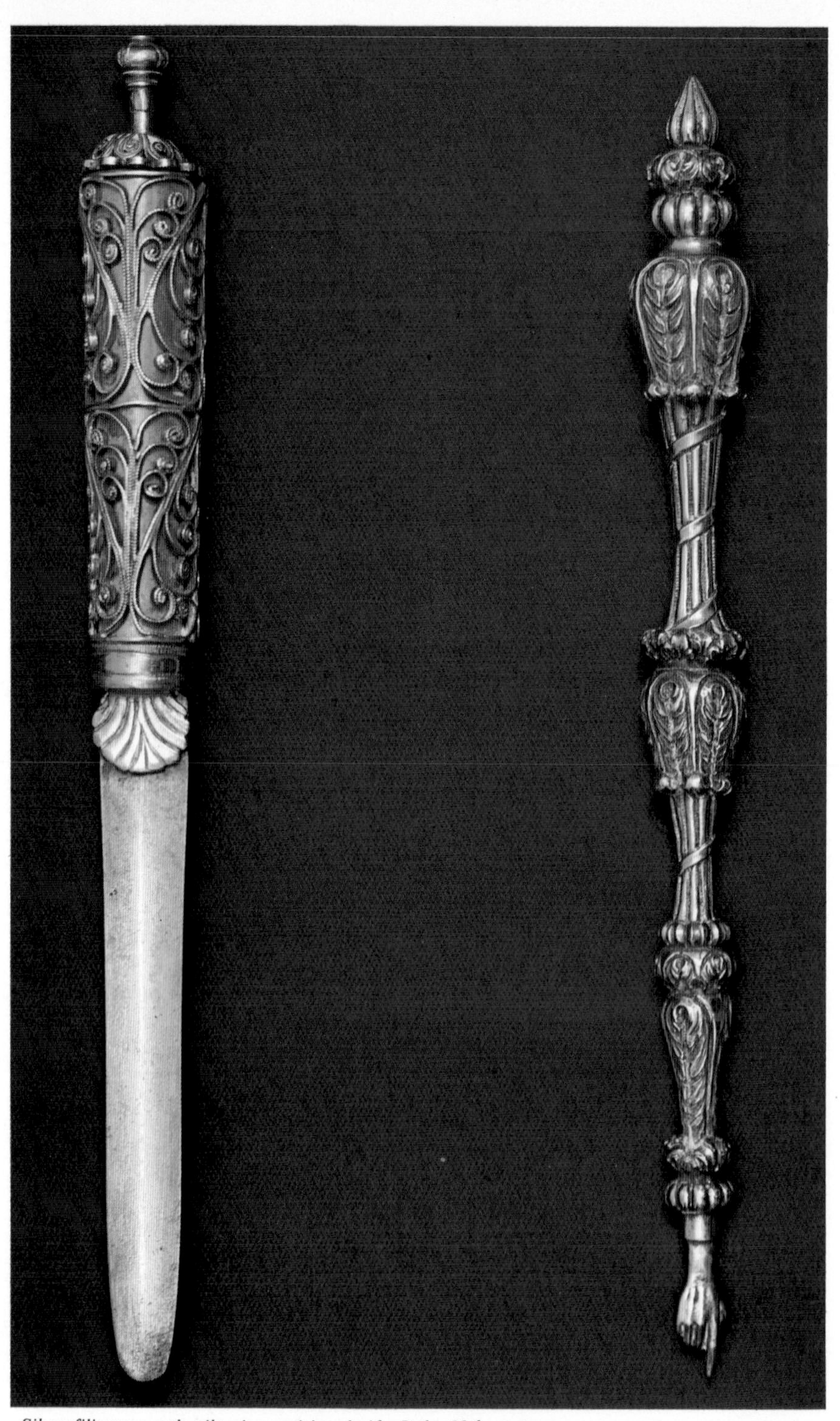

Silver filigree, partly gilt, circumcision knife, Italy, 18th century.

Silver gilt Torah pointer, Italy, 17th century.

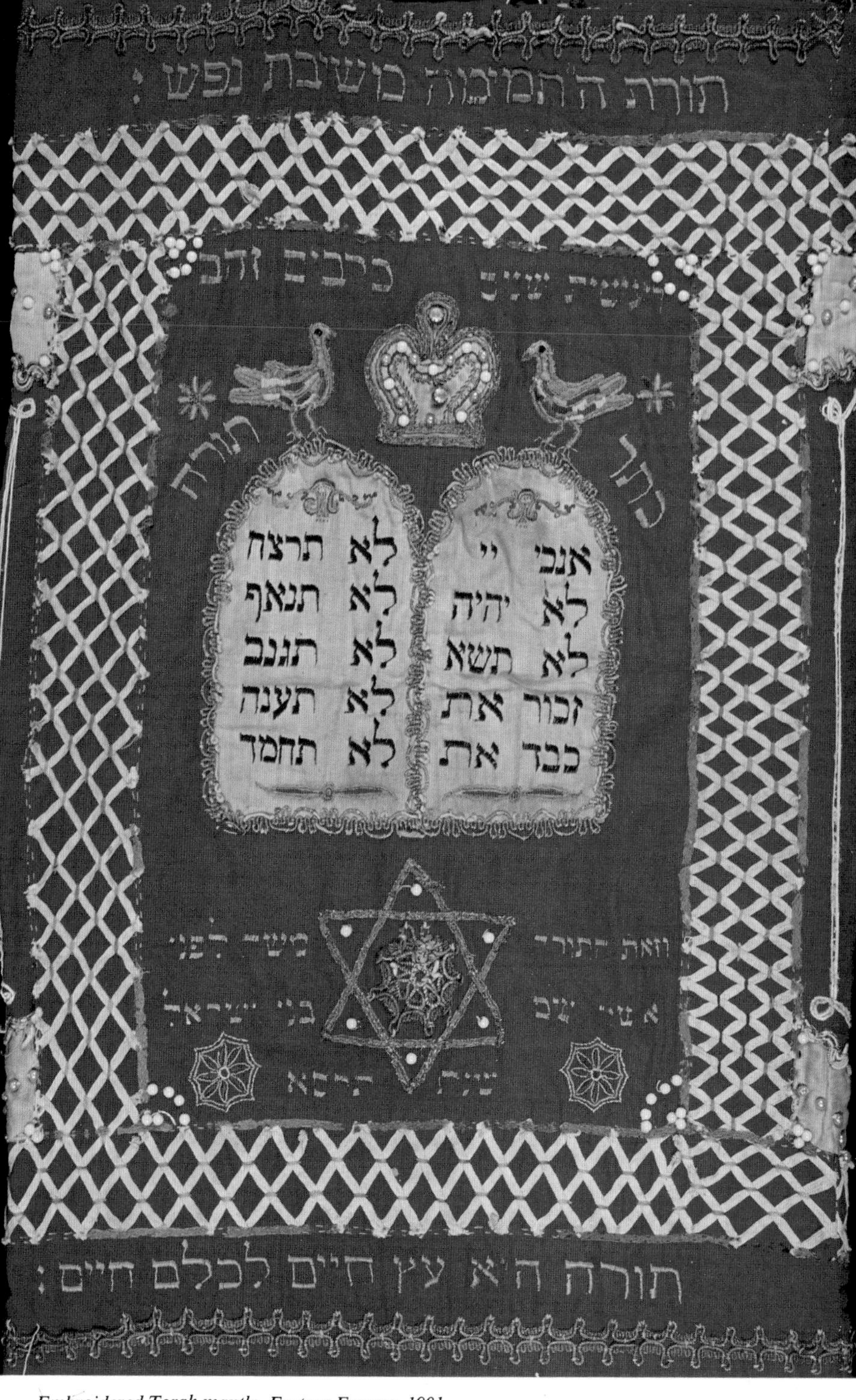

Embroidered Torah mantle. Eastern Europe, 1901.

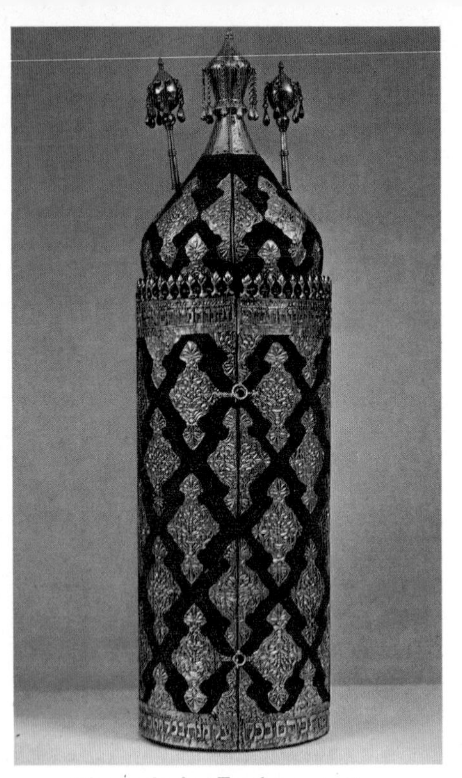

Silver and velvet Torah case. India, c.1840.

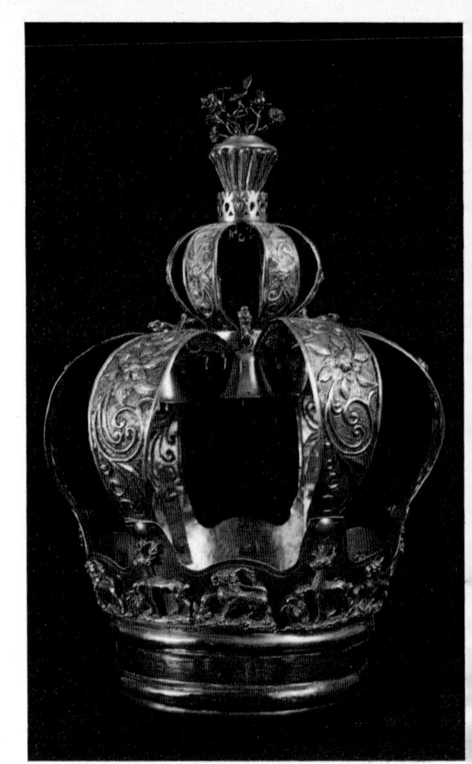

Silver Torah crown, with lions and stags at the bottom. Poland, 18th century.

Silver, partly gilt, Torah shield. Nuremberg, Germany, 18th century.

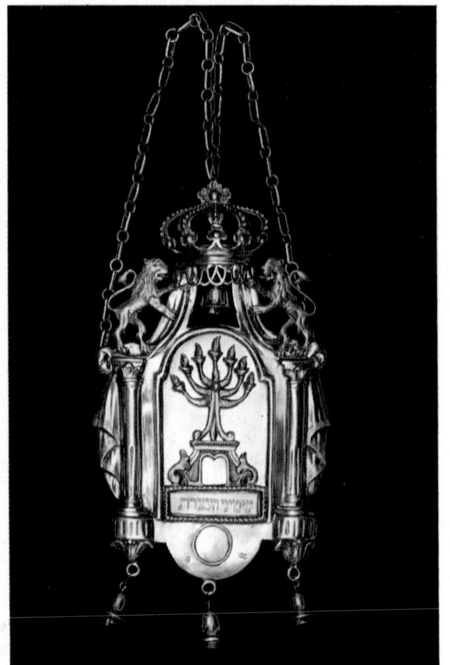

Silver, partly gilt, Torah shield. Germany, c.1800.

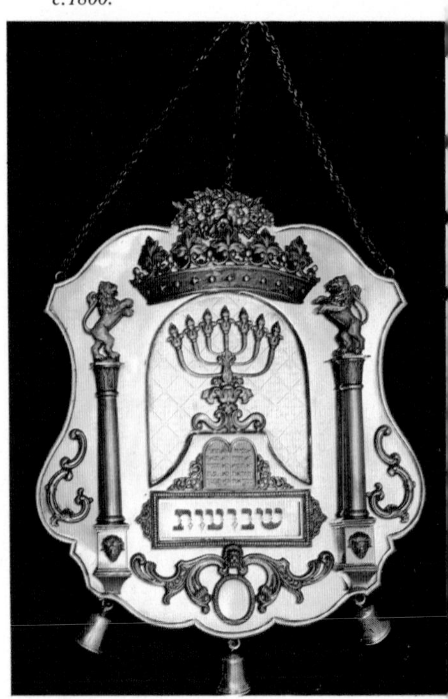

earlier, the Shofar appeared as a symbol and dominant Jewish motif in the mosaic floors of synagogues, fragments of Jewish gold glasses, ceramic oil lamps, seals, rings, amulets and tombs.

Also during Rosh Hashana and Yom Kippur, especially attractive Jewish prayer books called *Mahzorim* were used, in accordance with a tradition expressed by the nineteenth-century sage, Rabbi Hayim Palaggi, that 'an attractive prayer book is greatly effective to devotion'. But since a number of other sages held that figurative art in the prayer book itself would have the opposite effect and distract the congregant's devotion, the cover of the Mahzor was sometimes lavishly decorated instead. These covers were often fashioned of silver, some of them decorated with the scene of the Binding of Isaac, which is commemorated by the Rosh Hashana scriptural readings in the synagogue.

Over the pure white Holiday robe called a *Kittel* or *Sargenes*, the men sometimes wore a special High Holiday Belt. The Belt separates the lower portion of the body, associated with bodily functions, from the upper or 'purer' portion containing the heart and mind. Usually of silver, it was often decorated with Jewish symbols and motifs.

Succot and Simhat Torah

Four days after Yom Kippur comes *Succot*, the eight-day autumn harvest festival of thanksgiving, during which Jews traditionally reside in outdoor booths roofed with branches, as a poignant reminder of man's frailty and the better to appreciate God's bounty. The booth (*Succah*; pl. *Succot*) was always decorated attractively, often with special decorations, in particular the Jerusalem-oriented *Succah Tablet*.

A glimpse into a nineteenth-century Indian Succah is provided by a colourfully-embroidered velvet Succah Tablet. The door of the Succah is shown open to reveal a table covered with a gold-trimmed scarlet tablecloth bearing a wicker basket of fresh fruit, a pair of lighted golden candlesticks, a gilt wine decanter and a Kiddush beaker. The Succah itself is made of reeds or bamboo rods, covered by a canopy of fresh branches and autumn fruits and vegetables. The inscription, embroidered in gold-coloured thread, quotes the Biblical commands relating to dwelling in the Succah, being joyful during the festival, rejoicing with the 'Four Kinds' and praying with them.

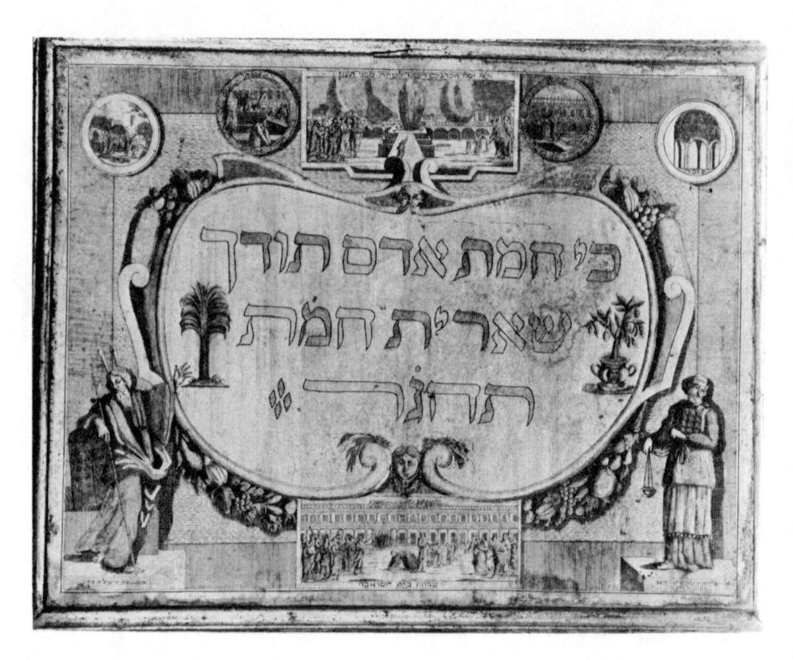

Above: *engraved Succah tablet, showing Moses and Aaron and Biblical scenes relating to the celebration of Succot in the Jerusalem Temple. By Francesco Griselini, Venice, Italy, c. 1740.*

Opposite, top: *silver etrog container in the form of a citron on a pedestal. Germany, 19th century.*

Opposite, bottom: *silver etrog container in the form of a melon on a leaf base. Germany, 18th century.*

The 'Four Kinds' – the palm (*lulav*), the myrtle, the willow and the citron (*etrog*) appear frequently as motifs in ancient Jewish art, particularly in synagogue mosaics and stone friezes, Jewish gold glasses and coins. To protect the etrog (pl. *etrogim*) while carried

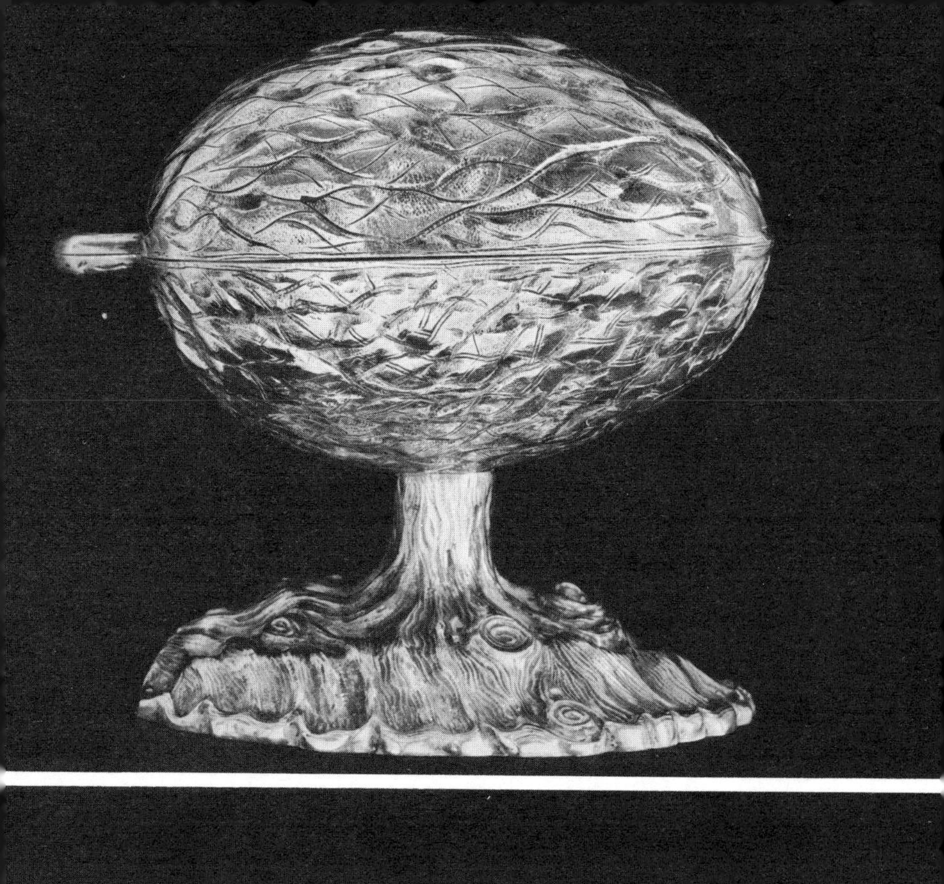

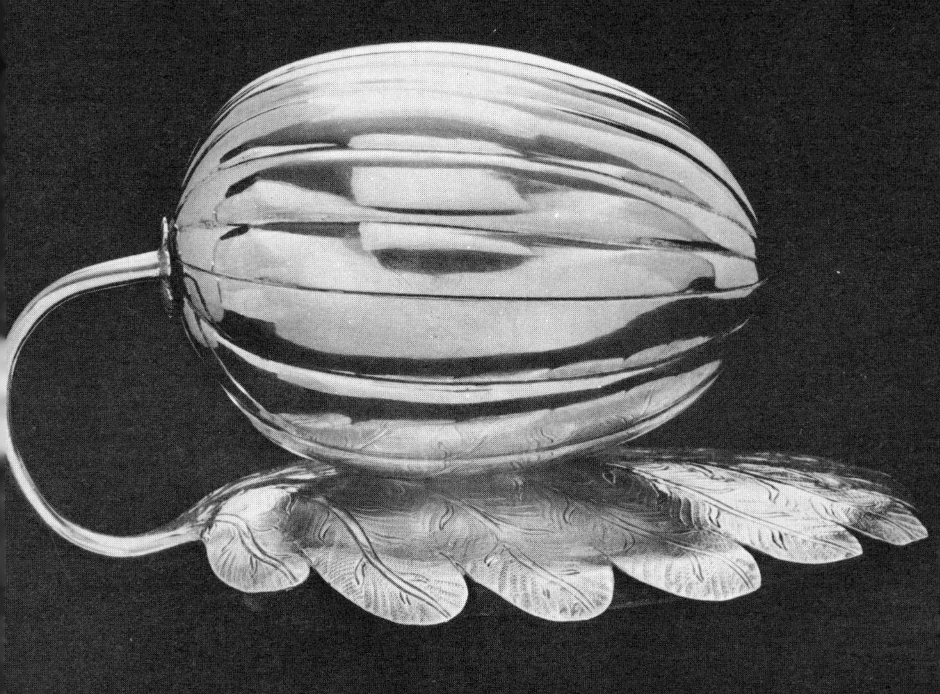

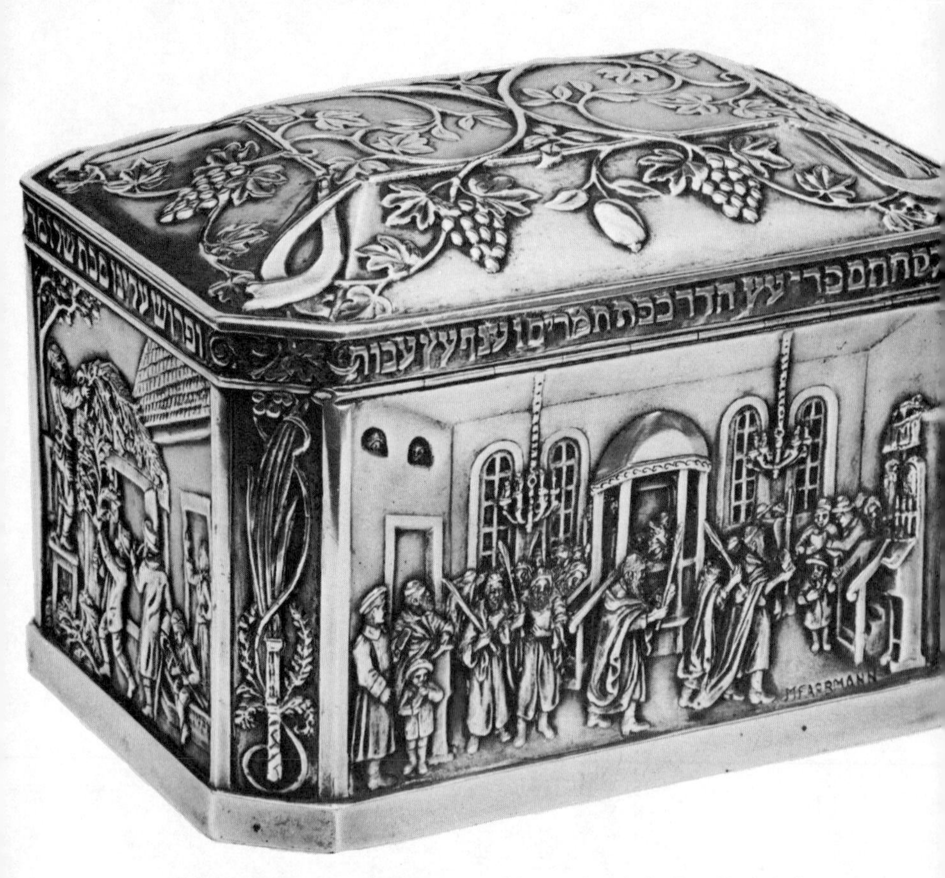

Silver etrog container showing scenes of the march with the Four Kinds in the synagogue, constructing the Succah, eating in the Succah and dancing with the Torah in the synagogue on Simhat Torah. Germany, 19th century.

to and from synagogue each day, etrog containers were used, sometimes in the shape of a large citron, and made from a variety of materials. The containers were usually inscribed with Biblical quotations relating to the command of the 'Four Kinds' and sometimes decorated with appropriate scenes.

Simhat Torah, a joyous one-day festival marking the end of the annual cycle of the reading of the Torah in the synagogue, concludes the Succot holiday. This day is celebrated by rejoicing and thanking

God for the Torah. All the Torah scrolls with their splendid adornments are removed from the Torah Ark and marched in a procession around the synagogue while the congregation sings and dances in the synagogue and in the streets. Although there are no ceremonial objects specifically associated with this occasion, it provides an excellent opportunity for appreciating the beauty and elegance of the Torah decorations.

Hanukah

Hanukah, the Feast of Lights, is an eight-day mid-winter celebration in remembrance of the liberation of Israel from the Syrio-Greeks by Judah the Maccabee in 165 BC. After the Syrio-Greek priests had been driven out, the Temple had to be cleansed and reconsecrated by the lighting of the Menorah. But only one vessel of the ritually pure olive oil – enough for one day – was to be found, and eight days were required to prepare additional ritually pure sacramental oil. Miraculously, the single day's supply of oil burned for a full eight days. This event is commemorated by the lighting of the eight-branched Hanukah Lamp, the *Hanukiah* (pl. *Hanukiot*) in a prescribed manner, whereby a ninth light, the *Shamash* or servitor, is used to light the other lights: one light on the first night, two on the second and so on until the eighth night, when all the lights are lit.

The Hanukiah, which is derived from the Temple Menorah, is one of the most distinctive ceremonial objects and is found in most Jewish homes. Often a home had several Hanukah lamps, one for each male member of the family. Originally an oil lamp, the Hanukiah remained so over the years, except for the introduction of candles relatively recently.

The earliest Hanukiot were probably single lamps with multiple apertures, possibly made of ceramic or stone and hollowed out. Lamps of this style were still used by the Jews of Yemen and the Atlas Mountains of Morocco until recently. Later on, 'bench-type' Hanukah lamps (so-called for their 'backs', 'seats' and 'legs') evolved which enable them to stand on window sills or to hang on walls in fulfilment of the requirement of publicly proclaiming the 'Feast of Lights'.

A native of Fez in Morocco, Rabbi Abraham ben Mordecai Azulai (born 1570) wrote that in his time no fewer than fourteen different

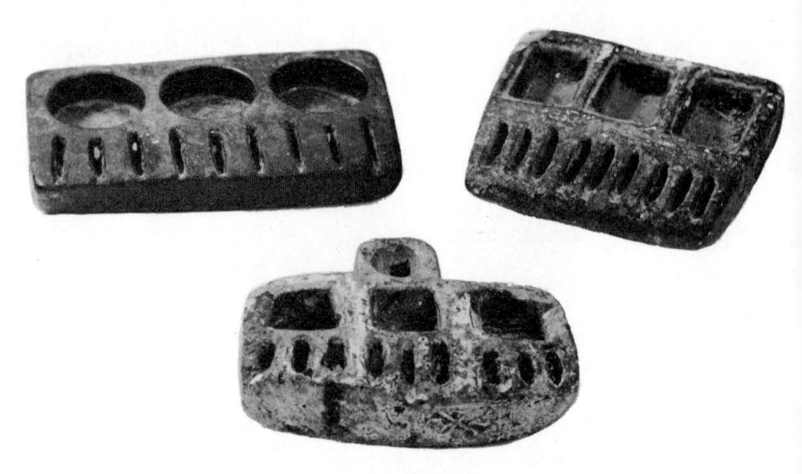

Stone Hanukah lamps from the Atlas mountains. Morocco, c. 15th to 17th centuries.

materials were used to make Hanukah lamps. One striking Hanukiah of Fez made of painted, enamelled ceramic is in the form of a Moorish synagogue, complete with courtyard. A popular Moroccan Hanukiah was one made of cast brass with a pierced and embossed back, featuring Moorish arabesque *mihrab* arches, with birds perched on branches at the sides. In some parts of North Africa, a small brass Hanukiah which had a triangular back formed of generally rounded openings created by the pierced brass design was used.

One interesting Hanukiah from Egypt is a tall, imposing example, featuring a seven-branched menorah in repoussé on its back, surmounted by twin Lions of Judah rampant flanking the Tablets of the Ten Commandments and a Star of David on top. The Hanukiah is framed by depictions of the Temple columns, Yachin and Boaz, and of olive branches. The *horror vaccui* to which the artist was prone, is reflected in the filling of all available space with Biblical passages and the benedictions for the lighting of the Hanukiah.

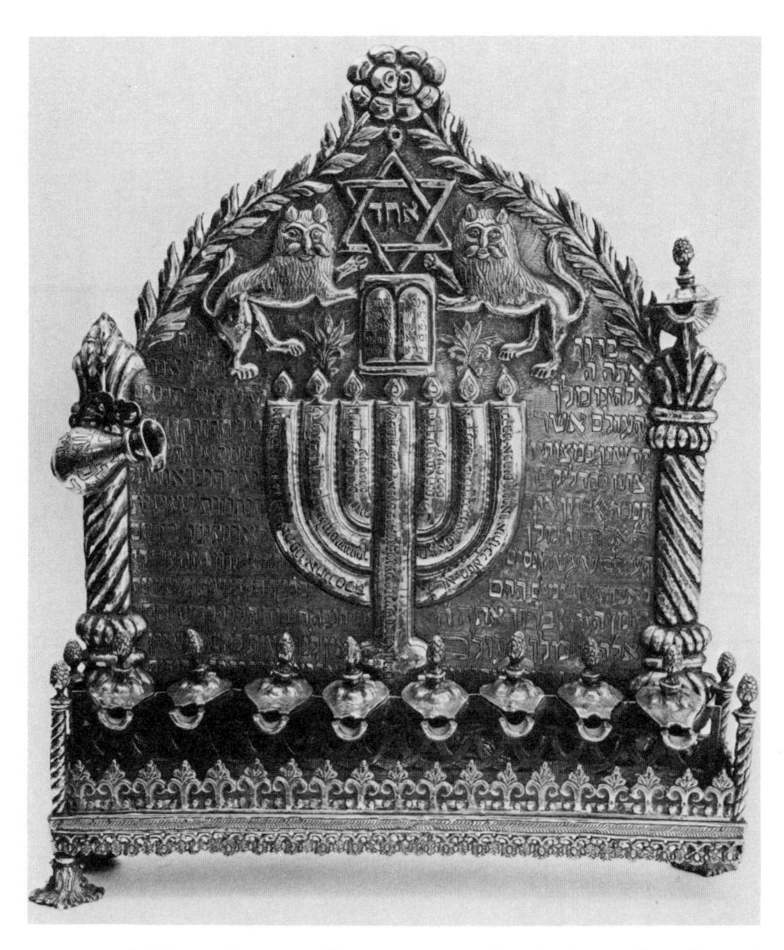

Silver Hanukah lamp. The rear wall contains a seven-branched menorah made up of the words of Psalm 67, surmounted by the tablets with the Ten Commandments, flanked by twin Lions of Judah rampant supporting a Star of David with the word 'One' inside. Alexandria, Egypt, 18th century.

In Baghdad the Hanukah Lamp usually had large glass containers for oil. Similar Hanukah Lamps were used by the Jews of India. They were usually made of brass and were attached to wooden backs designed in the form of Stars of David or shields.

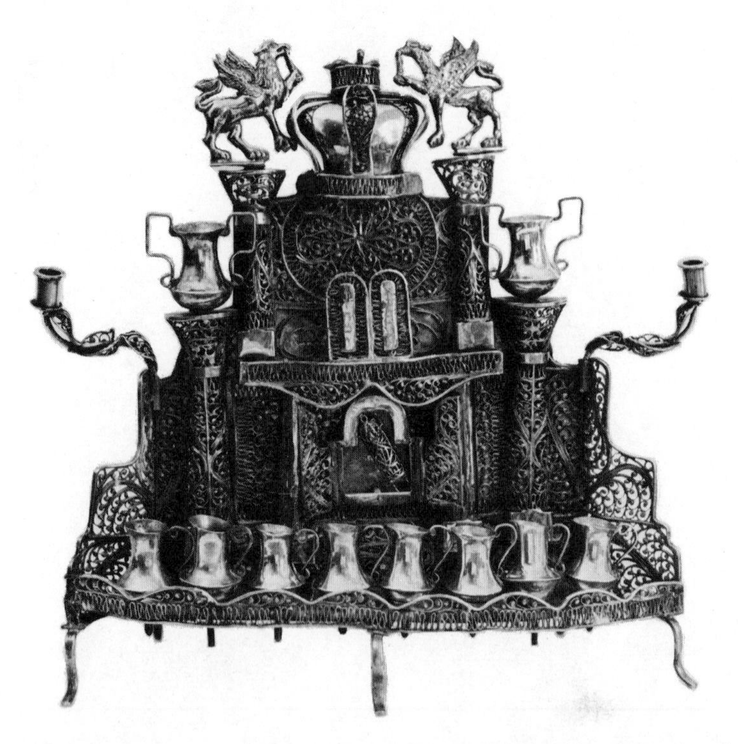

Silver filigree Hanukah lamp. The rear wall contains a miniature Torah Ark with a removable silver filigree 'Torah'. This is surmounted by the tablets with the Ten Commandments and twin griffins flanking a crown. The Ukraine, 18th century.

Renaissance and post-Renaissance Italian Hanukah lamps of silver and brass were often quite elaborate, with figurative and floral art, some with rear wall representations of lions, dolphins, tridents, mermaids, grotesques, masks and the like.

Eastern European Hanukiot were often of cast brass, and sometimes featured depictions of lions or stags on the rear and at the sides. Twin shamash lamps were standard features of many Eastern European Hanukah lamps, apparently because they provided stylistic balance and because they also served many households year-round as Sabbath and festival lamps. In Poland, the Ukraine,

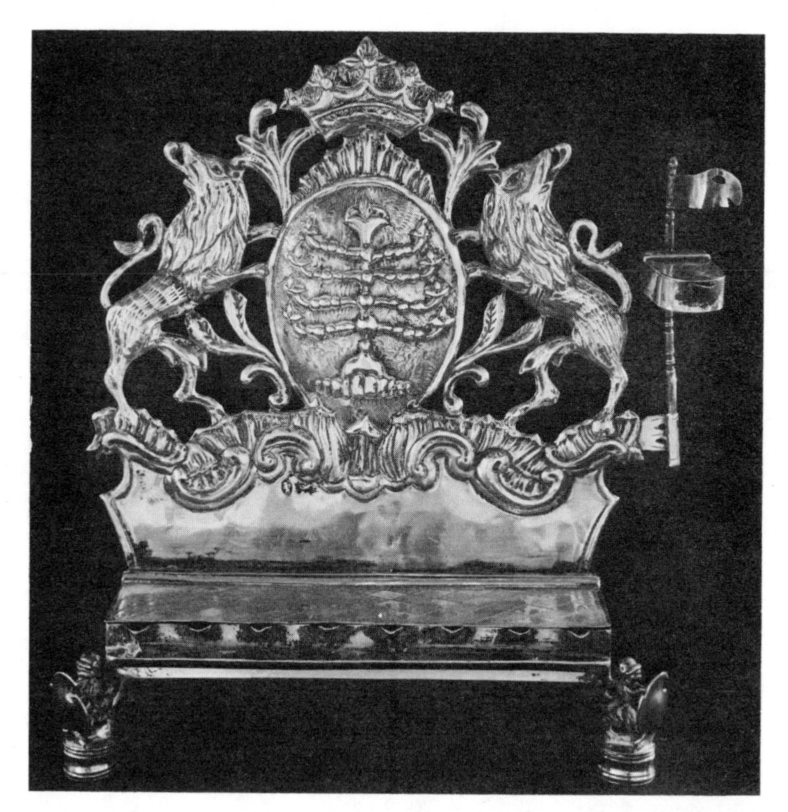

Silver Hanukah lamp. Resting on bases made up of Lions of Judah rampant holding shields, the rear wall is also made up of Lions of Judah flanking a medallion containing a Hanukah candlestick surmounted by a crown. Germany, 18th century.

and in parts of Bohemia and Moravia a silver filigree Hanukah lamp developed in the eighteenth century, the back of which sometimes resembled a Torah Ark, complete with doors which swung open to reveal a miniature silver filigree 'Torah'.

In Germany it is thought that early Hanukah lamps were hanging, circular ones, similar to the hanging Sabbath lamps suspended from ceilings, but with eight oil fonts. Later, silver bench-type Hanukah Lamps appeared in Germany, one popular eighteenth-century style

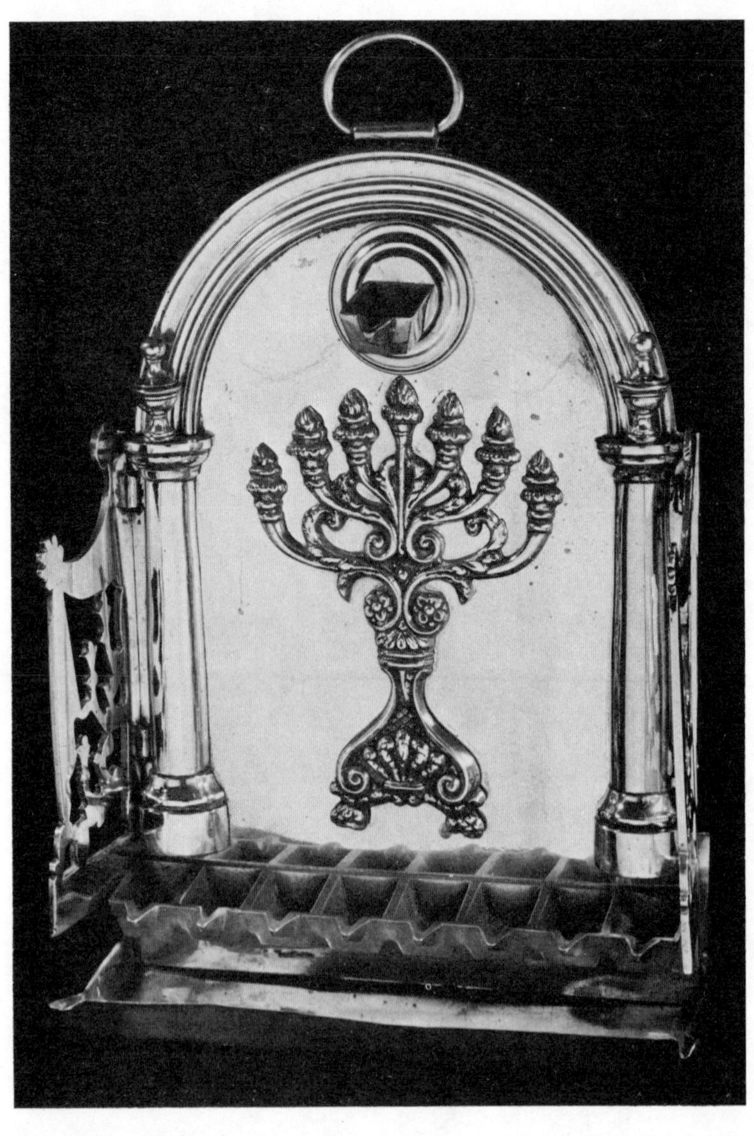

Brass Hanukah lamp, featuring a stylised seven-branched menorah at the rear. Italy, 18th century.

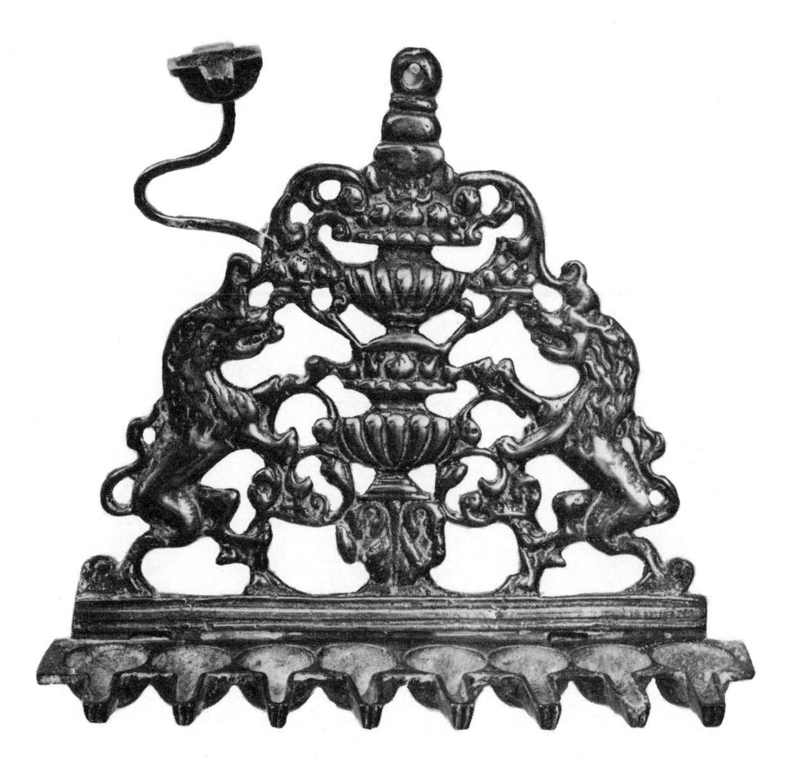

Bronze Hanukah lamp. Rampant Lions of Judah flank a vase. Italy, 17th century.

consisting of a lamp with a hinged plate covering the oil fonts, resting on a footed base made up of lions rampant holding shields, and on the repoussé back plate large twin rampant Lions of Judah support a cartouche containing a stylised nine-branched candelabrum surmounted by a crown. Figures of Moses and Aaron and other figures, such as Maccabee warriors, also appear on Hanukah lamps, especially German ones.

The introduction of a public Hanukah lamp-lighting ceremony in the synagogue necessitated the creation of a tall imposing candlestick-type of Hanukiah, which generally resembled the Temple

Menorah, and since depictions of the seven-branched Temple lamp were forbidden, these nine-branched Hanukah lamps often became the most specifically Jewish symbols in the synagogues.

Purim

As winter draws to a close, Jews celebrate the most cheerful day of the year, the *Purim* festival, commemorating an event that took place in Susa, capital of Achaemenian Persia in the fifth century BC, which is described in the *Megillah* (pl. *Megillot*), the scroll of the Book of Esther. The Megillah tells how Haman, vizier of King Ahasueros, plots to destroy all the Jews in the Persian Empire, only to be confounded by Esther, who had become Ahasueros' queen after winning a beauty contest. Revealing her identity as a Jewess and exposing Haman's scheme, Esther appeals to the king. Ahasueros grants the Jews the right to defend themselves and, instead of the predicted day of sorrow, there is a day of rejoicing.

Hence Purim is celebrated with parties, parades, masquerades, plays, jokes and games and the giving of gifts, especially to the poor. The Megillah is read in the synagogue and when Haman's name is mentioned, it is drowned out by the shattering din of the youngsters gleefully sounding their noisemakers.

Unlike Torah scrolls, Megillot are owned by families, who bring them to the synagogues for reading. The Scroll of Esther, like the Torah, had to be written by a scribe with a quill and plain black ink on parchment or leather made from skins of ritually pure animals, with the sheets hand-sewn together. Since there is no mention of God's name in the Megillah ornamentation was permissible. The dramatic and exotic Purim story naturally lends itself to illustration and thus has provided the master manuscript illuminator as well as the primitive folk artist with a wealth of material. Indeed, following the invention of the printing press, the Megillah became a main area of concentration for the decorators of Jewish manuscripts.

By far the most beautiful illuminated Megillot were those produced in Italy between the sixteenth and eighteenth centuries. Usually the artists would reserve the area of parchment above and below the text, and occasionally between the columns, to ornament the Megillah with floral, geometric or scrollwork patterns or with miniature vignettes illustrating the Purim story. If the illuminator was the scribe as well, the strict traditional patterns of rectangular

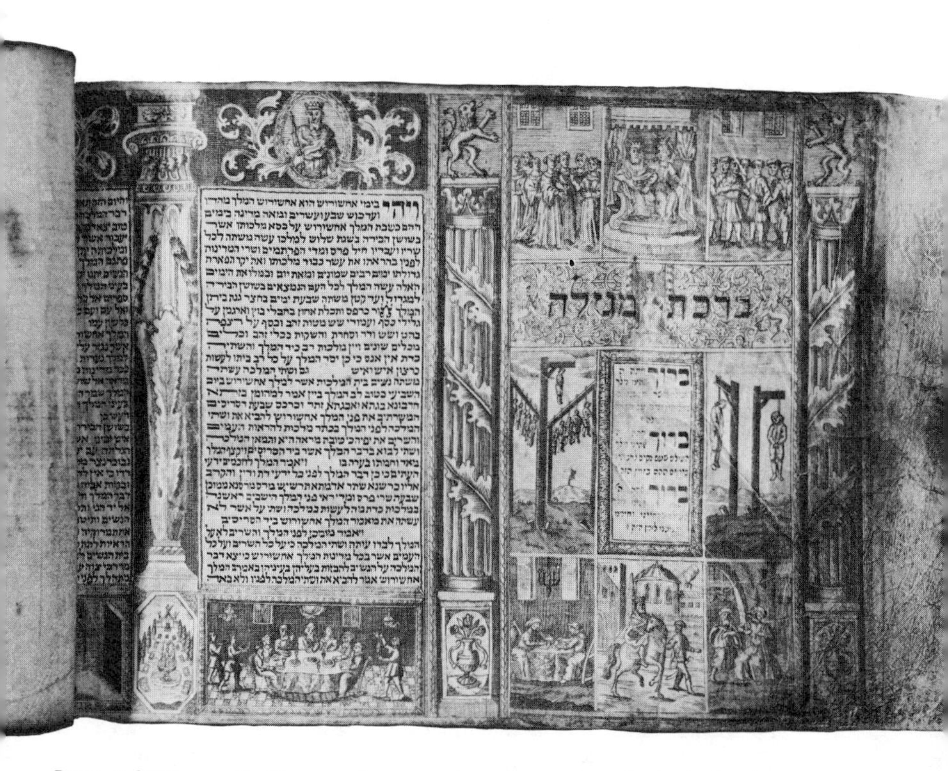

Decorated Esther scroll with copperplate engravings of scenes from the Book of Esther. Holland, 17th century.

columns of text, which tends to limit the artist's options, would be rejected in favour of a Hebrew text laid out in circular or other forms, giving greater latitude to the ornamentation.

A more 'formal' Megillah was achieved by painting tall, evenly-spaced and sumptuous Italianate architectural pillars to divide and frame attractively the rectangular columns of Hebrew script. Here, arches, cornices and vases full of flowers might embellish the text, with the sequential vignette-miniatures, also formalised, inserted between the bases or capitals of the columns, thus providing running pictorial commentaries and colourful depictions of the text above.

The stately appearance of the Megillah might be enhanced by representations of the heroes and villains of the Biblical drama in formalised poses, sometimes holding palms, sceptres or swords. Frequently, however, the figures would be in contemporary costume, themselves dividing the text instead of architectural and columnar dividers, like actors in a Purim play, who step out on the stage to introduce themselves at the start of the play.

In Moslem countries, where prohibitions against figurative art even affected the Jewish communities, Megillot were decorated only occasionally, and then only with floral motifs or geometric patterns.

At times Esther scrolls would be kept in handsome cases of carved wood or decorated silver, with a handle at the bottom of the case for winding or unwinding. In certain oriental lands it was customary for engaged girls to present them to their future husbands.

Passover

The Bible enjoins that Passover be celebrated in remembrance of Israel's redemption from Egyptian bondage and the triumphant exodus which took place in the middle of the second millennium BC. The *Seder*, a joyous and elegant ritual meal – observed on two evenings outside Israel (one by liberal and reform Jews) and one evening in Israel – highlights the eight-day Passover celebrations, its focal point being the reading of the *Hagadah* (pl. *Hagadot*).

The Hagadah is written in fulfilment of the Biblical injunction to the Jews to relate the story of the Exodus and the accompanying miracles to their children. Read aloud during the festive meal, with the participation of family and guests, it has become a storybook of unceasing popularity, containing Biblical quotations, narratives, songs, prayers and even riddles. Since the invention of printing, it has gone through some 3500 editions. Easily the most decorated of all Jewish books, it is usually illustrated with pictures designed to ensure children's continued attention during the long pre-feast reading.

In addition to the printed editions, approximately one hundred and fifty medieval illuminated manuscript Hagadot have also survived. A number of attractive illuminated Hagadot were also produced during the eighteenth-century revival of Hebrew manuscript

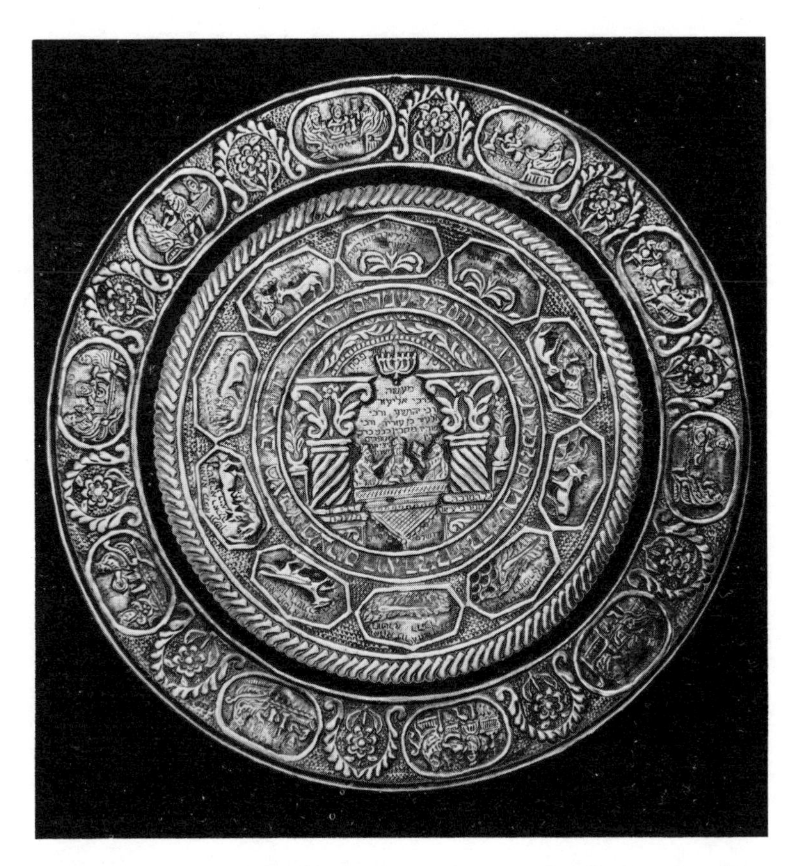

Brass Seder tray. In the centre the rabbis of the Talmud are discussing the exodus. Around this in heptagonal cartouches are depictions of the 'One Only Kid' song. On the outer rim oval cartouches depict the order of the Seder service. Probably from Jerusalem, 19th century.

illumination in Central Europe, mostly in Germany, Bohemia and Moravia. Since the Hagadah was a relatively small book, it was not a major expense at the time for a man of some means to commission an artist to decorate an attractive manuscript Hagadah with lots of pictures, designed as an instructional aid to the young. With but a few exceptions, most of the illustrations were hand-drawn copies of the popular pictures in the printed Amsterdam Hagadah of 1695–

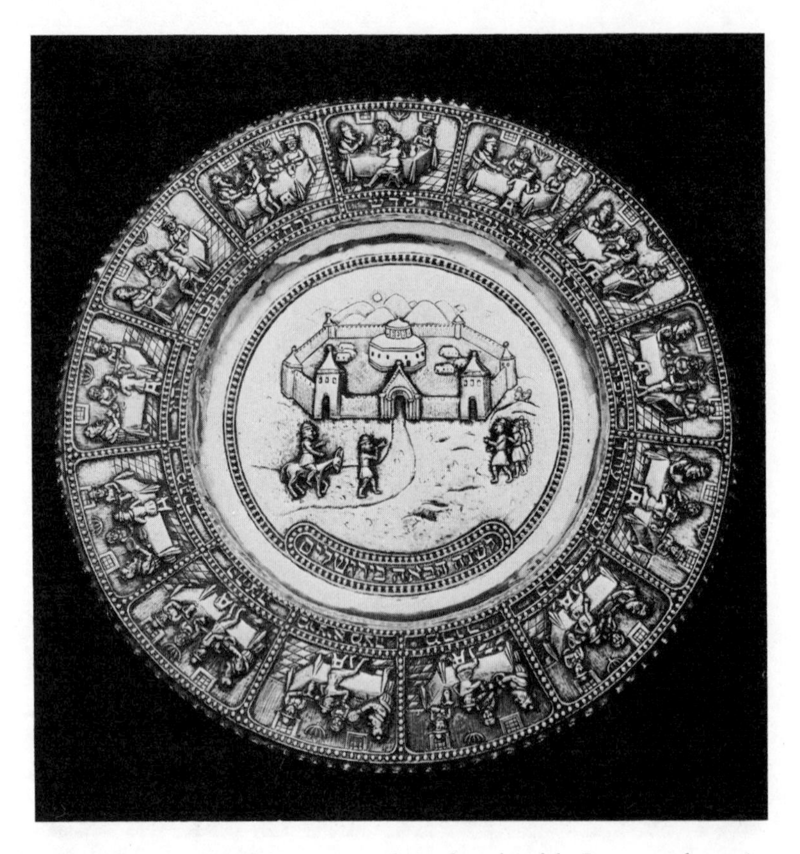

Silver Seder tray. Around the rim scenes depict the order of the Passover seder service. In the centre is the Messiah preceded by the prophet Elijah sounding the shofar of the redemption and about to enter Jerusalem. It is inscribed 'Next year in Jerusalem'. Italy, 19th century.

1712 (see Chapter 6). Notable among the miniaturists executing Hagadot during this period were Moses Leib ben Wolf of Trebitsch, Aaron Wolf of Gewitsch, Nathan ben Samson of Mezeritch, Joseph Pinhas of Ansbach, Uri Phoebus ben Isaac Segal of Hamburg, and the prolific Moravian-born Joseph ben David Leipnik of Hamburg-Altona-Wandsbeck.

The central ceremonial object at the Seder feast is the Seder tray. Designed to hold the five symbolic foods eaten during the feast, it

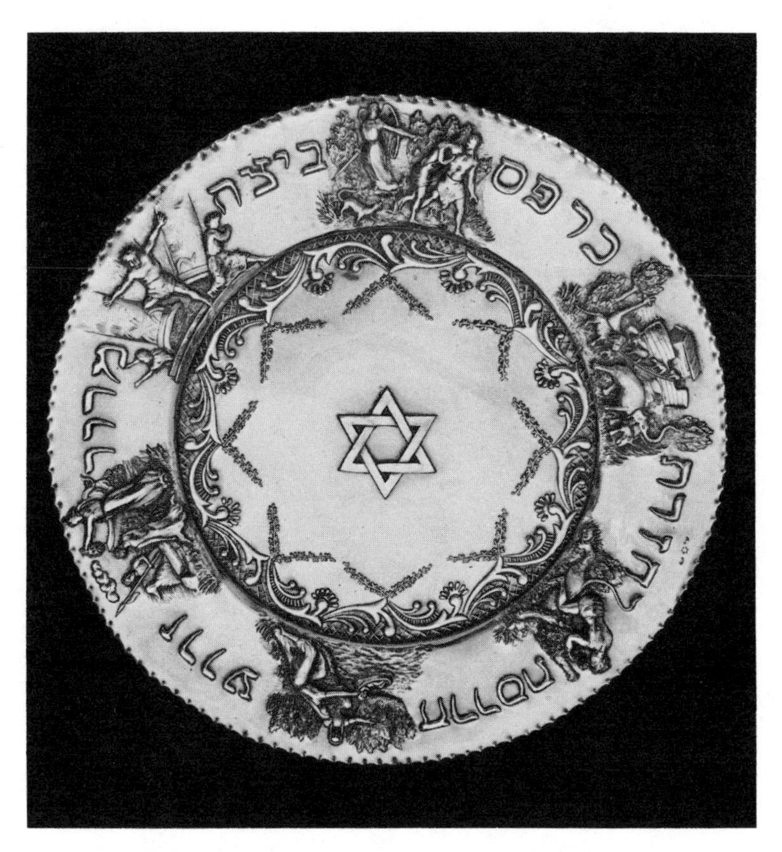

Silver Seder tray. Around the rim are six Biblical scenes, while in the centre is a Star of David. Italy, 19th century.

often has five or six compartmentalised sections. Sometimes it was tiered to hold three pieces of *matzah* (pl. *matzot*), the flat, perforated unleavened biscuits that replace bread during Passover week in the Jewish home. The Seder tray, made of silver, brass, pewter, carved wood or glazed ceramic, was frequently decorated with Passover scenes, often inspired by specific Hagadah illustrations or with scenes of Jerusalem and the Holy Land.

A special cloth is used for covering the matzah. The Matzah Cover

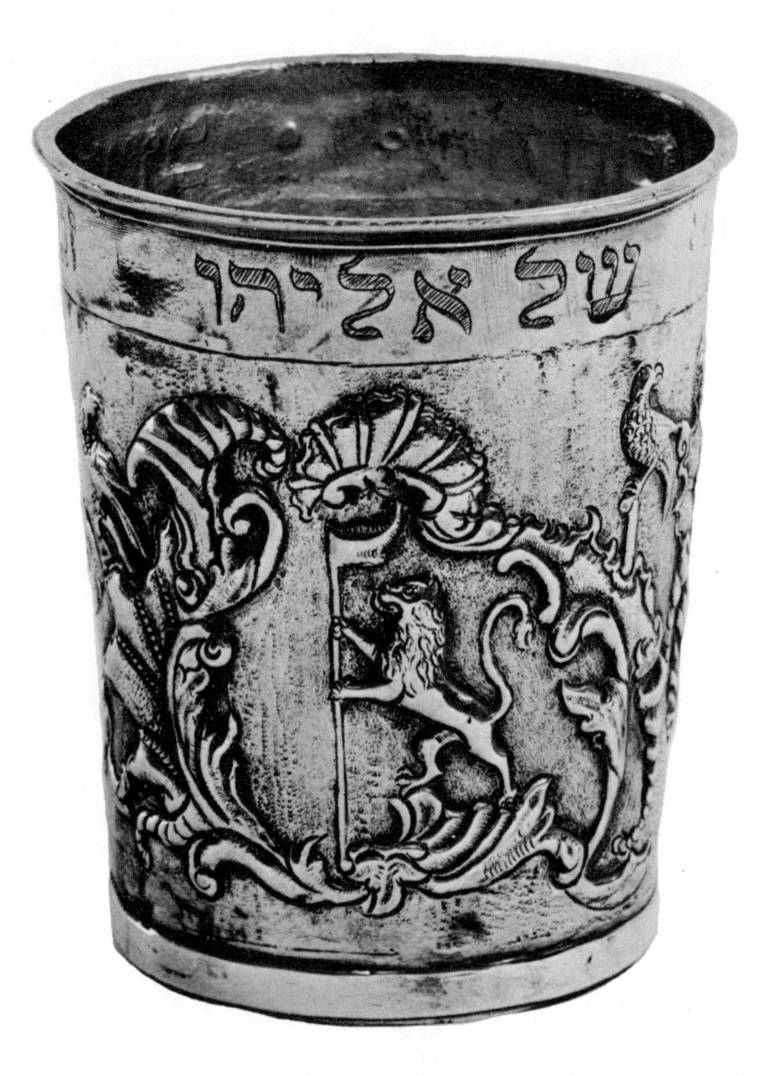

is usually made of cloth, velvet or silk brocade, often adorned with the benediction for matzah and with various Passover scenes.

For drinking the Seder's obligatory four cups of wine, Passover Kiddush Cups evolved, differing from Sabbath Kiddush Cups in their decorative Passover scenes and inscriptions.

The table is also graced with the Cup of Elijah, an imposing Kiddush beaker, usually silver, which is filled at the end of the Seder

Opposite: *silver cup of Elijah for Passover. Central Europe, c. 1700.*

and set aside for Elijah, the prophet of the redemption; he is a welcome guest at every Seder.

Shavuot

Shavuot, the late spring festival of first fruits, also marks the Revelation at Sinai seven weeks after the Passover Exodus from Egypt. Shavuot inspired an interesting art form in Eastern Europe – paper-cuts. Called *Shavuoslach* or *Raizelach*, they bore Jewish symbols and motifs, such as the menorah, the four 'Jewish folk animals', etc., and were pasted on windows during the festival.

11 The Life Cycle in the Jewish Tradition

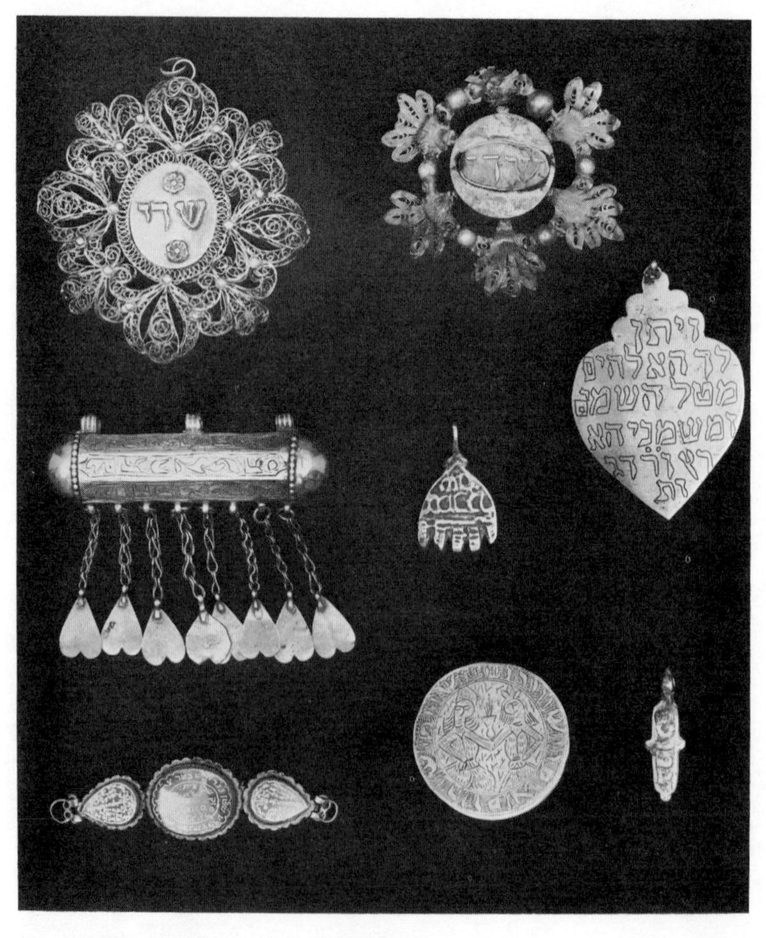

Silver amulets from Italy and the Middle East.

Birth

Before modern times many fears were aroused by and associated with pregnancy and childbirth. Understandably, the Jews, like other peoples, engaged in certain practices designed to allay fears and to ward off death during childbirth. Amulets bearing the names of God and protective angels or Biblical quotations were worn by Jews in many countries as a preventative of illness and for general protection and well-being. The rabbis' attitude towards the wearing of amulets was ambivalent. Many of those opposed to their use as superstitious and not based on authentic Judaism did not actively condemn the amulet because of the usefulness it served as a psychological placebo.

Silver amulets from North Africa and the Middle East.

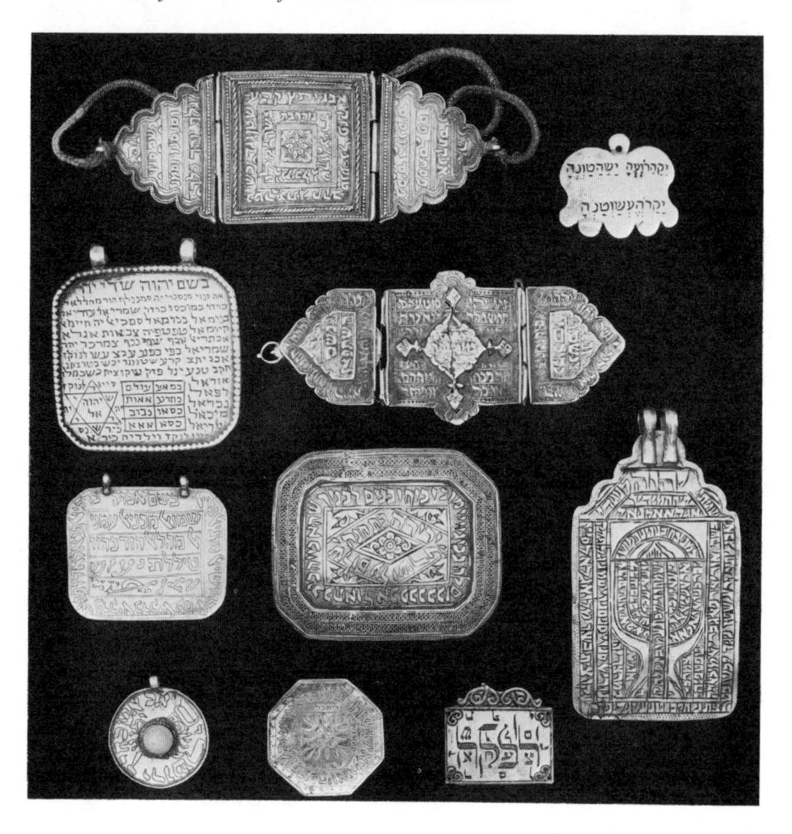

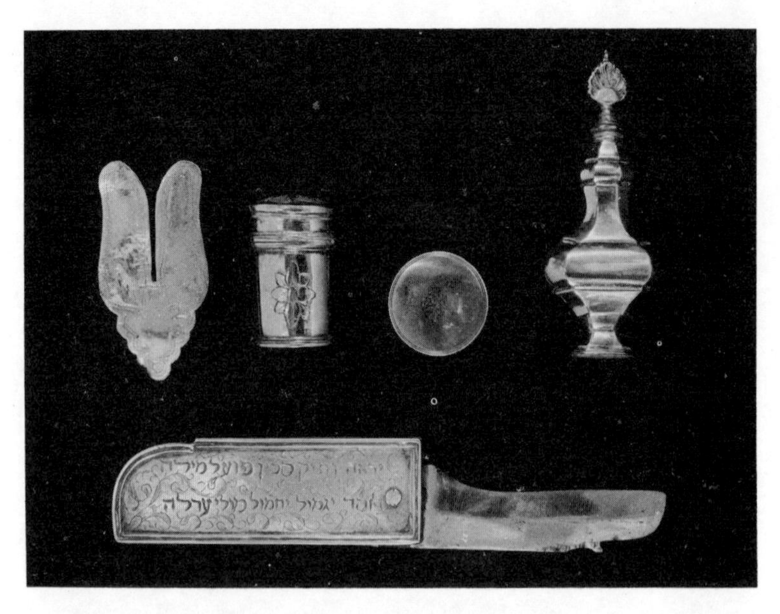

Silver circumcision knife and implements. Italy, 18th century.

Made of a variety of materials, especially of silver and brass (sometimes they consisted of inscriptions on paper or parchment and were inserted into metal containers), amulets were designed to be worn on different parts of the body and to be hung in the home, either near the door or above the bed of an expectant mother or a baby's crib. Sometimes they were exquisite miniatures, with the greatest variety coming from Persia, and Italy producing the most beautiful.

The Torah requires every Jewish male to be circumcised when he is eight days old. In this way each new generation reaffirms and reconsecrates the perpetual covenant (*Brit Milah*) God made with Abraham and the Jewish people (*Genesis XVII: 9–13*). The ritual circumcision, which is performed not by a doctor, but by a *mohel* (ritual circumcision surgeon), involves the use of a number of ritual implements, the most noteworthy being the circumcision knife.

This knife was at times a beautiful instrument, with handles

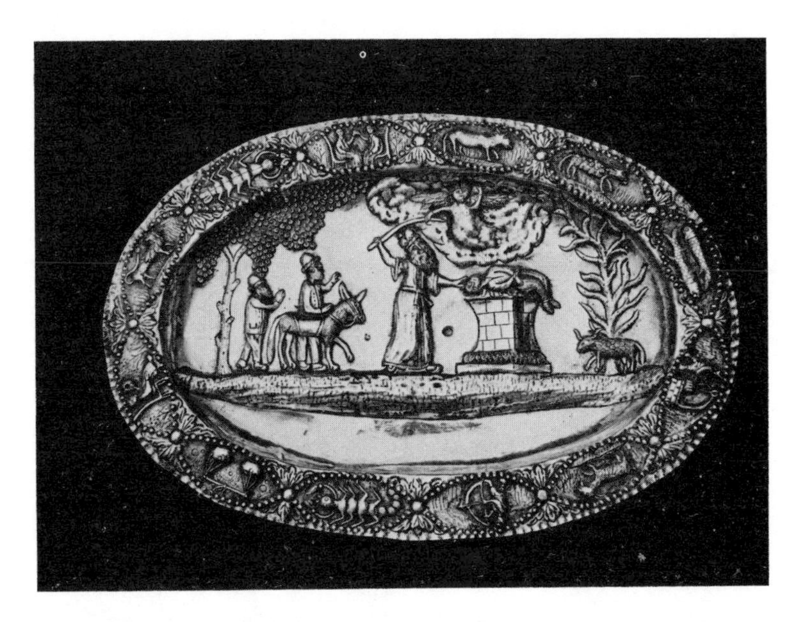

Silver circumcision tray. Around the rim are the signs of the zodiac and in the centre is the Binding of Isaac. Austria, c.1800.

Painted wooden box to hold the circumcision instruments. It is decorated with scenes from the circumcision ceremony. Italy, 18th century.

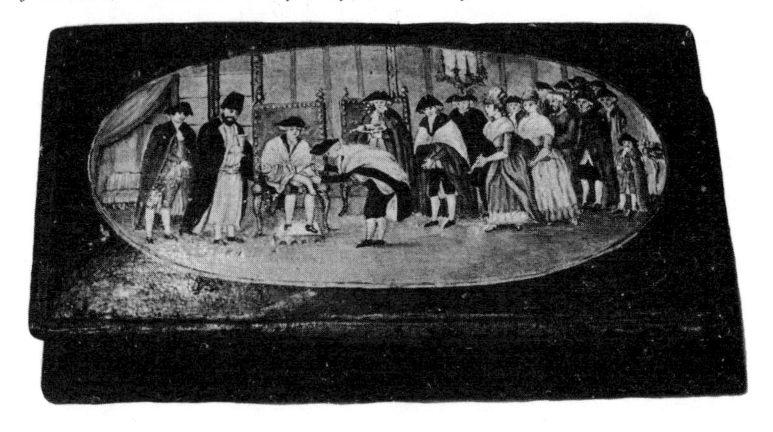

fashioned from either silver, ivory or mother-of-pearl, and sometimes set with precious stones. The mohel frequently kept a written record of his operations, a Mohel Book, which also contained the text of the accompanying religious services, and which were at times illuminated, providing charming examples of Jewish folk art.

Bar Mitzvah

Upon reaching thirteen, the traditional age of attaining religious majority, the Jewish lad becomes *Bar Mitzvah*, or 'Son of the Covenant', and is obliged to observe all of the Torah's commands. The transition has been traditionally observed by his being called up to the Torah reading in the synagogue and his donning of *T'fillin* when he recites his daily morning prayers, both rituals obligatory upon Jewish adult males, symbolising the passage from boyhood to adulthood. *T'fillin*, or phylacteries, are leather cubes which contain small parchment strips on which are inscribed Biblical verses containing passages about monotheism and some of the principal obligations of the Jew, as well as the Biblical command to wear T'fillin '... as a sign on your hearts and as frontlets between your eyes' (*Deuteronomy VI: 8*). The T'fillin are strapped to the upper left arm opposite the heart and to the forehead opposite the brain, to etch the message and significance into one's consciousness. T'fillin are sometimes housed in beautiful silver T'fillin cases when not in use, which in turn are kept in velvet T'fillin bags, often attractively embroidered and inscribed.

Upon reaching Bar Mitzvah (in some communities, upon marrying) a young man dons a *Tallit* (pl. *Tallitot*) or prayer shawl with fringes at the corners, during the morning services, in performance of the Biblical command (*Numbers XV: 37–41*) which requires the mnemonic device 'so that you may look upon them and remember all the commandments of the Lord and perform them'. Tallit containers were usually of velvet, often decorated and with embroidered inscriptions. A distinctive, purse-like Tallit container of velvet (occasionally with silver decoration) evolved in Morocco; it was customarily embroidered with the name of the Bar Mitzvah and ceremoniously presented to him.

Marriage

'It is not good that man should be alone', God says in the Bible

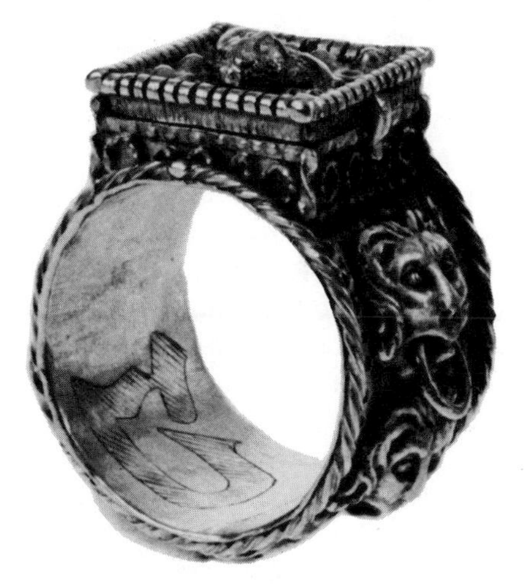

Gold marriage ring. Italy, 17th century.

(*Genesis II: 18*) and that has always been a guiding principle in Judaism. Every person is expected to marry and the unmarried state is considered repugnant to Judaism, especially in the case of a rabbi. The sanctity of marriage is reflected in the Hebrew word for marriage, *Kiddushin*, which is derived from the same root word as Kiddush, or sanctification, and in a word sums up the Jewish approach to marriage – the hallowing of a man and woman for the fulfilment of life's sacred purpose.

Marriage has two prime goals in Judaism – the perpetuation of the species and companionship. The duty of rearing a family is expressed in the Bible's very first command, 'Be fruitful and multiply' (*Genesis I: 28*), and is considered man's fundamental obligation and God's first and primary charge to man. Marriage was also designed to promote chastity and purity in life, the sexual urge having been given to man for the purpose of fulfilling the Divine command to perpetuate the species. In sanctifying marriage, Judaism at the same time sanctifies the family, which is the basic unit of social and religious organisation in Jewish life.

The *Ketubah* (pl. *Ketubot*) is a document which the Jewish bridegroom is required to present at the wedding. Its literal meaning, 'her writ', reflects the one-sidedness of this marriage contract, in that it details the basic obligations which the groom assumes towards his wife during their married life or in the event of death or divorce. It thus represented an early charter of woman's rights, especially in an age in which the woman was generally regarded as little more than chattel in other societies.

The Ketubah is an ancient document. A marriage agreement referred to in the third-to-second century BC apocryphal Book of Tobit is undoubtedly a Ketubah. The earliest Ketubah discovered was one from Aswan, Egypt, dating back to the fifth century BC, a document which indicates that the institution had already been in existence for a long time. Four Ketubot from the first and second centuries have been discovered by archaeologists in Israel's Dead Sea caves in the Judean desert.

Since the Ketubah was designed for the woman, who was considered to have a sensitivity for the beautiful, it was often decorated, especially in Sephardi lands and in Italy, and it is of particular importance to the study of Jewish art. The earliest remains of a decorated Ketubah are those of an Egyptian one, which dates back to the tenth or eleventh century, and contains remnants of decorative arches and Hebrew micrography. There is an incomplete *Ashkenazi*, or German Ketubah, from Krems in Northern Austria dated 1392, showing a man giving a large marriage ring to a woman.

The Krems Ketubah notwithstanding, the custom of decorating Ketubot was primarily a Sephardi and Italian one. Indeed, the fact that the custom of decorating Ketubot existed primarily in communities settled by Jews expelled from Spain and Portugal in the 1490's indicates that the tradition of decorating Ketubot had existed in medieval Spain and Portugal. One of the earliest examples extant is a fragment of a Ketubah from the Spanish town of Segura, near Saragossa, from the 1480's, which contains a wide band of decorative Hebrew lettering bordering the text. This form of decoration exists to this day for Ketubot where Sephardi Jews resided, and was a basic design element in Sephardi Ketubot. The lettering usually contained expressions of good wishes to the bride and groom and Biblical quotations.

A far more intricate method of Ketubah decoration is micrography, the painstaking art of minuscule writing to form ornamental patterns and designs. Another distinctive decorative style for the Ketubah was that of the paper-cut or, more accurately in most cases, the parchment-cut. As a rule, most old Ketubot from North Africa,

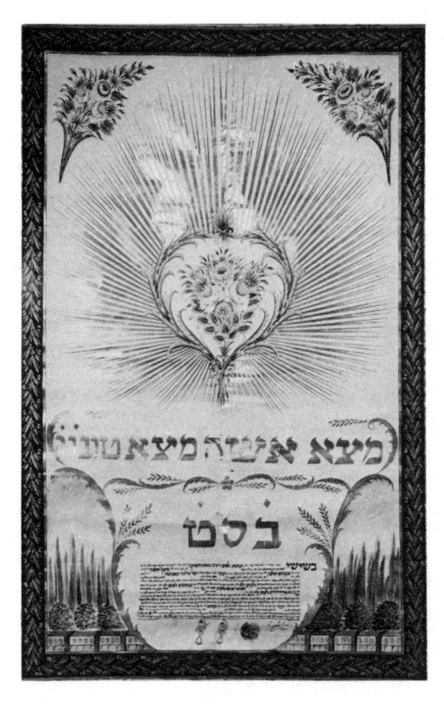

Ketubah on cloth. Turkey, 1849.

the Persian Gulf and the Middle East were written on paper, and most European Ketubot were written on parchment.

Floral motifs, the most frequently used decorative device, appeared mostly in Moslem countries, along with motifs of birds and geometric ornamentation. In Europe, figurative art was also used at times, especially in Italy and Holland.

Frequently the decoration would be accompanied by a suitable Biblical quotation. A vine-like decoration, for example, might be accompanied by the quotation that 'your wife shall be as a fruitful vine in the innermost parts of thy house' (*Psalms CXXVIII: 3*). Olive plants might indicate the following verse in Psalms: 'Thy children shall be as olive plants around your table.' The four so-called Jewish 'folk animals' (the leopard, the eagle, the stag and the lion) would often be accompanied by the Talmudic quotation which urges the

Jew to be 'strong as a leopard, light as an eagle, fleet as a stag and heroic as a lion to perform the will of your father who is in heaven' (*Chapters of the Fathers V: 23*).

Where figurative art was used, a bride and groom might be depicted, or Biblical couples in characteristic Biblical scenes. The decorative Hebrew text might then express the wish that the newlyweds be blessed as were the Biblical couples depicted. Similarly, if bride or groom had a name of a Biblical figure, a scene from the life of the Biblical namesake might grace the Ketubah. The signs of the zodiac, often accompanied by the phrases, '*Mazla M'alya*', '*Mazla Y'aya*' and '*Mazal Tov*' were frequently used to convey wishes for good luck.

The most beautiful and artistic by far of all Ketubot, are those of Italy. Carefully preserved over the years for their artistic as well as their historical value, these parchment Ketubot are prized as outstanding examples of Italian art of the seventeenth, eighteenth and nineteenth centuries. Grooms vied with one another for the Ketubah illuminators in the greatest demand at the time. Indeed, in at least one city, Ketubot became such an extravagance that a communal ordinance was issued which limited the amount of money one could spend. Centres for fine Ketubah illumination developed, with Rome, Ancona, Venice, Mantua and Ferrara producing the most beautiful ones.

Among the most folkloristic and most colourful Ketubot were those of Persia and Afghanistan. In every Persian city the tradition of decorating Ketubot was well developed, but each town evolved its own distinctive style, on occasion related to the history of the city. In Isfahan, the old imperial capital of Persia, prime decorative elements in the Ketubah included large twin rampant lions at the top, flanking a vase of flowers or a tall flame, and behind each lion, a rising sun with human features – parts of the national symbols of imperial Persia.

In Teheran, the 'book-form' Ketubah was often used, a colourful folio measuring about seven inches (17cm) wide by about nine inches (22 cm) high, usually containing five to ten leaves decorated in bright colours. The Jews of Meshed, who were forcibly converted to Islam in 1839 and who nonetheless continued to practise their Judaism in secret are commemorated in Ketubot written in Persian script, but which contain either parallel Hebrew text

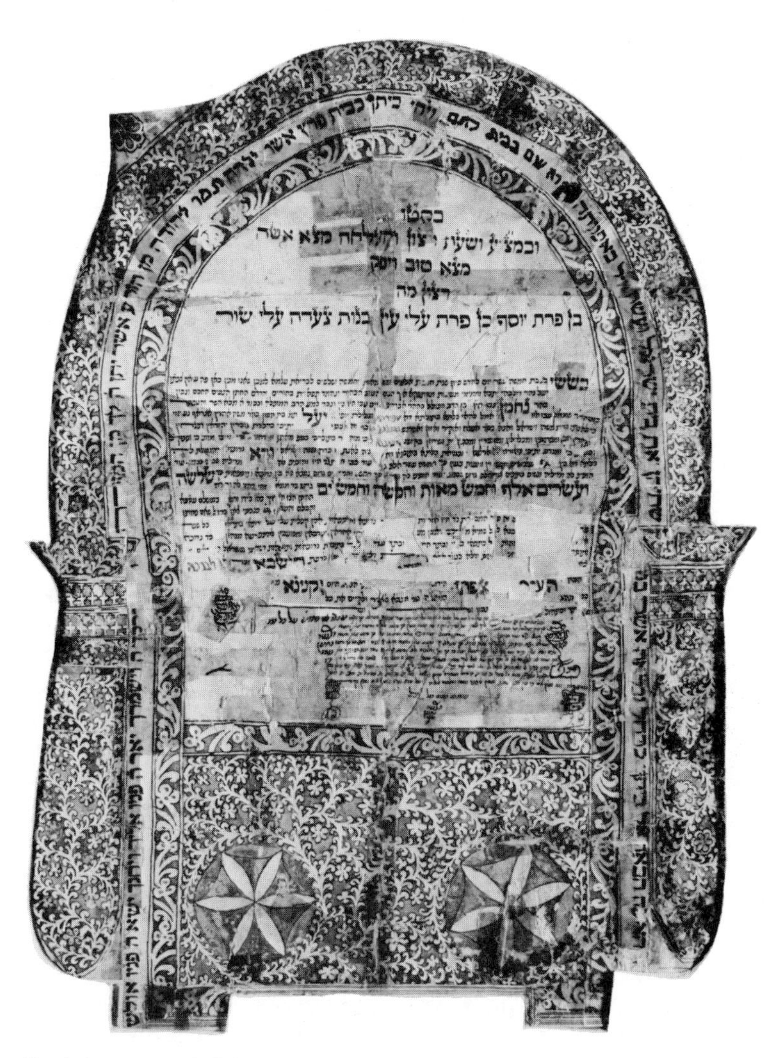

Ketubah on paper. Safed, Israel, 1875.

which has been subsequently added, or a few Hebrew words.

National elements also appear in the Ketubot of Gibraltar, the British Crown Colony. These Ketubot were distinguished by a scarlet crown at the top, sometimes above a wreath of flowers. In Tetuan, Morocco, where the members of the community are closely related in many ways to the Jews of Gibraltar, the Ketubot often featured three crowns at the top; these symbols may have been derived from the aforementioned Talmudic passage declaring that there are three crowns – the crown of Torah, the crown of priesthood and the crown of royalty.

Simple ornamentation was usually the rule in the Ketubot of Tunis, but occasionally birds, especially roosters, would be featured.

The Ketubot of Yemen were usually adorned only with rows of large decorative lettering containing good wishes to the bride and groom at the top of the Ketubah, but on rare occasions human figures, very primitively executed, also appeared.

The Ketubot of the Ottoman Empire were often large and filled with decoration, usually flowers and trees, with only the smallest portion of the space given to the actual Ketubah text, sometimes only about ten per cent. These were related to the Ketubot of Syria, which also were large and were allotted only a small percentage of the space to the text.

In the land of Israel, the Ketubot of Jerusalem, Safed, Hebron and Tiberias were limited to floral and geometric designs. Similar design elements make up the decorations of Ketubot in Soviet Georgia, Albania and Yugoslavia.

Death

The Jewish attitude towards death stresses its naturalness and inevitability as an integral part of the world order created by God. This is expressed by the well-known Biblical quotation: 'The Lord gave and the Lord has taken away, blessed be the name of the Lord' (*Job I: 2*), and by the Jew reciting the benediction 'Blessed be the true Judge' upon hearing that a loved one has died.

Every Jewish community had a *Hevra Kadisha*, a 'sacred society' which arranged all matters relating to death and burial. Membership in the Hevra Kadisha was considered to be a privilege. Annually, usually on the seventh of Adar, the day of Moses' death, the Hevra Kadisha would meet for a feast, and drink from special large silver wine cups, sometimes bearing the names of deceased members or officers. Occasionally they used tall drinking glasses or tankards. Examples of such glasses from Germany or the Prague area of

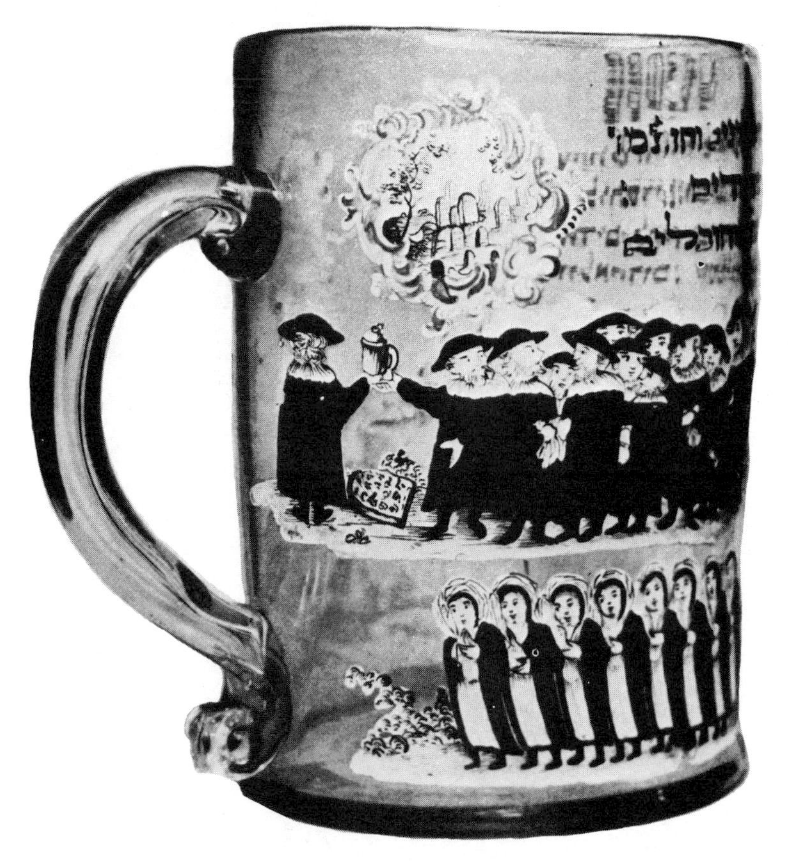

Burial Society tankard, showing groups of male and female mourners and the giving of alms during a funeral. Prague, 1784.

Czechoslovakia dating from the seventeenth, eighteenth and nineteenth centuries have been preserved. These bear depictions of

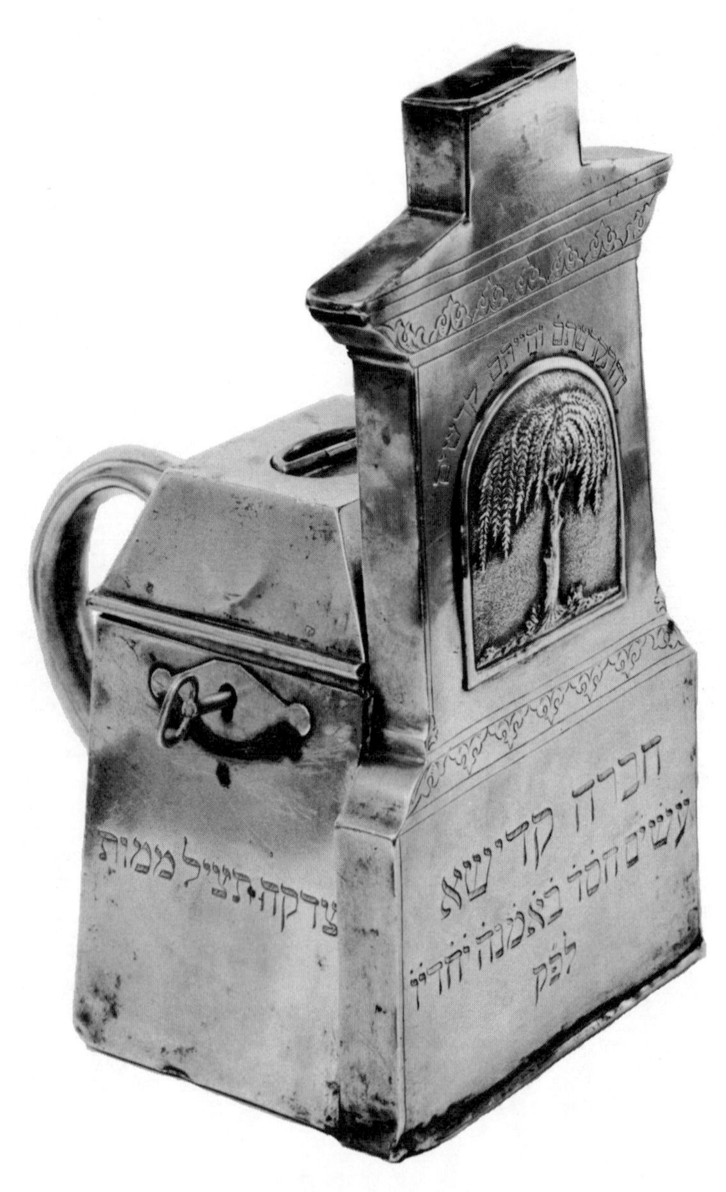

Silver alms box used by a burial society. Made in the form of a tombstone the front is decorated with a weeping willow tree. Eastern Europe, 1776.

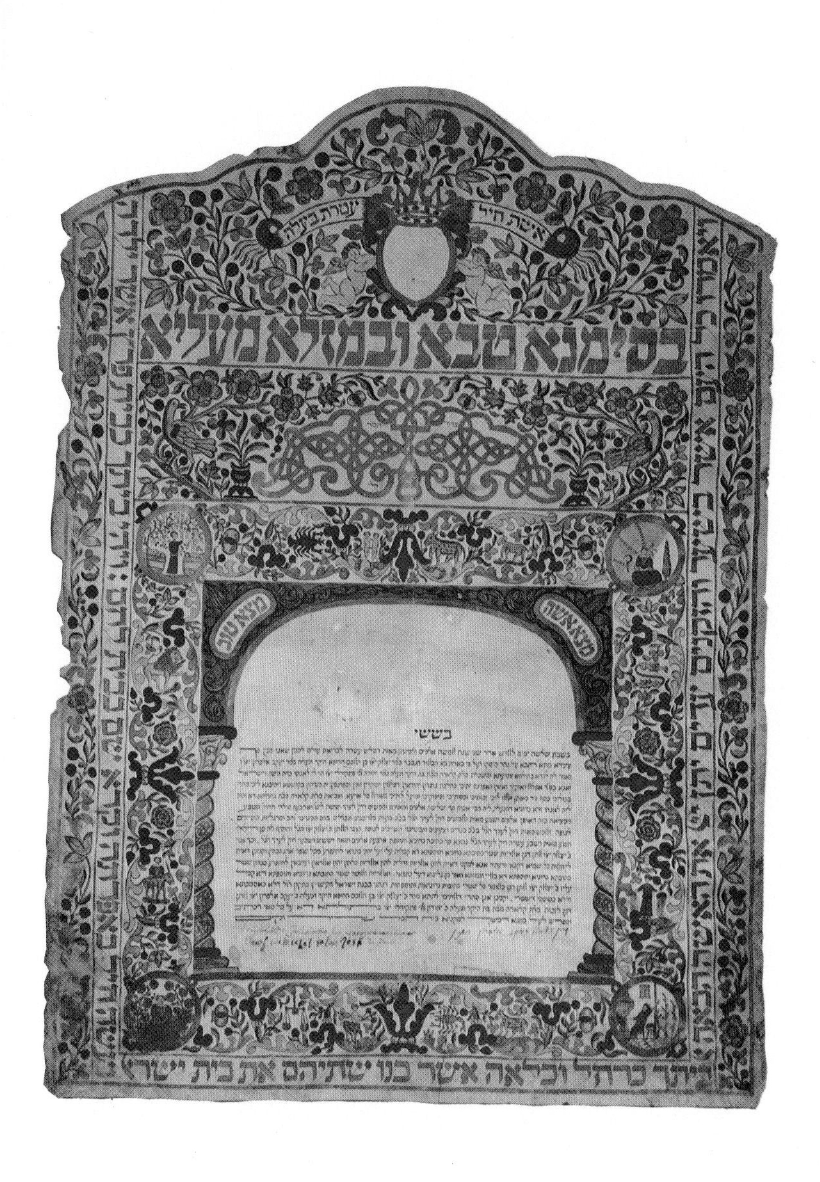

Ketubah on parchment. Vittorio Veneto (Ceneda), Italy 1753.

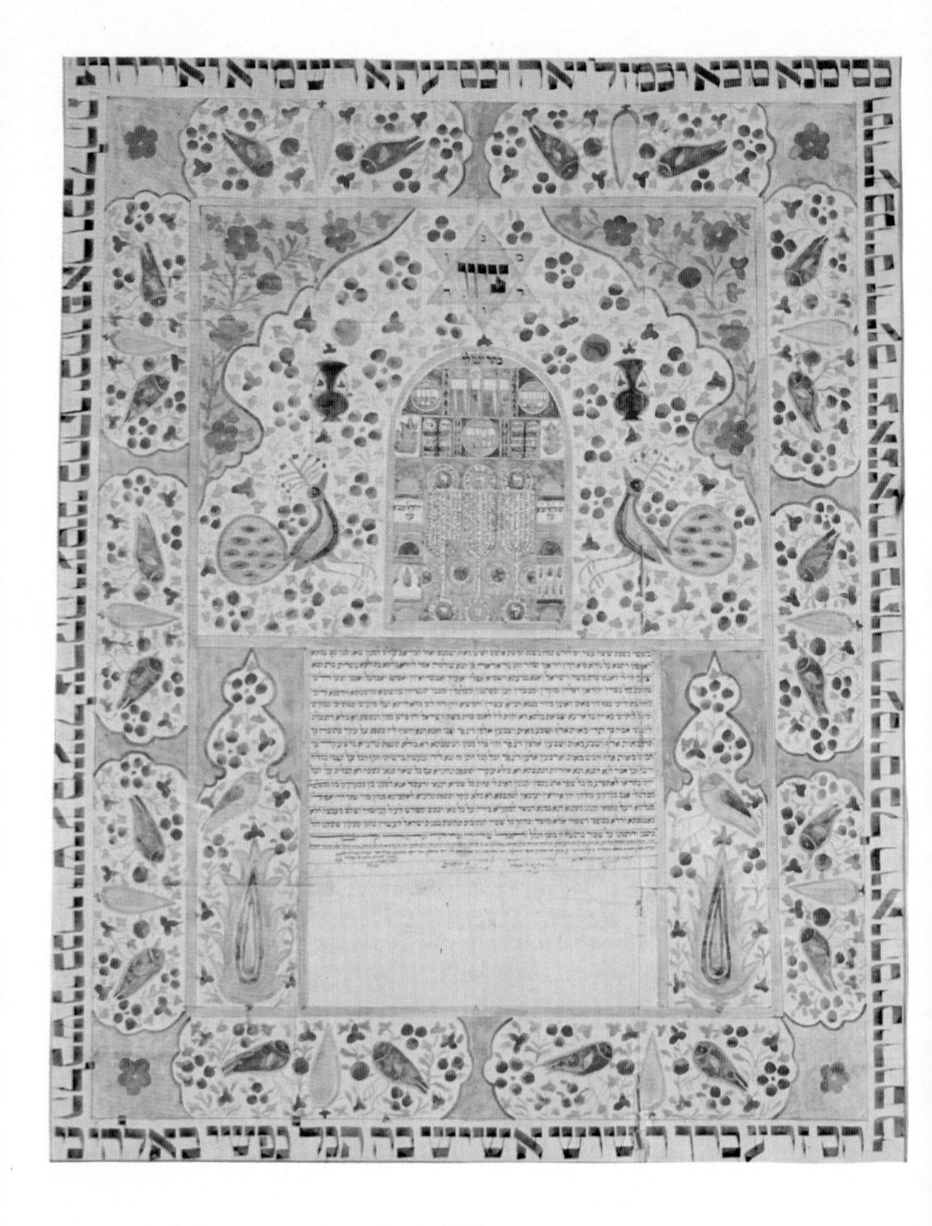

Ketubah on paper. Isfahan, Persia, 1921.

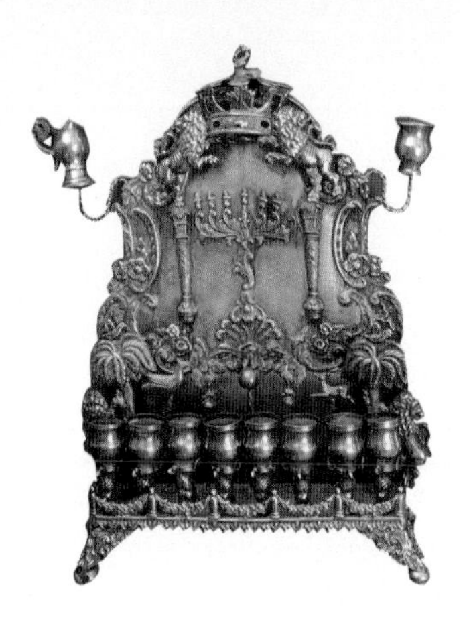

Left: silver, partly gilt, Hanukah lamp decorated with various animals and birds, a crown and twin columns representing those of the Jerusalem Temple. Poland, mid-19th century.

Below: glazed ceramic Hanukah lamp featuring twin lions of Judah couchant flanking a seven-branched menorah. Eastern Europe, 18th century.

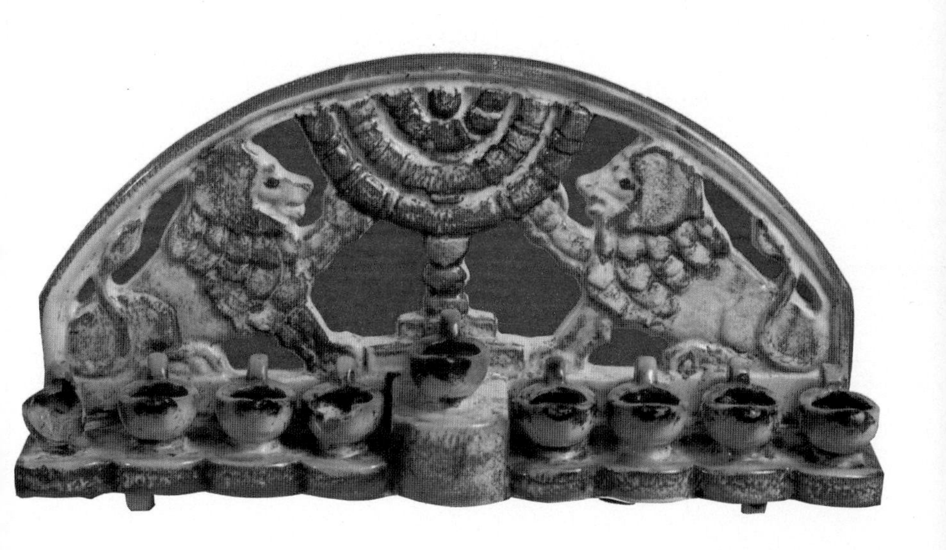

Right: glazed ceramic Hanukah lamp in the form of a Moorish synagogue complete with courtyard. Fez, Morocco, 1927.

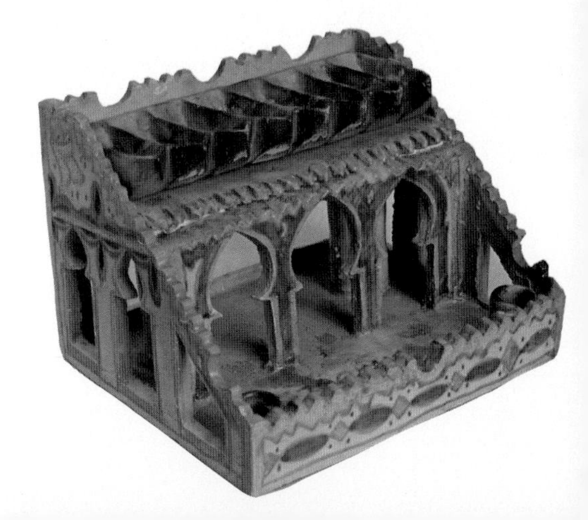

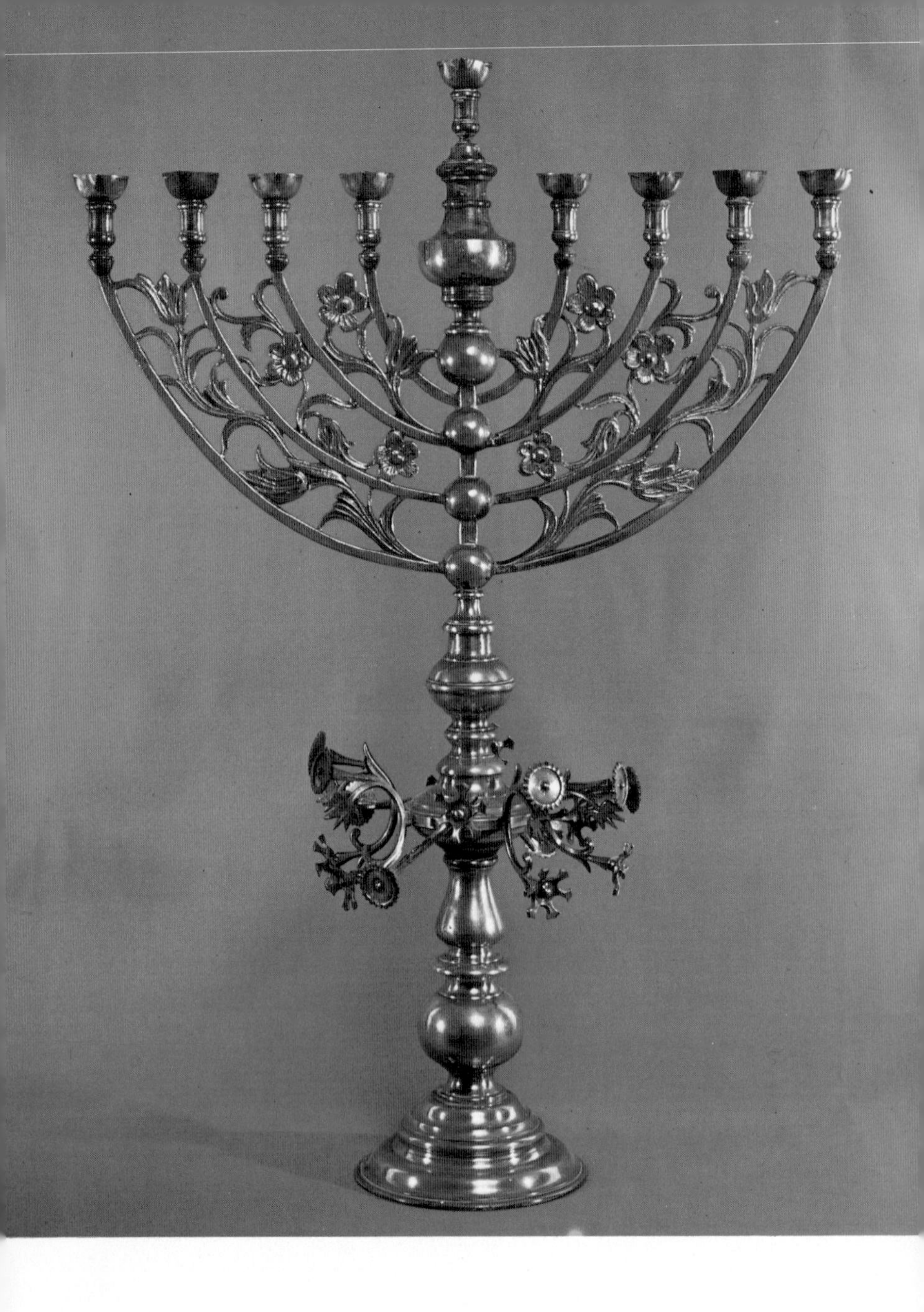

Tall bronze Hanukah lamp. Poland, 18th century.

Opposite, top: embroidered Passover matzah cover decorated with a seder tray surrounded by the symbolic Passover seder foods. India, 19th century.
Bottom: Bar Mitzvah. A Jewish lad, turned 13, reading the Torah for the first time in the synagogue. Detail of painting by Edouard Brandon (1831-97), Paris.

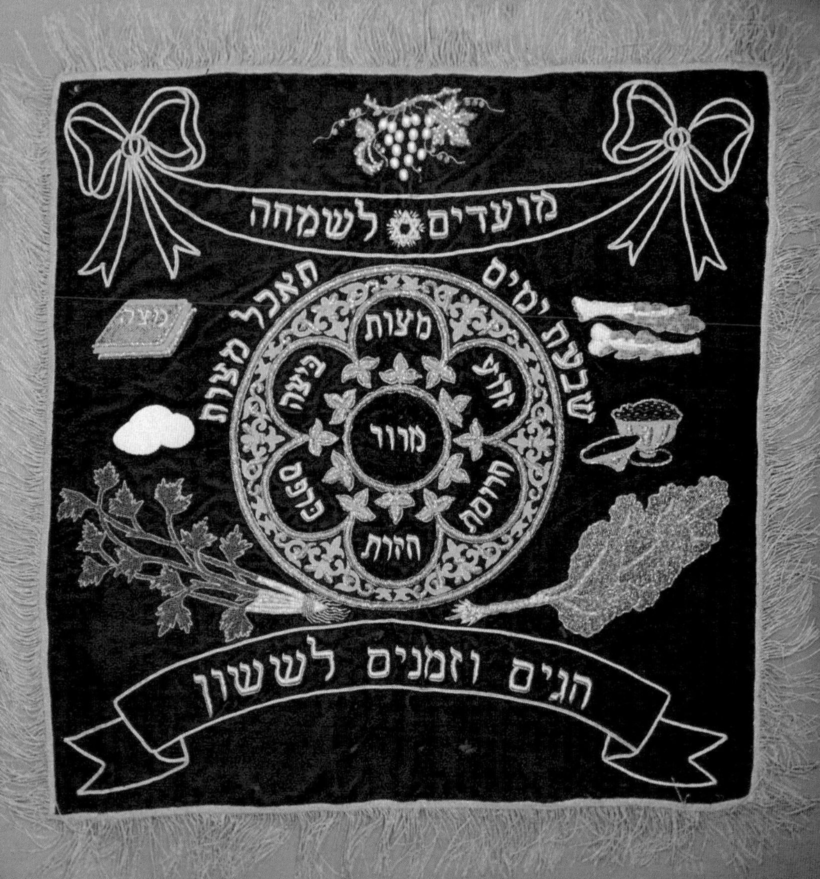
מועדים לשמחה
שבעת ימים תאכל מצות
מצה
מצות
זרוע
ביצה
מרור
חרוסת
כרפס
חזרת
חגים וזמנים לששון

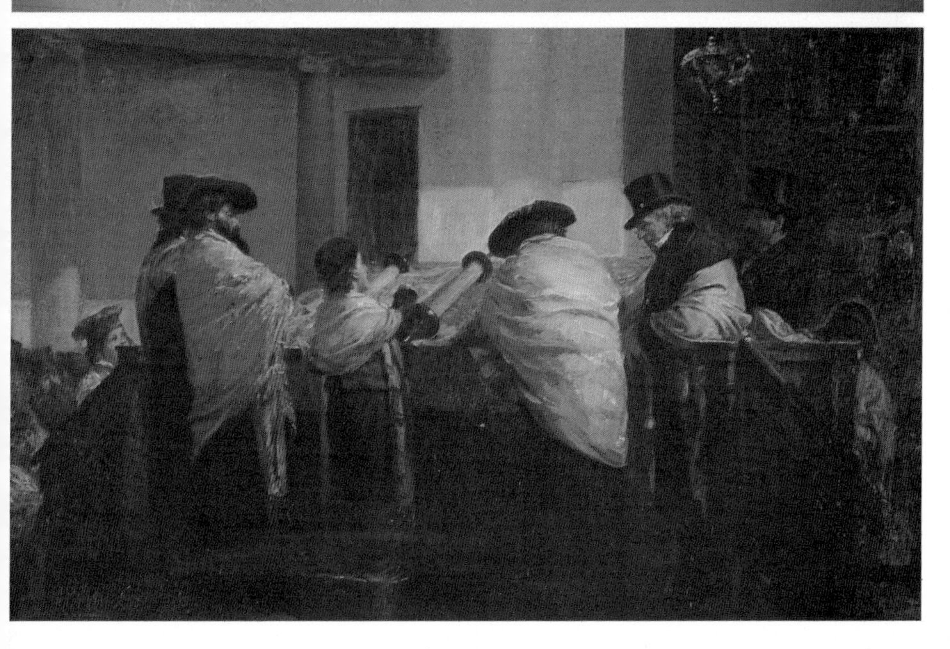

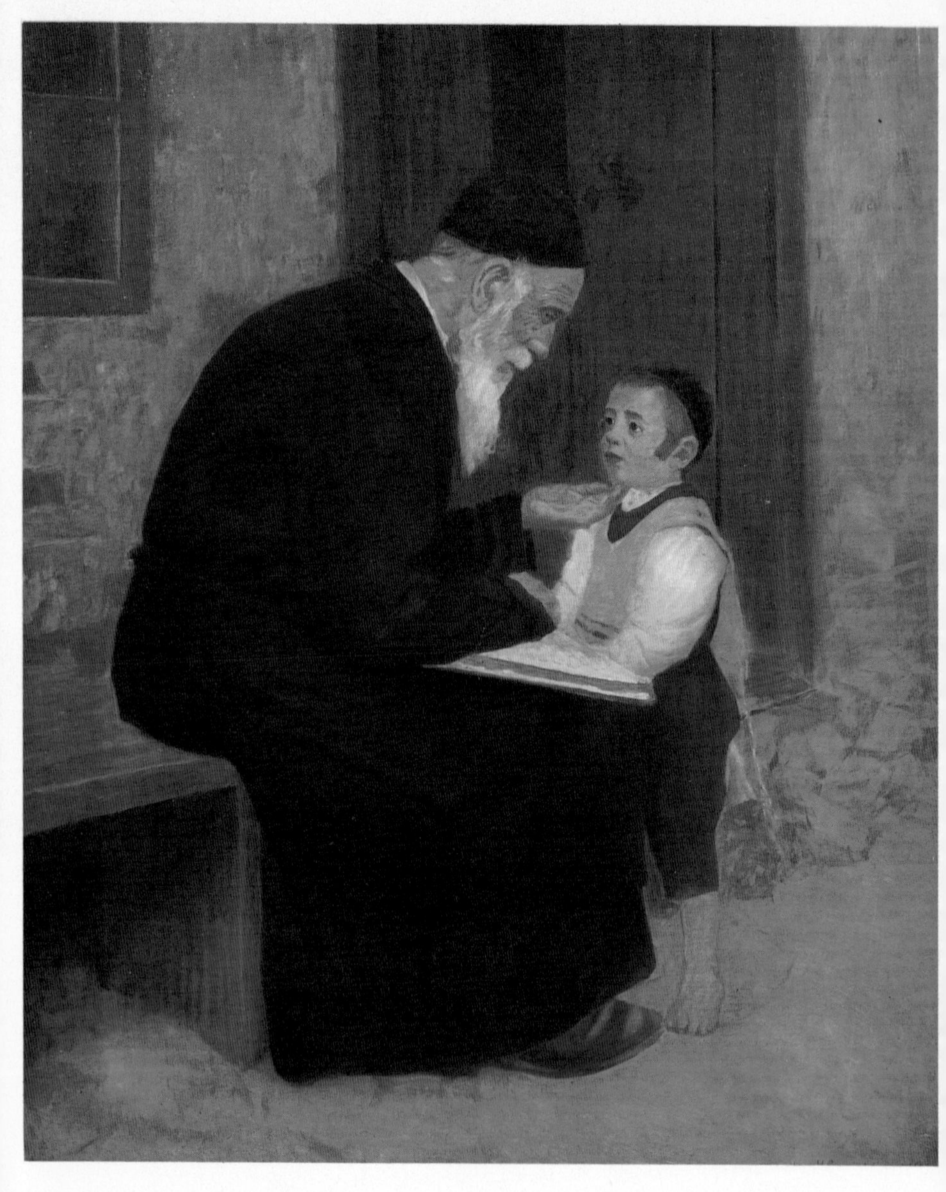

Transmission of the Jewish Tradition. Painting by Lazar Krestin, Vienna, 1904.

Opposite: silver, partly gilt, double wedding cup. Nuremberg, Germany, 18th century.

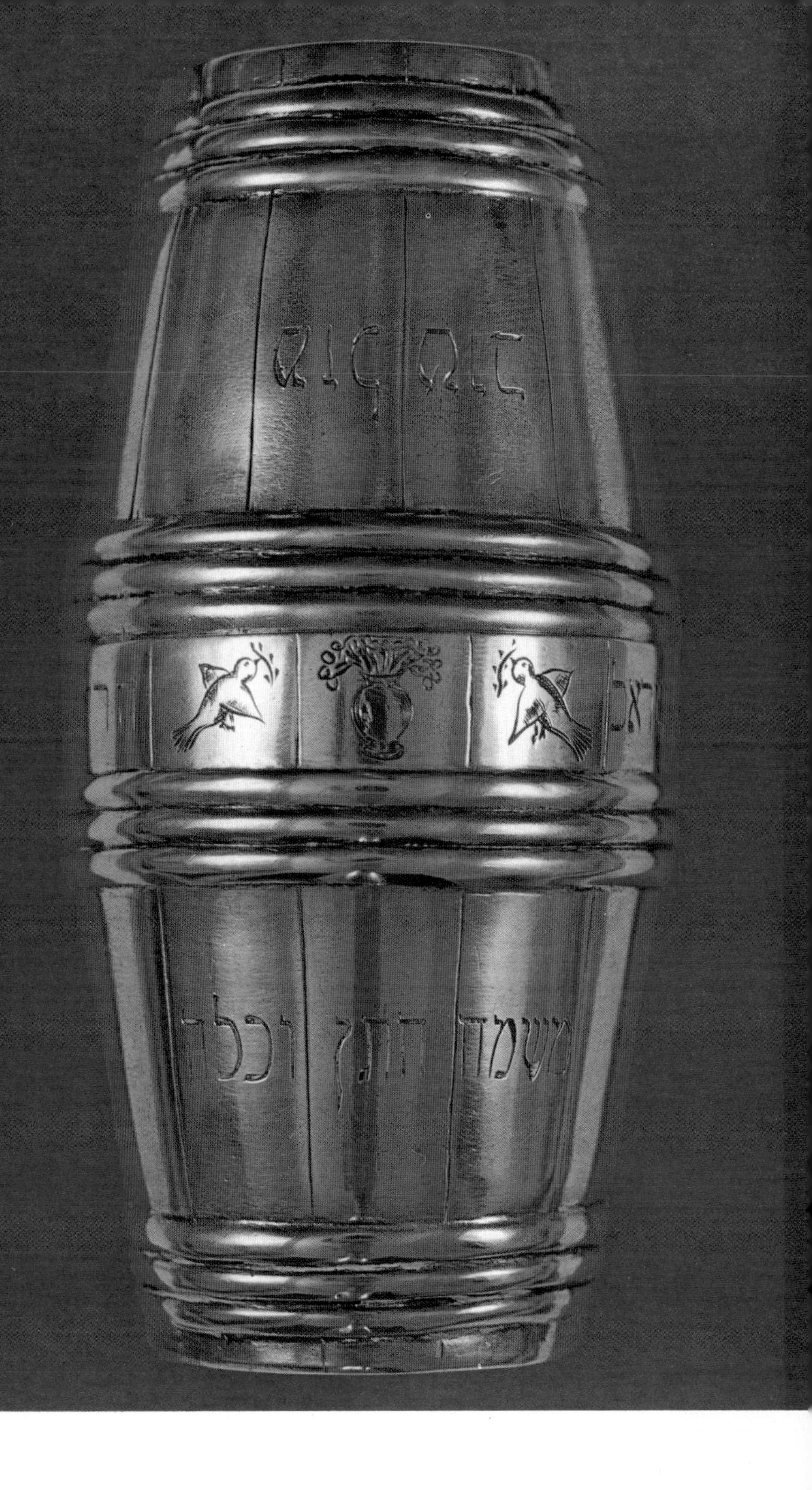

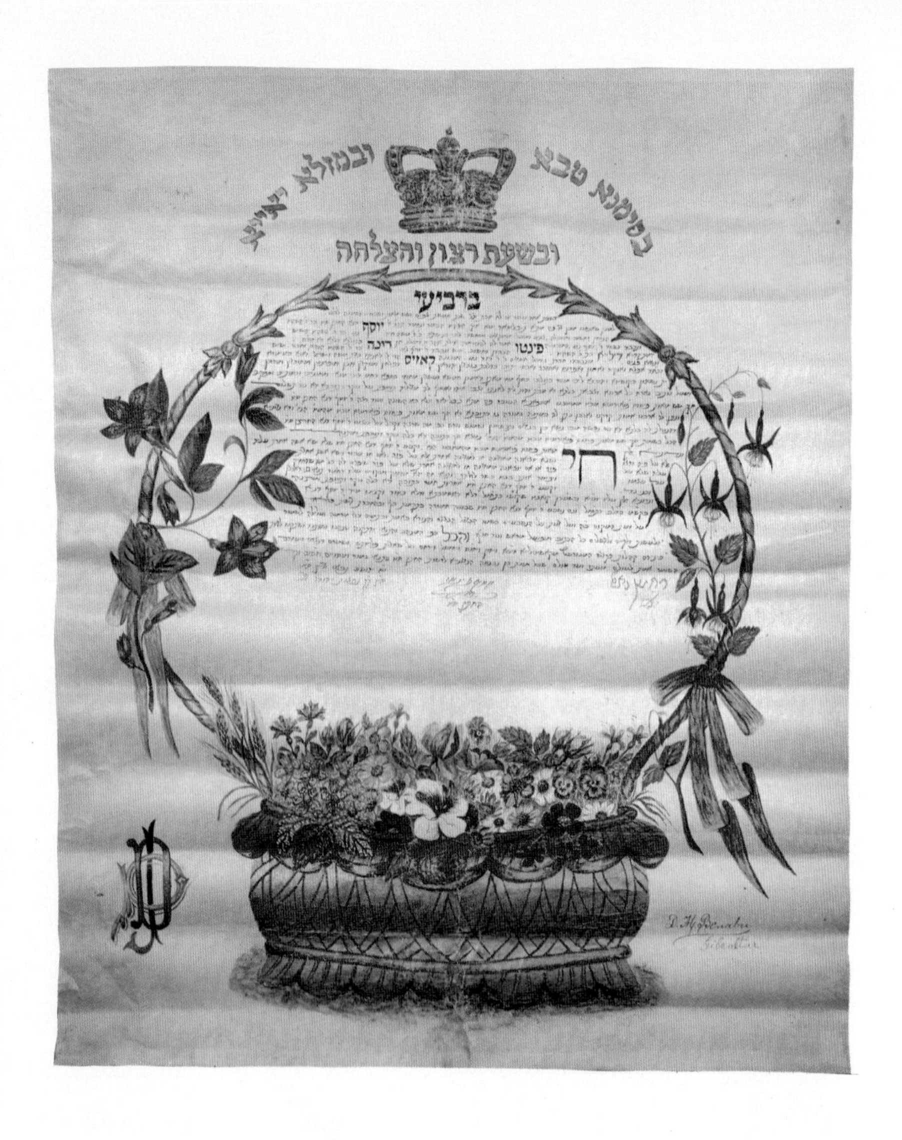

Ketubah on parchment. Gibraltar, 1887.

funeral processions attended by society members or by sombre male and female mourners. Some similarly decorated faience wine pitchers have also been preserved.

The prominent appearance of alms boxes at funerals is grounded in *Proverbs X: 2*, where it is written: 'Alms giving delivers from death.' At times the alms boxes, which were mainly made from brass or base metal, but occasionally from silver, would take the forms of burial tombs or gravestones. One outstanding example is a tall, silver alms box from Austria-Hungary. It is in the form of a tomb

Metal alms box with four separate containers for different charity causes. Eastern Europe, 18th century.

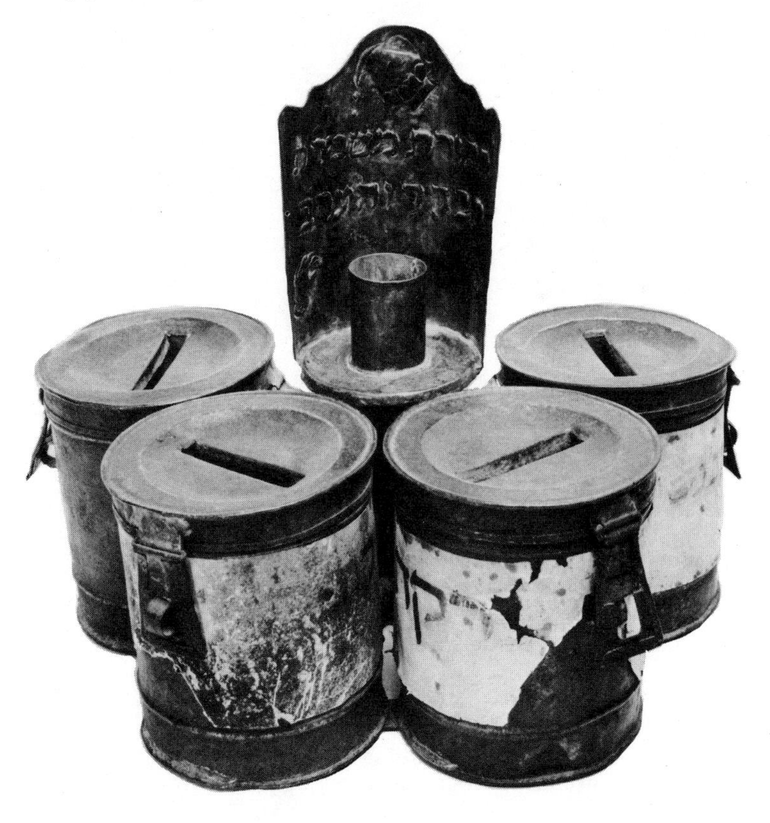

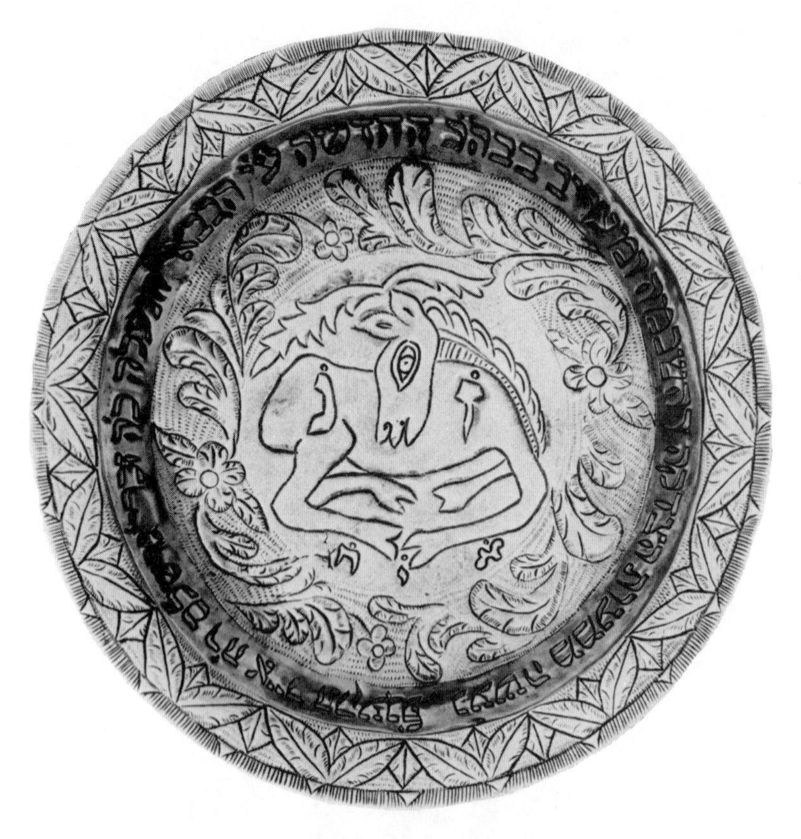

Silver alms tray. Probably from central Europe, 1813.

fronted by an imposing tombstone, which bears a repoussé depiction of a weeping willow. Biblical quotations on three sides and an inscription identify the alms box as one used by a Hevra Kadisha at funerals.

In many countries tombstones were decorated with carvings. Usually the decorations consisted of flora or fauna, often relating to the name of the deceased, or of appropriate ritual symbols. Sabbath candles would frequently decorate a woman's tombstone. Hands held in position for benediction would often be the symbols chosen for that of a *Kohen*, a descendant of the priestly family; and the tombstone of a Levite, whose family would ritually wash the hands of the *Kohanim* before the benediction, would often be represented by a laver. A man named Aryeh (lion) or Zvi (stag) or Z'ev (wolf) would be commemorated by a depiction of the appropriate animal. *Menorot* and Stars of David were frequently used.

Amongst Jews of Spanish and Portuguese origin representational art appeared much more frequently on tombstones, and even figurative art was often used. Frequently employed symbols included the hourglass, skull and crossbones (!), angels or putti, lighted candlesticks, ships (sculpted on the tombs of seafaring people) a censer with smoke rising, the *Kohanic* hands, doves and even masonic emblems. At times a tree, usually a palm or a cypress, chopped down by a hand coming from the clouds, would symbolise a premature death, or, in some cases, a forest is shown with a single tree felled. In the case of children, the tree might be replaced by a sheaf of wheat. It is in the depictions of Biblical scenes from the lives of the Biblical namesakes of the deceased where the sepulchral art of the Spanish and Portuguese Jews of Amsterdam and Curacao especially stand out. Fine examples of sculpture in relief in stone and marble of such scenes have survived, as well as depictions of scenes from the lives of the deceased.

The memory of the dead was also preserved by the *Yahrzeit* (annual) memorial held by the next of kin, and by *Yizkor* (memorial) services in the synagogue during the major festivals. In many Sephardi communities it was the custom for the children of the departed to donate oil lamps to the synagogues in memory of their parents. Indeed, some synagogues were distinguished by the large number of such lamps suspended from the ceilings, which at times blackened the ceilings and hid them from view.

Martyrs and noteworthy persons who contributed to the welfare of the community were often remembered by inscriptions in communal memorial books. Some of these, especially in Central and Eastern Europe, were attractively decorated, especially on their title pages.

12 The Synagogue

'Worship the Lord in the beauty of holiness' proclaims the Psalmist, and he continues: 'The voice of the Lord is in beauty' (*Psalms XIX: 2, 3*). Accordingly, many synagogues have been built and decorated to assure that God could truly be worshipped in 'the beauty of holiness'. But for a variety of reasons the Biblical quotation had to be interpreted more or less metaphorically through much of Jewish history.

Thus, when Rabbi Hama ben Hanina, a third-century Talmudic sage, pointed with pride to a beautiful synagogue built by his ancestors in Lydda, he was rebuked by Rabbi Hosea, who said: 'Were there no needy scholars whom that treasure would have enabled to devote themselves to the study of Torah?' The point is clear. Although Judaism does make *hiddur mitzvah*, the beautification of the Torah command, a significant adjunct to the command itself, one should never lose sight of the order of priorities whereby ethical concerns always take priority over beauty.

There were, of course, other reasons for building modest synagogues, such as the relatively small number of Jews living in many areas, or the low profile which the Jew was obliged to assume for his security and physical existence. And while Halacha, Jewish law, prescribed that the synagogue be built in a high place, there were usually very stringent regulations governing the size, nature and decoration of synagogue structures, imposed by the ecclesiastical authorities on those occasions when they did permit a synagogue to be built. More often than not, permission was denied altogether to build a synagogue or to enlarge an inadequate one. Strictures requiring that synagogues not exceed certain heights meant that builders often had to dig down deep to gain adequate interior height, thus inadvertently conforming to the Psalm which begins 'Out of the depths have I called to you O lord' (*Psalms CXXX: 1*).

The insecurity of Jewish life, the constant fear of the surrounding environment, borne out by the frequent persecutions, pogroms, massacres, wanton destruction of synagogues, physical expulsions from communities and forced migrations, combined to take away the incentive for lavishing money on beautiful synagogues which might well be put to the torch or end up being confiscated by the Church. Synagogues of modest dimension and exterior unpretentiousness did sometimes give way to edifices of imposing size and architectural significance in certain areas, but these were built during periods of relative tranquillity and respite for the Jews which were accompanied by the temporary relaxation of synagogue building restrictions.

There were certain intrinsic factors which affected the design and structure of the synagogue. While the Torah Ark was invariably at the front of the synagogue on the Jerusalem-oriented wall, the *bimah*, or Torah-reading platform-podium, would usually be placed at the centre, sometimes at the rear, and in recent times also in the front. The bimah, which also served as a teaching podium, was the most characteristically Jewish design element in the synagogue. A prominent focal point of the synagogue when situated at the centre or rear, the bimah distinguished the Jewish house of prayer. Another factor affecting the design of the synagogue was the women's section, sometimes located at the same level of the main prayer hall, and in others, in a gallery.

The oldest known synagogue in Europe is that of Worms, in the German Rhineland, a double-naved structure built in 1034 and rebuilt in 1175. Destroyed by the Nazis in 1938 and 1942, it was accurately reconstructed after the war. A surviving etching by Albert Altdorfer (1480–1538) depicts the double-naved synagogue at Regensburg built in 1227 and destroyed in 1519.

The Alteneuschul (literally 'Old-New Synagogue' or, Al-T'nai, 'On Condition') of Prague dating back to the fourteenth century is one of the oldest medieval synagogues. Surrounded by later annexes, it is double-naved, with high vaulted ceilings and two tall central columns. It was completely renovated in the 1960's.

Many medieval European synagogues were confiscated by the Church and traces of the origins of these structures are, by and large, no longer visible. In Spain and Italy, however, a number of churches which were originally medieval synagogues have been identified. While nine of Toledo's medieval synagogues were destroyed in anti-Jewish rampages in 1391, four synagogues were confiscated by the Church and survive as churches or chapels. One, the synagogue of

Joseph ibn Shushan of the second half of the thirteenth century, is of Moorish design, and typically modest on the outside but splendid within. Four long colonnades divide the building into five bays. The many columns and the oval arches give a feeling of spaciousness. It was turned into a convent, and renamed Santa Maria La Blanca. A second Toledo synagogue is that of Samuel Halevi Abulafia, built in 1357. It features Biblical inscriptions in large, decorative Hebrew lettering executed in exquisite calligraphic style on the walls, along with geometric ornamental Moorish patterns, somewhat reminiscent of Seljuk motifs. It is now known as the El Transito Church. Another Toledo synagogue containing a beautifully decorated ceiling is a chapel in the Franciscan convent of Madre de Dios.

In Avila, the Church of Todos los Santos was originally a synagogue. One can also see medieval synagogues in Segovia (the Church of Corpus Christi, which was until 1410 the Sinagoga Major), and in Ciudad Real (the Church of San Juan Buatista). Medieval Seville's Jewish quarter had many beautiful synagogues – in 1388, Ferrant Martinez, the Archdeacon of Ecija, listed twenty-three that he had destroyed – but the only one surviving today is the Church of Santa Maria La Blanca. An idea of the beauty of some of the medieval Spanish synagogues can be gleaned from a court case, in which the parish priest of Bembibre justified his confiscation of the synagogue on the grounds that it was rich and sumptuous. One surviving synagogue which was deconsecrated by the Church in 1887 and restored in 1900, is in Cordoba. The synagogue features richly decorated Mudejar stucco panels, many of which have deteriorated, with ornamental bands of Hebrew lettering. History has taken its toll, however, and in the one hundred and eighteen Spanish cities and towns in which at least one synagogue was known to have existed, very few can now be traced.

Of four synagogues in Trani, Italy, converted into churches in 1290 by Dominican friars, one (the Church of St. Ann) bore a tablet with a Hebrew inscription testifying to its construction as a synagogue in 1247. A number of Sicilian synagogues also became churches, in Palermo, Messina and Marsala. Few of the more than one hundred Italian synagogues brought into the Church's possession in 1569 by the Papal Bull of Pious IV decreeing the expulsion of the Jews from the Papal States except for Rome and Ancona and the elimination of fifty Jewish communities, have been identified. In Rome, the proximity of the Jewish community to the Vatican was the key factor to their welfare. The Papal Bull of Paul IV in 1555 which herded the Jews into the overcrowded Rome ghetto, limited them to a single synagogue. By 1581, however, there were apparently five synagogues for five separate rites, for Pope Gregory XIII ordered them to squeeze together under a single roof, thus forming the Cinque Scuola complex. This combined synagogue lasted for some three centuries, until destroyed by fire and replaced on the same site in 1900–4 by the imposing neo-Classical Great Synagogue on the banks of the Tiber, which with its large square dome and lavish decoration gave the synagogue a sense of grandeur.

In Italian synagogues the bimah was usually placed at the narrow western wall at the rear, opposite the Torah Ark, which stood at the narrow eastern wall at the front of the synagogue. This interior polar balance between the major design elements thus formed a latitudinal plan which left the entire long central portion open for seating. Usually the orientation was towards the centre, with rows of benches along the north and south walls facing each other. There was a women's gallery upstairs. By and large Italian synagogues were undistinguished externally so as to appear as unobtrusive as possible, but the interiors were usually richly furnished and adorned.

During the Renaissance and into the eighteenth century, many beautiful synagogues were built or reconstructed in scores of towns throughout central and northern Italy, from Leghorn to Trieste, and they provided examples of some of the finest baroque work of the period. Exceptional are the beautiful carved and ornately gilded Torah Arks and raised bimah platforms. The bimah platform was often considerably elevated, and sometimes reached via twin elegantly curved decorative staircases. Many of these synagogues no longer exist, and few of those remaining are still in use because of the very small number of Jews still living in Italy. A number of the ritual appurtenances and furnishings, especially Torah Arks, have been transferred to Israel, where they are being used once again. The Venetian suburban communities of Ceneda (Vittorio Veneto) and Conigliano Veneto had finely decorated synagogues which have been reconstructed in the Israel Museum and in the Italian Synagogue in Jerusalem.

Venice itself, long a commercial and cultural centre, had an active community concentrated in its ghetto. Five synagogues, some dating back four centuries, are preserved in the old ghetto, each a lavish expression of the high cultural and economic level of the Jews during the heyday of the Venetian Republic, and their desire to worship the Lord in the 'beauty of holiness'. While typically plain on the outside, the interiors and furnishings of the Italian, Levantine, Spanish, German and Canton synagogues are opulent and sumptuous.

The outstanding example of a rich synagogue interior in Italy is that of the synagogue in the Piedmont town of Casale Monferrato, which was built in 1595 and extended in 1664. On the outside the barn-like structure appears as intentionally mediocre and undistinguished as its drab neighbours. The dramatic contrast of the dazzling Renaissance splendour and sumptuousness of the Baroque–Rococo synagogue interior is a breathtaking surprise. Its lavish opulence is unparalleled in synagogues anywhere. The magnificent baroque Torah Ark, constructed in 1787, is imposing even by the standards of beautiful Italian arks. Enclosed by wrought iron grille work, the ark occupies a large area. Its doors open to reveal a small room in which the Torah scrolls are kept. The ornate gilding and painting characteristic of Italian Torah Arks of the period is lavishly extended in Casale throughout the synagogue interior; the walls, the graceful arches, the magnificent frescoed ceiling, the elevated rabbinic balcony-pulpit, are all richly decorated in a lush, florid manner. Two bas-reliefs, one of which depicts the Jerusalem Temple, face each other across two walls. Decorating the synagogue throughout are many Biblical quotations, each framed in ornate gilded cartouches. Quite appropriately, one of these reads: 'Greater shall be the glory of this latter house than that of the former' (*Hagai II:9*).

In the second half of the nineteenth century there was a revival in the design of synagogues in the Moorish style. Probably the best of these was the Florence Synagogue, completed in 1878. The elaborate relentlessly repetitive decorative detail of the ornate interior, in the walls, the domed ceiling, the bimah and the vestibule, successfully evoke a distinctive oriental grace and elegance. A large Moorish revival synagogue completed in Turin in 1885 to replace a monumental 'white elephant' synagogue, the construction of which had drained the Jewish community and had to be sold uncompleted, was less successful.

In Poland, in the early seventeenth century, a unique synagogue built of stone evolved to accommodate the bimah in the centre. Polish architects integrated the bimah into the very structure of the synagogue and made it an organic part of the building and, by thus accentuating the bimah, structurally created an architectural motif unique to the synagogue. Four columns rose up from the corners of an elevated bimah at the very centre of the synagogue to support a vaulted ceiling, forming a monumental concentricity and an imposing interior without having recourse to a high dome, a feature which would have violated synagogue building restrictions. The bimah itself was usually surmounted by a low canopy covering and when artificially lighted resembled a chapel within the synagogue, and had an emotional effect upon the congregation. Notable examples of such synagogues were to be found in Lublin, Zolkiev, Lancut, Vilna, Pinsk, Luck, Lvov, Ostrog and Novogrodov. Polish Jews settling in Eretz Israel transmitted this unique synagogue design concept to architects designing synagogues in Jerusalem, Safed and Hebron.

Characteristic of Poland during this period and earlier was a type of wooden synagogue, sometimes necessitated as much by the availability and low cost of the building material as by local building restrictions. A peculiar characteric of some of these was a façade built like a medieval fortress, a design feature made obligatory by local authorities in order to protect the towns in the event of attack. In some cases troops were garrisoned there at the expense of the Jewish community. Some of the wooden synagogues were somewhat pyramid-like structures which stood on top of square bases, while there were others which vaguely resembled Chinese pagodas.

Many of the wooden synagogues, as well as others in the Ukraine and in Romania, were distinguished by sumptuous folk art decorations in the form of multi-coloured walls and ceilings and tall, elaborately carved and colourfully painted wooden Torah Arks. Painted in water colours directly on to wood, the decorations often featured examples of the four 'Jewish folk animals', and a wide variety of other animals, including even the unicorn, and birds, plants, trees, vines and flowers. There were also the signs of the zodiac, geometric ornamentation and representations of the seven-branched Menorah and other Temple implements, and occasionally depictions of various musical instruments used in the Temple. Most of such synagogues in Poland and the Ukraine were among the 1800

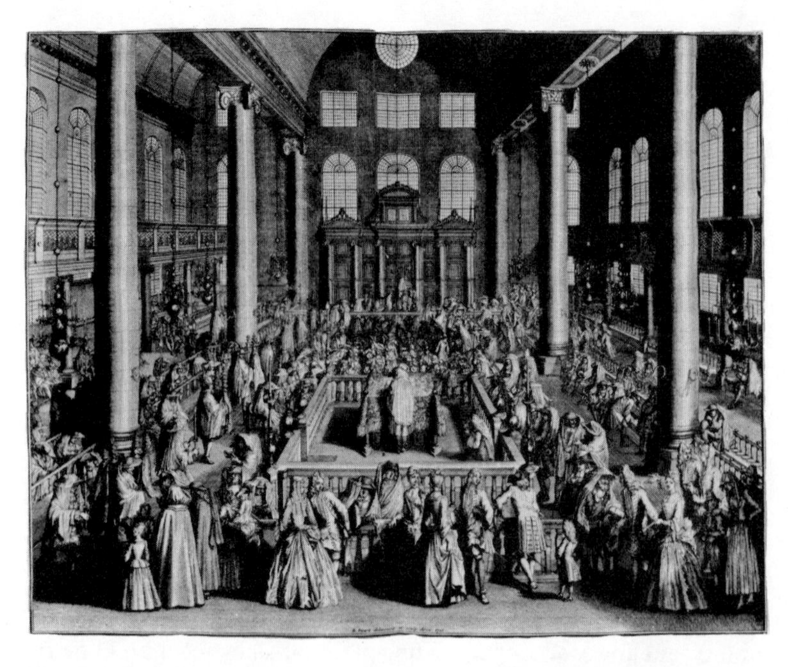

The interior of the Spanish and Portuguese Synagogue, Amsterdam. Copperplate engraving by Bernard Picart, Amsterdam, 1723.

destroyed in 1648 during the Cossack massacres of Zinoviev Chmielnicki, the nationalist hero of the Ukraine, which also took the lives of some 300,000 Jews. Similar wooden synagogues were built by East European Jews who migrated to Germany.

In the Diaspora in which Spanish Jews settled following their deportation from Spain and Portugal at the end of the fifteenth century, most synagogues were deliberately unpretentious and at times even camouflaged lest they attracted undue attention. A significant exception were the Spanish and Portuguese synagogues built by former Conversos or Marranos who had simulated Catholicism and secretly maintained their Jewish beliefs and practices for generations under the dread Inquisition, and were able to doff their disguises

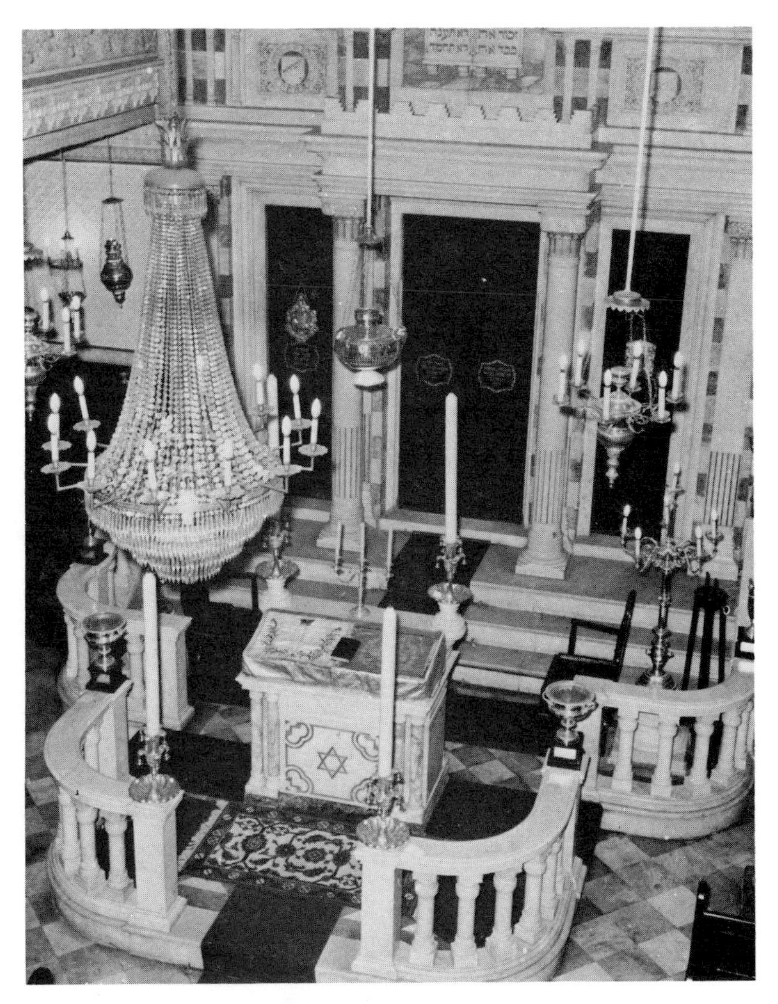

The Bimah and Ark of the Nefusot Yehudah synagogue, Gibraltar.

and practise their Judaism openly when they arrived in liberal, tolerant countries in the West. Outstanding amongst these was the large Spanish and Portuguese Synagogue in Amsterdam, built in 1675, and designed to resemble the Jerusalem Temple as it was thought to look. It became the mother synagogue of a number of other fine Sephardi synagogues built by former members who subsequently settled in London (Bevis Marks), Gibraltar (Nefusot Yehudah), Curacao (Mikve Israel), New York (Shearith Israel) and Newport (Touro Synagogue).

In North Africa and much of the Middle East, the tendency to hide synagogues was even more pronounced than in Europe. Often entrances would be unmarked, with only the initiate knowing that entry was via common courtyards or at times even through private residences. Synagogue interiors would reflect the poverty of the Jewish communities in Arab lands. In many areas, family-owned synagogues were the rule, the product of large, extended clanlike families. This was especially true in the *mellahs* of Moroccan cities such as Marrakech, Fez, Meknes and Tetuan.

The most widely known North African synagogue is La Ghriba of Djerba, an island off Tunisia, whose Jews trace their origins to the dispersion following the destruction of the first Temple in 586 BC. La Ghriba has been recognised by the Tunisian Government as a national shrine, to which thousands of Jewish, Moslem and Christian pilgrims annually flock from afar for the one-day Spring Jewish Lag Ba-Omer festival, because of miraculous cures associated with the synagogue. Tradition dates the synagogue back about 2500 years, but countless reconstructions, changes and additions over the years make it impossible to determine its age. A handsome structure, it features rows of columns supporting arches in the synagogue and the courtyard and it is decorated with multi-coloured tiles. The grounds also contain a caravanserai hostel for pilgrims. An architectural curiosity is a missing column under an arch suspended in mid-air, a phenomenon which is attributed to the Jewish tradition to leave buildings incomplete as a memorial to the destroyed Jerusalem Temple. Impressive oriental synagogues were built in a number of Jewish centres, notably in Baghdad, Isfahan, Sofia, Istanbul and Calcutta.

The emancipation in Europe in the nineteenth century removed many of the debilitating restrictions on building synagogues and gave Jewish communities the opportunity to construct synagogues outside the crowded confines of the ghetto walls. Until now forbidden, or only grudgingly tolerated, synagogues could now be built, even in monumental fashion, without the fear of their destruction or confiscation for use by others.

Simultaneously, the emergence of Reform Judaism effected revolutionary changes which significantly altered the character and design of the synagogue. The women's gallery was abolished and family pews were introduced. Seating capacity was increased as the bimah was removed from the centre of the synagogue and became an altar-like rostrum at the front. The ark, the bimah and a new elevated pulpit formed a single design unit, resulting in a frontal orientation and giving the Reform synagogue a distinctly Protestant church-like appearance. An organ was introduced for the service. To emphasise its divorce from the traditional synagogue, Reform christened its house of worship a 'temple'. The traditional synagogue had been egalitarian; the rabbi, whose role was primarily that of spiritual leader and teacher, was just another worshipper, and all congregants participated actively in the service. Many prayed and studied in the synagogue daily, making it a second home. Used for Torah reading and teaching, the central bimah helped engender an intimacy and informality in the synagogue. In contrast, Reform, seeking to draw closer to accepted Christian forms of worship, became minister-oriented, with the rabbi elevated to a pulpit and preaching to an audience-like congregation. The carefully orchestrated service in the vernacular, punctuated by occasional congregational participation in selected prayers, the emotional organ music and the distance separating rabbi from congregation in a cathedral-like temple, achieved an overwhelming formality which was a sharp departure from the traditional Jewish form of worship in existence for some two thousand years.

The interest of nineteenth-century architects in older architectural styles and forms expressed itself in the design of a variety of 'revival' style synagogues. Jewish communities unable to identify with the neo-Gothic, neo-Romanesque, and Greek-Revival styles favoured by churches, found in the Moorish Revival a style they could identify with. Perhaps it was because of pride in Jewish Middle East origins or, possibly, a new interest in the Jewish Golden Age of medieval Spain, but the Moorish Revival was adopted as a 'Jewish' style for many of the synagogues built in the second half of the nineteenth century in Europe and America.

Otto Simonsohn, architect of one of the first of these, the Leipzig

Synagogue completed in 1855, described the Moorish Revival style as characteristically Jewish. 'Judaism's ... whole substance', he wrote, 'is embedded in the east.' One of the most imposing synagogues built in this style is the Dohany Street Synagogue in Budapest. Seating three thousand, it is the largest synagogue in Europe, with internal measurements of 56 metres long and 26 metres wide, and 44 metres high outside at its twin onion-shaped cupolas. In a design competition in which some of Europe's leading architects participated, Ludwig von Forster's Moorish Revival style won, in part because it appeared more distinctly 'Jewish'. Writing about Budapest in 1891, an architectural historian called it 'the most striking building in that city'. Its success and enthusiastic reception inspired the construction of large Moorish Revival synagogues elsewhere. Forster designed another, the Leopoldstadt synagogue in Vienna, and one in Miscolcz, Hungary. In 1861 an imposing Moorish Revival synagogue was built in Cologne, the design of church architect Ernst Zwirner, who viewed Gothic architecture as an expression of the German spirit and Oriental architecture as innately Jewish. Arguably the most magnificent of all Moorish Revival synagogues was the one at Oranienburgerstrasse in Berlin, designed by Eduard Knoblauch and completed in 1866. Surmounted by a prominent bulbous cupola, the Oranienburgerstrasse Synagogue was an impressive example of monumental synagogue design in the Oriental manner. It was destroyed by the Nazis in 1938.

At the same time three American Reform congregations were building Moorish Revival synagogues, among them San Francisco's Temple Emanu-El, which was really a neo-Gothic structure with oriental elements. Completed in 1866, it was destroyed in the San Francisco earthquake of 1906. Cincinnati's B'nai Jeshurun (Isaac Mayer Wise) Temple, completed in 1866, also has Gothic elements, including a Gothic ark. New York's old Temple Emanu-El was also not pure Moorish Revival, and contained many Gothic and Romanesque elements. In addition, New York's Central Synagogue, completed in 1872, was a Moorish style synagogue which successfully combined Gothic elements. In 1889, New York's Park East Congregation completed a Moorish Revival synagogue which contained rich decorative detail in repetitive patterns.

At the end of the nineteenth century and the beginning of the twentieth century, large numbers of monumental structures were built in Hungary, no fewer than twenty-four of them the work of Lipholt Baumhorn, Hungary's outstanding synagogue architect, whose style was to influence significantly subsequent Hungarian synagogue architecture. Baumhorn's most important synagogue was that of Szeged, a house of prayer of majestic monumentality and one of the most beautiful European synagogues. Completed in 1903, it is basically a neo-Gothic structure with Moorish-Byzantine overtones. Together with its grounds it occupies a square block measuring 106,500 feet (9,893 square m). Its prominent cupola rises 159 feet (48.5 m from the ground). Using a more-or-less square central plan it was more successful in achieving a synagogue-like character than the long and narrow cathedral-like synagogues going up elsewhere at the time. From the inside, the lofty central blue-glass cupola with a background of the stars gave worshippers the feeling of being enclosed by heaven. The synagogue is extensively decorated throughout; colourful, ornamental stained glass windows and many drawings of Biblical scenes and Jewish symbolism, accompanied by appropriate Biblical quotations emphasising Jewish ethical concerns, fill the interior.

We have seen that in the art of Judaism aesthetics is the handmaiden of the divine ethic. While the creation of artistic works was indeed circumscribed in Judaism, the purpose was to channel artistic creativity towards the spiritual elevation of man. Through its philosophy and through the examples of its artistic production, the art of Judaism has profoundly influenced the development of Christian and Western art and has left the world a legacy of artistic creativity and aesthetic awareness designed to ennoble humanity.

תושלב״ע

Acknowledgements

The publishers wish to thank the museums, galleries, libraries and other institutions, and the author, who kindly made available illustrations of works in their collections.

Most of the colour and black and white photographs were taken by David Harris of Jerusalem, many of them especially for this book: pp. 8, 13–16, 18, 27, 29, 36, 38, 40, 46, 50, 53, 54, 59, 60, 64, 67, 72, 74, 77, 78, 79 (right), 81, 82, 83 (right), 85–87, 91, 94, 96, 98–102, 104, 108–110, 115, 116, 119, 121–124, 126–128, 129 (top), 133, 135, 138–140, 148.

Edgar Asher supplied the photographs on pp. 113, 114, 117, 131; Malcolm Varon: p. 68 and the colour photograph of the Torah Ark curtain: State Museum of Berlin, p. 33; State University of Hamburg (Library), p. 42; A. Strajmayster, p. 48.

Index

Aaron 97, 117
Abraham 62, 106, 128
Abraham bar Yaakov 55
Abraham ben Judah ibn Hayim 49
Abraham ben Mordecai Azulai 111
Abraham of Lunel 92
Absalom, Tomb of 31
Abulafia, Samuel Halevi 144
Abun, Rabbi 6
Aesthetics 9–10
Afghanistan 134
Ahasueros 118
Akiva, Rabbi 9
Albania 136
Alexander the Great 19
Alexandria 22, 34, 37
Alms boxes 66, 139
Altdorfer, Albert 143
Alteneuschul 143
America 151
Amsterdam 141, 149
Amsterdam Hagadah 55, 121
Amulets 63, 107, 127, 128
Ancona 134, 144
Anthropomorphisms 5, 16
Antioch 22
Antiochus 19
Aphrodite 4, 6
Appian Way 32
Arch of Titus 32, 63
Archaeology 6, 12, 21, 26, 28
Aristeas, Letter of 37
Ark of the Covenant 6, 19, 25, 63
Art 2–11, 16, 89, 153
Asia 101
Astarte 4
Athens 22
Augsburg 75
Austria-Hungary 139
Avila 144

Baal Pe'or 4
Baal Shem Tov, Rabbi Israel 10
Babylon 14, 19, 92
Babylonian Exile 6, 21
Baghdad 101, 113, 150
Bar Kochba 22, 73
Bar Mitzvah 130
Basmia 84–86
Bateman, Hester 70
Bateman, Peter, Ann and William 95
Baumhorn, Lipolt 153
Beauty 5, 7, 9, 10, 15, 19, 142
Bembibre 144
Berlin 152
Bet Alpha 2, 26, 28, 30
Bet Guvrin 28
Bet Shean 26, 29, 30
Bet Shearim 31
Bezalel 7, 9, 18, 63
Bible 2, 7, 9, 11, 16, 18, 26, 41, 64, 71, 73, 84, 90, 103, 106, 120, 130
Bimah 22, 95, 143, 147, 151
Binding of Isaac 28, 47, 70, 106, 107
Bird's Head Hagadah 47
B'nai Jeshurun 152
Boaz, Yachin and 97, 112
Bohemia 105, 115, 121
Bokhara 79
Boller, Johann Adam 69
Books 35, 50–55
Brazen Sea 19
Breastplates 90, 97
Budapest 152
Burning Bush 44, 64, 70
Byzantine Art 16, 17, 25, 26, 28
Byzantine Synagogues 6, 25, 26, 28

Cairo 35
Calcutta 150
Calligraphy 39
Candlestick 7, 64, 66, 67, 70, 71, 107, 141
Caporet 104
Carthagena 63
Casale Monferrato 146
Catacombs 31, 32, 34
Ceneda (Vittorio Veneto) 145
Central Europe 141
Central Synagogue 152
Ceremonial Art 7, 10, 11, 58–87, 103
Cherubim 5, 19, 32
Chmielnicki, Zinoviev 148

Christian Art 2, 12, 14, 16, 17, 32, 44, 153
Christianity 34
Church 143, 144
Church Architecture 25
Cincinnati Hagadah 47, 49
Cinque Scuola 145
Circumcision 9, 90, 128
Circumcision knife 32, 128
Ciudad Real 144
Code of Jewish Law 103
Coins 63, 73, 108
Cologne 34, 152
Conigliano Veneto 103, 145
Corinth 22
Corunna 41
Crackow Lamp 70
Crown of Torah 97, 103, 104
Curacao 141, 150
Curtain 104
Cyprus 22
Cyrus 19
Czechoslovakia 137

Damascus 22
Daniel 28, 62
Darmstadt Hagadah 47, 49
David 5, 28, 30, 41, 88
de Oliveyra, Abraham 70, 97
Dead Sea Scrolls 14, 35, 37
Death 136
Diaspora 32, 148
Divine Will 16, 62
Djerba 150
Dmitzehan, Andrea 51
Dohany Street Synagogue 152
Duke of Sussex Pentateuch 47
Dura Europos 2, 6, 11, 12–17, 28, 32, 34, 73

Egypt 12, 55, 63, 73, 125, 132
Elijah 80, 106, 125
Elisha ben Abraham Crescas 49
Elkone of Naumberg 105
El Transito Church 144
En Gedi 30
England 95
Ephesus 63
Esther, Book (Scroll) of 44, 118
Etrog 26, 28, 29, 32, 108, 110
Etrog Container 110

Europe 80, 103, 141, 150, 152
Exodus 120
Ezekiel 16, 62
Ezra 15, 19

Farhi Bible 49
Ferrara 47, 134
Fez 111, 112, 150
Figurative Art 14, 37, 120, 133, 134
Fire 61–62
Florence 47, 146
Florence Synagogue 146
Folk Art 90, 130, 147
Fostat 92
Four Kinds, The 107, 108, 110
Frankfurt 70
Frescoes 2
Funerary Art 31–34, 63, 103
Fust, John 51

Galilean Synagogues 25, 26, 28
Galilee 22, 23, 24, 31
Gamliel, Rabbi 6
Gans, Jacob Koppel 105
Garden of Eden 63
Gargoush 65
Gaza 28
Genizah 35, 37
Georgia 136
Germany 39, 44, 47, 95, 105, 115, 121, 137, 148
Ghetto 146
Ghriba, La 150
Gibraltar 136, 150
Gold glasses 34, 37, 63, 74, 103, 107, 108
Golden Hagadah 43–44
Great Synagogue 145
Greece 9, 15, 19
Gutenberg, Johannes 50–51

Hagadah 39, 41, 43, 47, 52, 55, 69, 120, 121, 123
Hai Gaon 92
Haifa 31
Halacha 35, 44, 142
Halicarnassus 31
Hallah 77, 78
Hallah cover 77
Hallah knife 78
Hallah tray 78
Hama ben Hanina 142

Hamam Lif 73
Haman 118
Hamat 28
Hamburg 70
Hamsa 97
Hanina 26, 28
Hanukah 20, 111
Hanukah lamp 111–118
Hasmonean 20
Hassidim 84
Hassidism 10
Havdala 60, 61, 79–87
Havdala candle 80
Havdala cup 80
Havdala tray 86–87
Hebron 136, 147
Helena of Adiabne 31
Hellenism 15, 19
Herod 20
Hevra Kadisha 136, 140
Hexagram 24
Hiddur Mitzvah 10, 58, 90, 142
High Holiday Belt 107
High Holy Days 106–107
Holland 95, 133
Hopkins, Clark 12
Horror Vaccui 30, 112
Hosea 142
Hungary 65, 84, 152, 153

Idolatry 2, 4–6, 11, 61
Illuminated Manuscripts 2, 35–49, 69, 71, 120–121
Incense shovel 25
India 84, 101, 113
Iraq 76, 84
Isfahan 134, 150
Isfiya 29
Islam 9, 21
Israel 2, 26, 32, 63, 120, 136
Israel Museum 49, 145
Istanbul 150
Italian Synagogue 145
Italy 14, 47, 84, 92, 94, 103, 118, 128, 133, 134, 143–146

Jacob 70
Jaffe, Meir of Ulm 49
Japhet 9
Jason, Tomb of 31
Jerash 28
Jericho 106
Jerusalem 5, 13, 18, 24, 31, 32, 49, 52, 62, 71, 73, 88–89, 92, 97, 104, 106, 123, 136, 143, 145, 146, 150
Jesus 15, 16
Jewish Art 2, 11, 14–15, 16–18, 28, 32, 34, 73, 102
Jewish Law 4, 35, 128, 142
Johanan ben Napaha 6
Jonah 41
Jonathan ben Uziel 5
Joseph ibn Hayim 41
Joseph ibn Shushan 144
Josephus 21, 22, 65
Joshua 43
Judaism 2–11, 21, 51, 58, 62, 63, 86, 127, 131, 153
Judenstern 67–69
Judgement of Solomon 70

Kandil 71
Kaufmann Hagadah 43
Kennicott Bible 41
Ketubah 39, 131–136
Kiddush 73–76, 84, 131
Kiddush Cups 34, 73–76, 80, 84, 107, 124–125
Kidron Valley 31
Kitttel 107
Knoblauch, Eduard 152
Krems 132
Kurdistan 71

La Ghriba 150
Lancut 147
Laud Mahzor 47
Laver 76
Leghorn (Livorno) 52, 145
Leib, Moses 122
Leipnik, Joseph 122
Leipzig 151
Leopoldstadt Synagogue 152
Light 60, 61–62, 63, 66, 67
Lions of Judah 26, 29, 34, 70, 92, 97, 103, 104, 112, 117
Lisbon 43
London 70, 150
Lublin 147
Luck 147
Lulav 26, 28, 29, 32, 108
Lvov 147

Maccabees 117
Mahzor Lipsia 44
Mahzorim 39, 107
Maimonides 4, 5, 39, 47
Manna 77
Mantua 47, 52, 103, 134
Marianos 26, 28, 30
Marrakech 150
Marranos 148
Marriage 130–136
Marsala 144
Martinez, Ferrant 144
Matzah 47, 84, 123, 124
Matzah cover 123–4
Mayer, Gerson 105
Mayim Aharonim 79
Megillah 118–120
Meir Baal Hanes 66
Meir of Heidelberg 49
Meir of Rothenburg 44
Meknes 150
Menorah 7, 13, 19, 25, 26, 28–30, 32, 34, 62–65, 66, 74, 111, 112, 141, 147
Meshed 134
Messiah, Messianism 30, 52, 64, 106
Messina 144
Mezuzah 89
Michael, Erna Hagadah 47
Micrography 39–41, 132
Middle East 133, 150
Midrash 43, 44, 61, 62, 63
Minhagim Books 52
Miscolcz 152
Mitzvot 10, 58, 63, 103
Mizrach, Mizrach Tablet 88–89
Mohel 128
Mohel Book 130
Moloch 4
Monotheism 4, 16, 19
Monteverde 32
Moorish Revival 151–152
Moravia 105, 115, 121
Morocco 70, 71, 111, 112, 130, 150
Mosaics 2, 6, 26, 28, 30, 37, 108
Moses 7, 10, 12, 15, 21, 43, 58, 62, 63, 64, 70, 75, 97, 117, 136
Moses ibn Zabara 41
Motifs 32, 33
Mount Carmel 29
Mount of Olives 31
Mount Sinai 62
Myers, Meyer 97

Na'aran 28
Naro 30
Nathan ben Samson of Mezeritch 122
Nathan ben Simon Halevi of Cologne 49
Nazareth 31
Nebuchadnezzar 6, 19
Nehardea 6, 14, 21
New York 150, 152
Newport 150
Noah's Ark 9, 28
North Africa 92, 97, 101, 112, 132, 150
Novogrodov 147
Nuremberg 75
Nuremberg Hagadah 47

Old Testament 7, 14, 32, 37, 41, 69
Oranienburgerstrasse Synagogue 152
Ossuaries 31
Ostia 22
Ostrog 147
Ottoman Empire 136
Oxford 41

Pagan motifs 6, 33–34
Palaggi, Hayim 107
Palermo 144
Palestine 75
Palma de Majorca 95
Papal Bull 144, 145
Paris 35
Park East Congregation 152
Parochet 103
Passover 39, 44, 47, 55, 69, 88, 120–125
Paul 22
Paul IV 145
Pentagram 24
Persia 76, 79, 84, 118, 128, 134
Philo 22, 65
Phoenicia 34
Pinhas, Joseph of Ansbach 122
Pinsk 147
Pisa 47
Pogroms 142
Poland 70, 92, 103, 114, 147–148
Pompeii 12, 13
Portugal 132, 148, 149
Prague 137, 143
Prague Haġadah 52, 55
Ptolemais 21
Ptolemy 21, 22, 37
Purim 44, 118–120

Raizelach 125
Rav 6
Red Sea 44
Reform Judaism 151
Regensburg 143
Regensburg Pentateuch 47
Renaissance 41, 52, 103, 114, 145, 146
Representational art 3, 32
Revelation 62, 125
Rimonim 92, 94–95, 97
Ritual objects 7, 19, 26, 30, 32, 34, 39, 40
Roman art 15
Romania 147
Rome, Roman Empire 13, 22, 31, 32, 34, 47, 63, 134, 144, 145
Rosh Hashana 44, 106, 107
Russia 75, 103

Sabbath 34, 58–87, 90, 97, 115, 140
Sabbath lamp 60, 65–71, 115
Sabbath tablecloth 79
Safed 75, 136, 147
Samson 70
San Francisco 152
San Juan Buatista, Church of 144
Sanctum Sanctorum 19, 103
Sanhedrin 9
Santa Maria La Blanca, Church of 144
Sarajevo Hagadah 43, 92
Sarcophagi 31
Schueler, Valentin 69
Sculptors 9
Sculpture 5, 141
Seals 63
Seat of Moses 24
Second Commandment 2, 11
Seder 88, 122, 125
Seder tray 122, 123
Segal, Uri Phoebus 122
Segovia 144
Segura 132
Seleucids 19
Seljuk motifs 144
Septuagint 37
Seville 144
Shavuoslach 125
Shavuot 125
Shechina 65
Shem 9
Shiviti 89
Shmuel 6
Shocken Bible 47
Shterntichel 65
Shulhan Aruch 103
Sicily 63, 144
Silversmiths 75, 84, 97
Simhat Torah 107, 110–111
Simonsohn, Otto 151
Sinai 97
Sofia 150
Solomon 18
Solomon, Judgement of 70
Spain 41, 92, 95, 132, 143–4, 148, 149
Spice containers 80–85
Star of David 24, 87, 113, 141
Strasbourg 50, 51
Succah 107
Succah Tablet 107
Sukkot 84, 107–110
Susa 118
Symbols 3, 13, 32, 34, 63, 73, 84, 92, 103, 107, 141, 153
Synagoga Major 144
Synagogue 6, 7, 11, 12–14, 17, 21–30, 32, 37, 39, 63, 73, 86, 90–105, 107, 110, 118, 142, 144, 145, 146, 149–153
Syria 12, 22, 73
Szeged 153

Tabernacle 7, 18, 63, 104
Tallit 130
Tallit container 130
Talmud 5, 6, 9, 10, 20, 21, 22, 26, 37, 51, 58, 65, 90
Teheran 134
Temple 5, 19–20, 21, 25, 29, 31, 32, 37, 40, 62, 63, 65, 73, 76, 88, 92, 94, 97, 104, 111, 112, 117, 118, 146, 147, 150, 151
Temple Emanuel-El 152
Tetuan 136, 150
T'fillin 130
T'fillin bags 130
T'fillin cases 130
Thessalonica 22
Tiberias 136
Tik 101
Titus 32
Todos los Santos, Church of 144
Toledo 92, 143, 144
Tombstones 66

Torah 2–5, 7, 13, 16, 22, 24, 32, 34, 37, 63–64, 89, 90, 92–105, 110–111, 118, 130, 142, 151
Torah Ark 24, 26, 28, 32, 34, 74, 92, 95, 102, 103, 111, 115, 143, 145, 146, 147, 151
Torah Ark Curtains 103–105
Torah Crowns 92, 94
Torah Mantles 90, 92, 101
Torah Pointers 97, 100
Torah-shields 90, 97
Trani 144
Transito, El 144
Tree of Life 63
Trieste 145
Tripartite Mahzor 47
Tunisia 30, 71, 73, 136, 150
Turin 146
Tyre 18

Ukraine 114, 147, 148
Unicorn 147

Venice 52, 105, 134, 145
Vienna 152
Villa Torlonia 32
Vilna 147
Vine 73
Vittorio Veneto (Ceneda) 103, 145
Von Forster, Ludwig 152

Wall paintings 12, 13–14, 26, 28, 34
Washington Hagadah 47
Western Art 2, 14, 17, 153
Western Wall 88
Wimple 90
Wine 71–76, 124
Wine decanter 73, 107
Wolf, Aaron 122
Woodcuts 69
Worms 143
Worms Mahzor 47

Yachin 97, 112
Yahrzeit 141
Yahuda Hagadah 47
Yaknehaz 47
Yemen 65, 100, 111, 136
Yemenite Manuscripts 39
Yizkor 141
Yom Kippur 88, 106, 107
Yugoslavia 43, 136

Zecharia 31
Zeus 4, 19–20
Zodiac 26, 28, 29, 134, 147
Zwirner, Ernst 152